Advance Praise for *The Frugal Book Promoter*

"At last—a solid, sensible, systematic guide to the ins and outs of promotion and publicity. Written by a writer, *for* writers—Carolyn Howard-Johnson proves that she's not only an accomplished poet, essayist, and novelist, but also a marketing maestro!"
~ JayCe Crawford, *Cup of Comfort* author, copyright professional

". . . until now I didn't have many other staples to recommend to new authors looking for publicity."
~ Jenna Glatzer, author of *Make a Real Living as a Freelance Author* (Writer's Digest)

"[Carolyn Howard-Johnson is] an incessant promoter who develops and shares new approaches for book promotion."
~ Marilyn Ross, founder Small Publishers of North America and coauthor of *The Complete Guide to Self-Publishing*

"*The Frugal Book Promoter*! I love it. Most authors don't have deep pockets for publicity, promotion, and marketing. The chapter on perks offered by Amazon is a perfect example of the kind of practical advice offered—the kind that took me months to discover."
~ Rolf Gompertz, author, veteran publicist for NBC, and UCLA instructor

"*The Frugal Book Promoter* is excellent. . . . It has given me ideas that would never have occurred to me and has changed the way I think about book promotion."
~ Mark Logie, award-winning poet and short-story writer

"Interesting, informative, readable. Easy to follow quotes and technique mixed together wonderfully. This is an A-one job. I'm going to have to put it under my pillow. "
~ Leora Krygier, author of *First the Raven* and *When She Sleeps*

"While brainstorming marketing ideas with one of my authors, she informed me she had just purchased the book *How To Do What Your Publisher Won't*. My immediate reaction was an internal "oh no." Then I clicked to Amazon to order it and read up on what it was I wasn't going to be doing! When the neon yellow book arrived, I devoured it. I was hooked from the  first line in Carolyn's acknowledgement: 'Oh, to remember all those who have been instrumental in the birth of a book!' By the time I was done there was as much neon-highlighter yellow inside as it was outside, and, as a fan of Post-its, I made the book look like a yellow-feathered peacock! Carolyn Howard-Johnson has "been there, done that" in marketing her own books and she packed all her hard-earned wisdom into this Frugal Book series."
~ Nancy Cleary, publisher. Photo also by Nancy Cleary.

". . . chock full of ideas that even seasoned book promoters will not have tried . . ."
~ Dallas Hodder Franklin, writer

Careers that are not fed die as readily as any living organism given no sustenance.

The
Frugal Book Promoter
(Second Edition)

**How to get nearly free publicity
on your own or partnering
with your publisher**

By Carolyn Howard-Johnson

Careers that are not fed die as readily as any living organism given no sustenance.

Dedicated to . . .

. . . my first demanding teachers in the fields of journalism and publicity, including Mary Chachas, former society editor of the *Salt Lake Tribune* and the late Eleanor Lambert of the Eleanor Lambert Agency, New York. It is also dedicated to *you*, the author-publicist of the new millennium.

In Memoriam . . .

Hazel McElroy Cutler
1923–2004
whose chosen career centered
on libraries, the drivers
of all things literate

and

Trudy McMurrin
1944–2009
university press director
and editor extraordinaire.

Other Books in the Award-Winning HowToDoItFrugally Series of Books and Booklets

The Frugal Editor:
Put your best book forward
to avoid humiliation and ensure success

Great Little Last-Minute Editing
Tips for Writers:
The ultimate frugal booklet for avoiding word
trippers and crafting gatekeeper-perfect copy

The Great First Impression Book Proposal:
Everything you need to know
to sell your book in 20 minutes or less

Frugal and Focused Tweeting for Retailers:
Tweaking your tweets and other tips for integrating
your social media

A Retailer's Guide to Frugal In-Store
Promotions:
How to increase profits and
spit in the eyes of economic downturns
with thrifty events and sales techniques

Your Blog, Your Business:
A retailer's guide to garnering customer loyalty and
sales online and in-store

Careers that are not fed die as readily as any living
organism given no sustenance.

The

a. 1. A word placed before nouns to limit or individualize their meaning.

Fru´gal

a. 1. Economical in the use or appropriation of resources; not wasteful or lavish; wise in the expenditure or application of force, materials, time, etc.; characterized by frugality; sparing; economical; saving; as, a frugal housekeeper; frugal of time.

Book

n. 1. A collection of sheets of paper, or similar material, blank, written, or printed, bound together; commonly, many folded and bound sheets containing continuous printing or writing and now digitally produced books for e-readers.
2. A composition, written or printed; a treatise.

Pro`mot´er

n. 1. One who, or that which, forwards, advances, or promotes; an encourager; as, a promoter of charity or philosophy.
2. Specifically, one who sets on foot and takes the preliminary steps in, a scheme for the organization of a corporation, a joint-stock company, or the like.

This book is an updated edition of *The Frugal Book Promoter: How to do what your publisher won't*, first in the HowToDoItFrugally series of books, one series for writers, one for retailers. It comes to you with the gentle reminder that in the publishing world authors *are* retailers. That is nothing new, but in the quickly changing world of publishing, writers are more responsible than ever for the sales of their own books and, therefore, need marketing skills more than ever.

The cover of this book, designed by Chaz DeSimone, uses the font American Typewriter from International Typeface Corporation to suggest a writer's typewritten manuscript, and ITC's Century Condensed to emulate the typeset composition of a printed book. The interior of this book is set in Times New Roman, a highly legible font traditionally used for books and newspapers.

Careers that are not fed die as readily as any living organism given no sustenance.

The Frugal Book Promoter
(Second Edition)

How to get
nearly free publicity on your own or by
partnering with your
publisher

By Carolyn Howard-Johnson

HowToDoItFrugally Publishing
Los Angeles, California

Acknowledgements

. . . traditional marketers count dollars; guerrilla marketers count relationships. ~ Jay Conrad Levinson, author, the Guerilla Marketing series

Oh, to remember all those who have been instrumental in the birth of a book! Once, at a writers' seminar, I overheard a well-known author deride writers who include many thank yous to mentors and helpmates. He thought the process a ridiculous name-dropping tradition. He is a wonderful writer, but he must have an inflated opinion of his own abilities if he believes he writes books by himself. He may also have no knowledge of marketing, for the nourishing elements of PR are helping others, accepting help from others, and being grateful for the growth that comes from that exchange. My thank-you list is long, but probably not long enough. My apologies to the many others who contributed to my success but are not noted.

Thanks to members of my most enduring critique group, Leora Krygier, Phyllis GeBauer, and JayCe Crawford; to Emily Heebner who was made to nourish others; to my talented cover designer Chaz DeSimone; to my photographer Uriah Carr; to publicists Debra Gold and Rolf Gompertz; and to all those who cheerfully gave me permission to relate their PR successes and disasters.

Thank you, too, to Joyce Faulkner, Kristie Leigh Maguire, T.C. McMullen, and members of the writing and marketing organizations I belong to who have been generous with their time. Oh! And to my teachers. Writing is a never-ending learning experience.

Special thanks to my husband Lance G. Johnson, author of *What Asians Need to Know About America from A to Z.* He is never too busy to apply his organized and unrelenting passion for detail to editing my work.

Before We Get Started

Knowing the rules of promotion is like knowing the rules for writing. When you have mastered them, you have the confidence to break them when you need to. ~ CHJ

Don't misunderstand the above quotation. I'm not suggesting that an author run willy-nilly breaking the rules of public relations (PR). That will not benefit his reputation as either an author or someone who knows how to brand himself. Many books give you PR essentials, but once you know the rules, you are better able to let your writer's imagination loose so you can promote yourself and your book with confidence. When you do that, even our rule-oriented culture will appreciate your creativity rather than criticize you for it. Rather than the tinkle of bells, your efforts will be the sound of timpani to the ears of gatekeepers—you know, folks like editors, producers, and anyone else in a position to help you get your message out there.

It is a myth that authors—especially the greats—lack the ability to promote. In some circles it appears to be stylish to eschew promotion as vocally as possible. However, many of our most famous and literate authors were very good promoters and some did it without PR classes (or books!) to tell them how. Mark Twain was one of the best.

Laura Skandera Trombley, president of Pitzer College in Claremont, California, and a noted Mark Twain scholar, says the image we have of this American icon is the one we have "because that's the image [Twain himself] wanted people to have," and that Twain was a man "so gifted at marketing himself that nearly a century after his death, his name still evokes his white-haired likeness." Branding works so well that Trombley was moved to add, "And [Twain's image has] been so co-opted, it sells everything from pizza to banks to luggage. You know, Twain and Elvis, two symbols of American cultural life that are just indelible."

As important as branding is, building relationships (that might be read as networking) is even more important. Certainly networking is part of branding, but it can obscure the definition. Branding is all you do to encourage people to think of you favorably and often.

We all know what building relationships is. The thing is, with the advent of the Net the possibilities for relationships are so much greater than they were. Relationships have become—if not a more important part of a good promotion campaign—at least more widespread. "Social networking" is the new term for some of that relationship building and I don't neglect that concept in this book. Having said that, the basic concepts and tools of public relations are still the drivers behind promoting with new media.

Marketing and all it encompasses (PR, branding, promotion, building relationships, and more!) works. And it works better if the author is proactive. A publisher's publicist can only do so much without an author's cooperation. Further, most publishers assign no publicist or, if they do, she may have access to a very slim Rolodex, an even thinner budget, and hardly any experience or none at all.

This book is for authors who want their books to soar and do not want their careers to languish. It is structured so authors can select chapters that address aspects of their marketing plan most needed at any given time.

If a reference is made to something covered in depth elsewhere, the reader is given a prompt, and the Index is edited to make it easy for authors like you to find tips for different kinds of promotions as you need them. As an example, when you look up "TV," you'll find information on how to get TV appearances, how to prepare for them, and how to make the most of them.

The Frugal Book Promoter is not a textbook. It contains opinions—some as black and white as the page you find them on. It is me talking to you, sharing with you. I had no desire to write a tome that would make people hearken back to their boring (and heavy!) high school texts.

I may not have covered every possible promotional idea out there. In fact I avoid anything I have not tried as a professional publicist or in promoting my own books. You will, however, find some new (or rarely used) ways to promote that have not been scorched, stirred, and then warmed over.

What is important is that you find a path for promoting that fits *your* interests, skills, pocketbook, and your book's title. I expect you to pick and choose. Only

Carolyn Howard-Johnson

someone who had no guidance (like me in the days right after my novel was published) would attempt to use them all. I hope that my experiences will save you time, money, and heartache.

Novelist and political powerhouse Hill Kemp and I had a conversation about how interesting it is that writers scorn something so commercial and practical as marketing, but when they sign with a fine traditional publisher (or any other publisher!) who doesn't market their books, they are most put out. That is one of the reasons the first *Frugal Book Promoter: How to do what your publisher won't* came to be and why I am expanding it in this edition. Marketing is essential. It is also creative. Hill suggests that both nonfiction and fiction writers can help themselves overcome their aversion with this exercise:

> "Pretend you are writing a novel. Create a character who lives to market something—anything. Put that character into situations you might face in promoting your own book. You'll then have in this character a mentor for furthering your writing career."

Contents

Section I
Getting Started and Getting On with It

The aim of marketing is to make selling superfluous. The aim is to know and understand the customer so well that the product . . . sells itself. ~ Peter Drucker, management theorist

As making a living from selling books has gotten tougher for publishers and budgets have gotten slimmer, big and small publishers alike have put a greater priority on marketing.

Even as publishers shift more of the responsibility for marketing to the authors, many authors are convinced there is something déclassé about the words "marketing" or "selling." We coyly say "submitting" our work or "shopping" our books, even though we sense we must build platforms, regardless of the words we use. We know we must submit the most professional proposal, synopsis, and chapters we can, but the idea that the image we are creating is part of a promotion plan sort of gets lost in . . . well, the language.

Ever-changing technology has also made authors fearful of what we must do—what we must learn—to carve a successful career.

As they say, we need to "just get over it." This first section of *The Frugal Book Promoter* helps assuage your fears. Trust me. Great marketing is merely sharing your passion with others. And it's lots of fun.

Chapter One
Excuse Me! I Have To Do What?

No matter how authors publish—on their own or traditionally—their books may live or die at the hand of their own marketing skills. ~ CHJ

True publishing includes the marketing of a book. That means your writing (and you!) will be *exposed* to the public no matter how it is published. If you managed to find a great agent or publisher, you are probably aware you succeeded because your résumé (or platform) shows you write well *and* know how to market yourself and your writing. Once we authors realize how important these skills are, we understand that we must come to terms with fears that keep us grounded when we should be flying high.

Doubt and uncertainty about the publishing world are in the air. My clients and students say things like, "If I let people see my work, will it get stolen?" or "Is it safe to send my work to an agent or publisher?" or "I'm a writer, not a publicist and I'm scared."

Now just about the time we've finally decided to follow our dreams, we learn we must also do something most of us are not suited to or something we expected someone else would do for us. That is, we must market our books.

This is how we deal with it. Though the world of publishing is very different from our expectations, those differences will open doors for us. Just as writing has made a difference in our lives, so will the entire publishing process.

For the first time we writers can take complete charge of our own careers—or not. It's our choice. Technology lets us aim at niche markets that were once economically unfeasible. There are more ways to publish than we could have imagined a decade ago. We can reach more people with news of our book than was ever possible, and less expensively. We are living in miraculous times for writers.

Some successful authors have natural talent, some don't. Some talented authors have never taken their manuscripts out of a drawer. Though a few writers get lucky and soar to the bestseller lists with no effort outside having produced a manuscript, it is foolhardy to expect we will be among the fortunate few. The good news is we can have successful writing careers if we are motivated, if we have patience, if we persevere.

Even then, the prospect of facing the publishing world is daunting. Myths and exaggerations circulate. It is easy to be fearful. We can get over that. We can grab at success and we can do it our way. Wasn't it Roosevelt who said, "The only thing we have to fear is fear itself?" So let's get rid of our fears so we can "just do it." Wasn't it Nike who said that?

-∞-

BIG WORRY NUMBER ONE: Plagiarism

Fear of plagiarism is a topic of discussion among the writers I meet on the Web, in my critique groups, in my classes or wherever authors get together to further their careers. Some writers are so crippled by the fear that someone will steal their idea or plagiarize their work, it keeps them from sending their manuscripts to publishers and agents. Even from trusting professional editors and teachers. Mostly it deters them from seeking the spotlights that will assure the success of their books.

The most important part of writing, after the process itself, is to be read, to *share*. Worry about plagiarism keeps inexperienced writers from doing that and produces anxieties that interfere with their creativity.

An author must take precautions, of course, but worry about plagiarism or giving away an idea instead of an interest in sharing their talent with others, is destructive to both their creativity and to the business of building a career. I would rather have a million people read one of my poems in a Dear Abby column credited only as "Anonymous" than have it read not at all. Having our voices heard is more important than selling books. Having our voices heard is sharing our souls. I fervently hope more writers will come to share this view.

The kind of plagiarism that authors worry about is quite rare—that is, having an agent or someone in a writing class steal an idea. It's hard to steal an idea. For one thing, there are no truly new ideas in the world. If you don't believe me, read Joseph Campbell's works (which you should do anyway). He divides all of literature from Greek plays onward into a few categories with a few basic elements. It's unlikely that your work is so unique that it doesn't fit into one of them.

Further, ideas cannot be copyrighted. A recent court case reaffirmed this notion. If it had not, much of Shakespeare's works would be considered plagiarism and, because science fiction writers often borrow theories from those who win Nobel prizes in physics, that genre could no longer exist as we know it.

Many kinds of borrowings are not plagiarism but the result of the similar way our brains function. You've probably heard the story of monkey colonies on one island who take up the same habits of monkeys on another island with no understandable way for them to have communicated.

You should know that anyone who used your idea would surely write a different book than yours. Bolster your confidence by trying this exercise: Ask three writers to pen a piece using a very specific subject— maybe even something you've considered writing yourself. My critique group used a story about how, as a child, one of our members sneaked into a neighbor's house and ate frosted strawberries out of the Fridge. We then set a lunch date and read each work aloud. In spite of the similar plot lines, the voices, characters, and details were so different we wondered why we had been concerned about a fellow writer stealing an idea. Usually, a writer won't be interested in writing someone else's stuff, anyway. Writing, after all, is about *self*-expression.

Often when a case of plagiarism occurs among those who have the public trust, it gets lots of press. However, by the time the perpetrator is found innocent, the case has lost its news value, and we never hear about the accused's exoneration. Thus, authors feel bombarded with reports of plagiarism-that-never-happened.

Careers of a few writers have been broken into kindling when plagiarism was uncovered, but sometimes the opposite happens. Near-anonymous writers or those relegated to the obscure halls of academia become household names when they are found to have picked clean the bones of others' words. When controversy threatened to tarnish names like Stephen Ambrose and Doris Kearns Goodwin they became known among people who would never have heard of them before.

Many times plagiarism goes unnoticed because the thief is not caught or his work is so poor that even stealing cannot make it star-worthy. But think! Think! How much is written, published, put out into the world. The chance that your story might be *the* one stolen is minuscule.

Plagiarism is most rampant in academia. If you need proof, Google "plagiarism." Yep, a few famous cases and lots more stories about kids trying to make the grade at school. We cannot condone such theft, but we authors should not allow the idea of plagiarism to doom the progress of our writing careers. Generally it is only the poor young schmuck who grabbed down someone else's work who suffers—whether or not he is caught.

Another consideration. If someone should swipe a few of your words or an idea, his chances of becoming rich, famous, and envied because of them are no better than yours. If he should, that sets him up for legal action worth pursuing. If he doesn't get rich on your work, you have the satisfaction of knowing he didn't, and won't need to bother your talented head about chasing after a pauper. You might even benefit. The publicity surrounding such a case could be the lucky stroke that makes *you* the rich, famous, and envied author.

Worries about readers accessing our books free also plague some of us. The prospect keeps us from publishing e-books or from using the "search inside" functions offered by online bookstores, Google, and others. But books have been passed around for centuries. And books were Xeroxed long before computers let us download them as e-documents. These practices deprive authors of their royalties, but they also drive word-of-mouth exposure. In any case, these borrowings are impossible to control completely no matter how you publish. It's another fear you must conquer rather than let it handicap you.

Publicity is what makes a book a commodity. Sometimes the worst possible scenario you can imagine can be a blessing. Any excellent public relations professional knows how to make a sweet drink out of very sour fruit.

In the meantime, there are ways you can protect yourself. Mind you, these are not official, lawsuit-tight methods. There are lawyers for that, and *they* can't make guarantees. These ideas, rather, are meant to help writers feel more comfortable about deciding when such help is required.

- Know that once any work has been published (made permanent), it is protected by copyright law. Make yourself comfortable, if you must, by adding the © symbol to your copy.

- Officially copyright your large works with the copyright office. It isn't inordinately costly if you don't let the "lost copies" disclaimers you find on so many sites tempt you to use a third-party service. Go to copyright.gov for instructions. Titles can't be copyrighted, but research your title so you can consider the pros and cons of using one someone else has used. Register screenplays with Writers Guild of America (wga.org).

- Most writers can't afford to copyright every poem or short piece they write. Make yourself feel more comfortable with these stopgap measures:

  o Print your piece and put it in a sealed manila envelope. Label the outside of the envelope with your title and the word "Copyright," and send it through the mail to yourself. Don't disturb the seal when it arrives. File it. In some courts this untouched envelope and contents may be acceptable proof the material is yours. Lawyers hate the idea—probably because it is far from foolproof—but I suspect it is also because they can't invoice an author who uses this method.

31

I include this work-in-an-envelope idea as a way to put your mind at ease, and I'm going to keep recommending it to authors who need to relax enough to enjoy writing.

> **Caveat:** This method does *not* replace the need for an official copyright when your book is ready for print.

- o Some suggest that smaller works like poems and short stories be bundled into a single manuscript and registered with the copyright office. It isn't as frugal as the work-in-an-envelope method, but if you ever decide to bring suit, you may have a sounder case.
- If you must, waste a few minutes every ninety days or so to surf the Web. Type a phrase from one of your pieces into the search engine with quotes around it. If those exact words have been used, you will find them. You may find that these words were used in something other than a duplicate of your work, but this process may reassure you that all is well.
- If your fear of plagiarism is a hurdle that minor fixes will not assuage, hire a copyright lawyer. A good attorney can be worth her pounds in sterling.

Some writers have been known to ask an agent or publisher to commit to secrecy before reading their proposal or written work. This is not the brilliant idea it appears to be. Agents and publishers may be less than interested in an author who seems too suspicious and litigious or doesn't understand the industry's traditional submission process.

Many authors give away their work or barter it. They do it in trade for exposure of their names and titles, to help build their platforms (their résumés), and to encourage writers to buy their other works.

Some consider this trend unfortunate. They forget that a no-pay model has been used for decades by many of the most reputable poetry, literary, and academic anthologies and journals. Some literary entities "pay" with only a few copies of the finished book.

Some well-known authors like James Patterson have updated that model. Patterson is no newbie to marketing. The once-chairman of one of United States' major advertising agencies made free e-copies of his old novels available to publicize his new work. He doesn't need a career boost, but marketing like this will do that, even for him.

I offer free content directly from my Web site (howtodoitfrugally.com/free_content.htm) with the stipulation that those who use articles include my byline and credit line (the mini bio at the end of the piece that I provide with each article). I may use Patterson's free e-copy idea when my next novel is released.

Building a platform is what all this writing and publishing and giving away your work is about. It's also about something called branding. (You'll learn more about both in Section II of this book.) For now, suffice it to say that when you have built a great platform one plank at a time and kept your branding in mind as you do it, it becomes easier to snag a great agent or publisher.

You've probably heard of the old-fashioned term, "clips." Clips are tear sheets (your work in print that is actually torn from a newspaper, magazine, or other printed matter) or a photocopy of that piece. They prove to a gatekeeper that you have been published. Today your "clips" may be hardcopies like these, but they will probably also include printouts or links to your work.

Your clips are part of your branding and branding is part of the book promotion process. Every time your byline appears on subjects related to your book, you make at least some gatekeeper aware of what you do.

Every time you are published—for pay or not—you have a new clip. A credit appears beneath the published piece that tells something about you and it often links to your Web site, your e-mail address, or the online buypage for your book. Each one becomes part of your résumé, part of your media kit, part of the confidence you need to promote with your chin up and a brave smile on your face.

So, what is the worst thing that could happen if you don't get paid for something you write? Whatever that is, it's worse to be paralyzed by something that may never come to pass.

What if your work is plagiarized? We can make lemonade from the bitter fruit of plagiarism by making it into a win-win situation. When one of my articles for *Home Décor Buyer* showed up on a Web site, that magazine's lawyers didn't care to pursue the problem (probably because two hours of a lawyer's time would cost more than what they had paid me for the article). So I pointed out to the offending Webmaster that they had used a story that this magazine had paid good money for and suggested that they give both the magazine and me a little publicity in trade. The Webmasters were apologetic and happy to make amends. That's an example of good public relations, by the way. Nonconfrontational. Willing to communicate. Willing to compromise.

-∞-

BIG WORRY NUMBER TWO: Oops! Swiping Others' Work
Plagiarizing other's work is something that should be a bigger concern for you than that *your* work might get filched. Sometimes our memories don't serve us, our minds absorb something so completely we don't remember where we first saw something, or our researchers don't take accurate notes. To protect yourself, research carefully, keep accurate records, and assiduously credit others.

We should also take care when we quote others, though it is legal to quote for certain purposes and in certain amounts without getting permission. Generally you may quote without permission if you write commentary, satire, criticism, academic material, or news reports. The number of words you can use without permission depends upon the size of the copyrighted work as a whole. Guidelines differ from genre to genre. Find specific guidelines at the Library of Congress Web site, loc.gov, or let a research librarian help you. The online bookstore division of Amazon protects itself by allowing quotations and blurbs of up to twenty-five words.

If you borrow a theme or idea from someone, read *Literary Law Guide for Authors: Copyrights, Trademarks and Contracts in Plain Language* by Tonya Marie Evans, Susan Borden Evans, and Dan Poynter, or check with a lawyer familiar with literary law. Freelancers or those employed by newspapers and other publishers can look to their companies' legal departments for advice.

> **Caveat:** Sometimes getting unnecessary permission is cumbersome and counterproductive. Balance your decision-making process. If you're writing an unofficial biography (which often means the person you're writing about isn't thrilled with your project), you probably need a good lawyer. If you're writing a piece for a newspaper or academia, research their policies. In many other cases, asking permission can slow you down but also earn you friends.

-∞-

BIG WORRY NUMBER THREE: Being Sued

Many of you worry—a lot—about legal suits. Fear of litigation can help you protect yourself, but it can also be a creativity spoiler and lead you to make counterproductive marketing choices.

To avoid lawsuits (and sometimes to avoid being in the limelight), some of you consider writing under a pseudonym. That is certainly an option. Doing so, however, will make it much harder to promote your work and won't necessarily protect you from litigation.

It surprises first-time authors to find that it is at least as important (sometimes more important) to promote the author than the title of his book. Frequently the identity of the real author becomes known very quickly anyway.

Many are familiar with Joe Klein's *Primary Colors*, a book he published anonymously to great media fanfare. It quickly began to die. After the initial promotion putsch there was no one to interview, no story, no driving personality. He may deny this motivation, but it appears the author came out of the closet to save his baby from a quick death of slow—then no—sales.

Pseudonyms are useful for branding a separate series or genre. If you're determined to use a *nom de plume*, study the techniques Nora Roberts used for her romances and the mysteries she wrote under the name of J. D. Robb. Both Roberts and Robb are pseudonyms, but this author has a team of marketers and lots of experience to make the juggling process easier.

-∞-

BIG WORRY NUMBER FOUR: Success or Rejection
Fear of success and fear of rejection are mirror image twins that can be fatal to the writing process. Psychology journals are full of information about both. You worry that you won't be successful. Then

something inside your head screams, "Gulp! What if I am?"

If you suffer from disabling fears of success or failure and want to be published, you must learn to at least mitigate them. This book gives platform-building methods that will help even the shy writer shop her book effectively and, once published, give her a chance at topping bestseller lists. She can't completely avoid the public, though. Her publisher will (at a very minimum) expect a writer to meet her adoring public on book tours and book launches. It is true that a few reclusive authors appear to do very well, but that is mostly a myth perpetrated by the media. Louise Glück, the famous and well-respected poet, is one of those. Yes, she avoids media exposure but she is no recluse. She teaches and teaching is an excellent way to build a following. And teaching certainly requires some crowd-pleasing skills.

A good therapist can help you with worries like these that often run deeper than the writing problem at hand. A book for writers that addresses several of the psychological intricacies of writing is Bruce Holland Rogers' *Word Works* (budurl.com/HollandRogers).

Try a few exercises on your own. Affirmations and baby steps help us get over some fear because the subconscious absorbs what it is exposed to and little steps are less daunting than big ones.

Affirmations work better when you say them out loud. Here are some that may get you toddling. Look in the mirror and say them once a day:

- The universe protects the work I send out.
- The universe lets my career progress surely and comfortably.
- The universe is infinite; there is space enough in it for everyone to succeed, including me.

It also helps to divide the submission process into baby steps, like digging into the bowels of your computer for something you wrote years ago one day, editing it the next, finding a magazine that publishes similar material the next, and so on. Once you have taken several tiny steps, you have taken a giant step. You begin to overcome your fears because good things begin to happen. All you need add is love and a pat on your own back.

> **Tip:** Repeat these baby steps at least five times for five different submissions. It is hard to worry about any one of them with so many submissions out there working for you.

-∞-

BIG WORRY NUMBER FIVE: I'm Not Enough
If that little voice in your head keeps telling you that you don't measure up, there are remedies for that, too. Knowing you are a fine writer and have other skills required to support a writing career will help dissipate fear. Here is what you can do to build confidence.

- Take classes from a reputable college that specializes in classes for writers. Pick some classes in writing craft and some that cover the business of publishing. I chose UCLA Extension Writers' Program (UCLAExtension.edu) and now teach there.

- Join a critique group or assemble one from members of classes you have taken. They have demonstrated an eagerness to learn more about their craft and already have experienced the delicate nature of the critique process.
- Read books. Books on editing. Books on grammar and the elements of writing. I love June Casagrande's *It was the best of sentences. It was the worst of sentences.* Read books on marketing other than this one, too. The more you know, the more you are able to pick up on advanced ideas. Check the Index for some books I've mentioned in these pages. We all know good books are one of the thriftiest ways to learn.
- Utilize experienced support people:
  o Joyce Faulkner can teach you how to structure a professionally written manuscript and provide other services. Reach her at katieseyes@aol.com.
  o Eve Lasalle Caram (ecaram@roadrunner.net), one of my first teachers at UCLA and one of their award-winning instructors, teaches and critiques privately.
- Read Milli Thornton's book *Fear of Writing* to help you with other mental blocks.

> **Caveat:** Choose the best of mentors, especially at first. If you must rely on the Web to find seminars or editors, try to get referrals from folks who are not new at writing. Use the same analytical skills you would use to hire a contractor to build your dream home.

-∞-

BIG WORRY NUMBER SIX: Fear of Marketing
The most pressing fear of all seems to be the fear of marketing. It's amazing that in a capitalist country where money, success, and entrepreneurship are admired, many of us don't value the very skills that energize our economy. That cultural disapproval leads to a fear of marketing and is the most destructive fear for the future of a manuscript that's already been written. When you have finished reading this book, marketing techniques and principles will feel like old neighbors. You'll know exactly which ones to embrace and which to avoid.

If you read this from front to back, rather than use it as a tutorial on specific promotion basics as you need them, you may come away with a new anxiety.

"How will I ever find the time to do everything the *Frugal Book Promoter* says to do?"

Just know you don't have to.

You get to pick and choose from this book what fits your pocketbook, your book's title, your personality, and the time you have available. You'll even find that as you learn one skill, new ones seem to come naturally.

Just know that you can do it.

The more you work at it, the more baby steps you take, the easier it becomes. Your fears will fall away.

Plutarch said, "Go on, my friend, and fear nothing: You carry Cæsar and his fortunes in your boat." As writers, we carry a valuable cargo. We, too, should go without fear.

Chapter Two

Marketing Basics: The Short Course

In a few short years the Internet changed the world of marketing, but, at its best, it still relies on understanding, caring, and passion. ~ CHJ

In Chapter One you learned you must market your book to give it its best chance for success and, I hope, you committed to learning what you must do to give your baby—your book—the best start in life. That's the hard part. The next hurdle—learning the marketing essentials—will be easy for you. I know because you're creative and have perseverance. That's what it takes to market a book.

Getting over the I-don't-want-tos is the next step. So pick any excuse or scary marketing word from the list below. Go ahead. Have your little tizzy fit. Then we can get to work:

- Marketing: I don't want to "market." It's an ugly word. Reminds me of selling pigs at a renaissance fair.
- Promotion: The word "promotion" gets paired with "self" way too often. I get embarrassed just thinking about it.
- Publicity: Give me a break. "Publicity?" What is *that*? Sounds expensive and I haven't figured out how it's different from "public relations."

- Advertising: That sounds expensive. I have big hopes for my book but no assurances my book will make any money, so how can I spend money on advertising?
- Branding: My book isn't published. It's too early to do any branding, much less learn what it is.
- Platform: Don't even mention the word. I'm a writer, not a politician.
- Public Relations: Oh, gosh. Does that mean I have to get out from behind my computer and relate to people?

All the misunderstandings, prejudices, and concerns expressed above are why you hold this book in your hands. You know you have to do something so readers know about you and your book. Indeed, to convince them they *need* your book.

Putting off your marketing is dangerous to your book's health. The arguments most destructive to the success of your book usually go something like this:

- I don't need to learn this stuff. I'll have a team behind me—everyone from an agent to the whole marketing department of a powerhouse publisher. My writing career will just naturally follow.
- It's too early to begin worrying about promotion. I've got a book to write.
- I'm willing. I'm able. Maybe I don't even need this book on marketing. I'll start soon. Maybe tomorrow.

No, no. Please don't delay! It gives me an Excedrin headache to think of the time you are wasting rationalizing away the need to learn to market. It gives me a migraine if you really think you can wing it. If you've even breathed these objections, it's very nearly certain you're living in the last millennium.

It's unlikely that even if you snag a big publisher they will allot much of a budget to what used to be called a midlist author. Now "midlist" merely means a new author with a publishing house—one who'd better be able to market his book to stardom on his own if he wants another book contract.

Here's why you must start using some marketing tools right now rather than later.

- When you build your credibility, your experience, and your ability to help market your book, you're building a platform. You begin to build it the moment you decide to be a writer. A great platform includes what you know about marketing and that works in your favor when you go after an agent or publisher.
- Elements of marketing, like writing query letters, taglines, and knowing how to pitch, is the power behind your entire writing career, not just your book's marketing campaign.
- To be effective, publicity must build.
- You can't possibly learn all you need to know about publicizing your book in one evening. Publicity is like practicing piano. The more you do it, the better it will play in Peoria and everywhere else.

-∞-

A **MARKETING UMBRELLA** is my gift to you. Picture a big red umbrella with the words
"S-E-L-L-I-N-G S-T-U-F-F"
printed around the edge in pristine, white letters. It helps if you add
"E-V-E-N B-O-O-K-S."

This umbrella is your map. Each of the ribs of the umbrella represents a division of marketing similar to those the marketing departments of universities and corporations use. One rib might be "market research." One might be "advertising" (something you may want to avoid—but more on that later). One is "public relations." "Publicity" is one of the happiest ribs because—as you will learn—it's about getting *free* ink. There may be further divisions right down to the ever dreadful "statistics."

"Branding" is what you do so your reader will call to mind a certain image when *you* (notice I didn't say "your book") come to mind. Hang in there. We'll talk a lot about branding.

You might hear the word "promotion," but you probably won't find a class dedicated to it in any university catalog. It's not that "promotion" won't get discussed in some classes, but authors tend to use that term inaccurately, just as the title of this book does. In its strictest sense, a promotion is an individual gimmick that businesses use to sell a product. Esteé Lauder has frequent gift-with-purchase promotions to coax women to buy their anti-aging creams. An author offers his

book packaged with another author's book at a book fair. Magdalena Ball and I offered the Christmas chapbook we coauthored to our readers at a discount so they could use them as greeting cards. See how we structured that offer at
howtodoitfrugally.com/more_on_blooming_red.htm#greeting_card_offer.

I'll probably use the word "promotion" incorrectly in this book again—just for convenience's sake. "Promotion"—the way we use it—is important for authors, so we're going to designate one of our umbrella ribs to it whether academics or marketing professionals like it or not.

You'll also hear the word "campaign." A campaign is all the promotions that a business carefully crafts into an overall plan for the success of a product. McDonald's offered coupons for free cups of latté to promote its McCafé line when it was new. Later it did the same thing for its real fruit smoothies. Those promotions, combined with others, fit its overall "campaign" to boost its image as a cool place with more healthful food choices. We authors are in business whether we like to think that way or not, and we need to work on a plan for the progress of our writing careers.

The publishing world has sort of co-opted the word "platform" in the sense of résumé. Even though business people need to build platforms to get jobs just as authors must, the word "platform" may never come up in the marketing classes at USC's Marshall School of Business. Still, authors must be business people, too. We must start building our platforms in high school when we begin to collect tangible evidence that we're motivated, talented, and persistent. All that good stuff. We start building a platform for our writing with the first article or story that comes out in print or on the Web. We also build platforms when we show in verifiable ways that we know how to market. Publishers have always needed their authors to be good marketers, but authors need those skills now more than ever.

One of the most important ribs in our marketing umbrella for building our platforms (or careers) is "public relations." The initials PR are short for public relations or your relations with the public and the media, relationships that help you get "publicity." You know. That free ink or exposure you need to get your book read.

"Public relations" is neither advertising nor free ink. It is the part of your marketing that builds the right relationships between you and your readers and those folks who can give your career a boost. It is, in part, dissemination of information that sets a standard for how you would like to be perceived. First and foremost, your public relations must be undertaken with the highest ethical standards.

Public relations helps advance your career and, done well, keeps you from chasing down and putting out brushfires. You avoid ticking people off (readers, editors, radio hosts, your providers, and a host of other folk associated with your career) by using great PR. When you do, you have more time and energy to market your book.

To have great relations with the public, you must never assume the worst about any situation. Think of yourself as the best coach in any league. You rally support. You *know* that people want what's best for you. That means no chips on shoulders, no low esteem for yourself or others, no thoughtlessly flying off the handle. It means viewing every challenge that arises as an opportunity.

When it comes to what aspect of marketing is best for your writing career, we're playing Pickup Sticks. Sometimes the sticks intersect. Sometimes they mess with each other. "Branding" and public relations are a little like those two sticks that can't be pried apart without jiggling the other. What you do to create an image for yourself as an author and for your books can be ruined in an instant if your public relations goes awry. What you do to better your public relations (like remembering the thank-you notes your mother taught you to write) contribute to both your branding *and* your public relations.

You've been practicing PR most of your life. Getting along with family. Impressing a new boss or teacher. You've been a customer and know why you like some products and businesses better than others. All it takes is some examination of the processes that influence you to get a grip on public relations—even on marketing as a whole. You may still have lots to learn in terms of your book but you will begin to understand the basics so you can go forward. It's mostly about the golden rule.

Branding, publicity, and PR are thriftier and more effective than most other means of selling. This is one time we don't have to give up quality to save money. Other aspects of marketing are important but all the above divisions are the essential freebies.

Jerry D. Simmons, a former Time Warner executive who developed a social network called nothingbinding.com that supports independently published authors, thinks publicity is one the most important ribs in your big, red umbrella, and so do I. Publicity is the most frugal way to make a great public impression for your book—and for you. In fact, except for supplies and your time, publicity is free and not that hard to learn. Sound good? Keep reading.

You now have the definitions down and will soon have all the essentials you need to carve out a writing career for yourself and a niche among those most likely to read what you have written. Now it is time to think about hiring a publicist—or not.

Chapter Three

To Hire or Not to Hire a Publicist

A publicist, like an artist, must have the proper brushes, paints, and thinners to do her work. For your PR person, the credentials you have built and the contacts you make are the palette from which she works. ~ CHJ

You may be asking why you need to know marketing and promotion stuff if you're going to hire a publicist or if your top-flight publisher will be assigning one to you. That you, the author, must still work your marketing campaign diligently—even if you have a publicist—is part of what makes the decision to hire one so difficult. If you still have to face your fears and toil like a worker bee on a hot day—even after spending thousands of dollars on a publicist—what is the point?

I'm inserting a disclaimer here. I worked as a publicist. I hired one for my novel *This Is the Place.* You would think that makes me an unbiased giver of advice because I've seen it from both sides. It doesn't.

Even with a journalism, marketing, and publicity background, my experience with a publicist did not go so well. That makes me wonder how well it will go for an author who doesn't have any marketing- or journalism-related experience. Or worse, how will an author without that background even know if she is getting full value for her money?

Here is what a good publicist will do for you:
- You'll have a partner to share the work.
- You'll have her expertise and assurance.
- You'll have access to her contacts.
- You'll have a credible voice other than your own to laud your talents.
- You'll benefit from the prestige of having your releases and other marketing essentials go out under the letterhead of a professional.

Some publicists specialize and some are full service. Some have tiered levels of service and charge only for what you want or need, and some expect that to reap the benefits of their profession you must give them the freedom to run in whatever direction they feel is best for your book. Find out exactly what the publicist you are considering will do and what she won't. Here are some services offered by publicists.
- Most publicists disseminate media releases and query letters *en masse*. They may have no knowledge of your local media possibilities outside of your city's daily newspaper.
- They probably have lists for libraries, bookstores, editors, producers, and charity and professional organizations, but you must provide your list of personal and local contacts.
- A publicist who specializes in representing authors may produce a catalog or newsletter for a targeted group of bookstores (usually independent stores) or editors.

- Some publicists concentrate on getting book-signing tours at bookstores, blog tours (an online version of book tours), print, or TV or radio appearances.
- Some larger publicity firms have many associates. Ask who you'll be working with.

> **Hint:** A mailing service that collates, stuffs, manages lists, and has a close working relationship with an excellent printer can be a reasonably priced partner for some of your direct-mail promotions.

Only you can decide whether or not to hire a publicist. It will depend on:

- If your publisher has assigned a publicist to you, and, if so, her expertise and workload.
- The budget your publisher assigns to promoting your book. Remember, what *seems* like a big budget may not cover much. Ask what she will *do* with that budget.
- The time you can give over to marketing.
- The calorie quotient of your wallet. How fat is it? How willing are you to spend your own money or use your advance to publicize your book?
- How you feel about the skills and projects outlined in this book, especially those of traveling and speaking. If your fear limits your publicist too severely, she won't be able to do as much for you. Catch 22. If you are eager to hit the campaign trail, you might be less likely to need a publicist.

- If you can find a publicist who is familiar with books. Nay, not just books but the kind of book you have written.
- If you can find a publicist who already has contacts. If she doesn't, her query letters and releases will be hardly more effective than if frugal you sent them out yourself.

Even if you hire a publicist, you need to know marketing basics. When *Publishers Weekly* writer Judith Rosen interviewed Lissa Warren about publicity efforts for her book, the seasoned publicist and author emphasized that, at a very minimum, the author needs to be "actively involved—even proactively involved."

You should be prepared to do those tasks that only the author can do. Your book will also benefit if you determine to do the jobs that, no matter how savvy your publicist, you can do better. Here is a quick run-down of where your publicist (or your publisher's publicist) will need *your* expertise:

- She'll need your personal mailing list and the list of contacts you've made with editors and producers. See Chapter Eleven on building contact lists.
- She'll need you to be willing to speak, to workshop, to travel, and to back up her efforts at organizing events.
- She'll need your input on current news that relates to your book so she can work on coverage apart from other aspects of your campaign like getting reviews and pitching acquisition librarians.

- She'll want the media kit this book helps you put together (see Chapter Eleven). If you've hired your own publicist, having that kit will save you money. If you don't have a kit ready to go, your publicist will ask you to provide a bio and a sample interview page or FAQ suggestions and more. She can't manufacture information out of the air so you'll end up doing lots of the work anyway.

   Hint: Publicists familiar with the book business are not easy to find, and most authors are reluctant to recommend them because they are acutely aware that the publicist who worked their book well might not work for yours. Contact university public relations departments and PR organizations for recommendations. Ask for references. Ask why they liked that publicist. Their expectations may differ from yours.

   Caveat: Don't be surprised if hiring a good publicist feels like a reprise of what you experienced finding a good agent. You may be required to submit a marketing proposal and a copy of your book. Also beware the sticker shock. If a publicist is reasonably priced, the scope of her services or experience might be limited.

Chapter Four

Promoting Ethically

It's easy to get roped into unethical behavior
when we're the new kid on the block. We're naïve,
and everyone else professes to know what they're
doing. ~ CHJ

Promoting ethically online or off is a must. Authors
often get tricked into buying (and participating in) all
kinds of promotional services that are unethical, don't
sell many books, and aren't useful as lasting marketing
practices. I could mention them, but I don't want to
give them any traction. As they say, "Buyer beware."
Now you know they are rampant you'll be more likely
to know 'em when you see 'em.

Review-and-opinion sites, online bookstores, and
online popularity contests like the annual one run by
Preditors and Editors, seem to attract unethical
practices. Often these involve getting bestseller status
for one's book. Mind you, there is nothing wrong with
coordinating a launch or promotion to try to propel your
book to a top ranking, but much depends on how it is
done. There is a difference between buying up a slew of
your own books to skew numbers versus working a
joint viral promotion campaign with an expert like
Denise Cassino (wizardlywebdesigns.com/JVPartnerships.html), just
as there is a difference between asking for a review of

your book and telling the reviewer how to rate it. If it smells fishy, it probably is.

When authors participate in unscrupulous behavior, they often do a disservice to the publishing industry as a whole. I've seen benefits offered by Web sites like Amazon.com disappear after authors abused them.

Occasionally people react to these abuses by appointing themselves watchdogs for these sites. Vigilante groups often go overboard and these folks are no exception. Authors caught in the web find themselves at the brunt of a campaign against them. Sometimes the fight against unethical behavior becomes as destructive as the practices they were meant to curtail.

Be alert to anything that feels manipulative. If your book is going nowhere, do something positive for it instead. Take a writing or promotion class or buy a book to learn more about the publishing industry. Learn the time-honored publicity techniques outlined in the next few chapters of this book. Your career will soar—ethically.

Section II
Plunging In: Publicity Basics Now

Publicity is a not a sprint but a marathon. As any coach knows, you start training slowly and build up steam. ~ CHJ

Maybe your book isn't written yet. Or you haven't decided how to publish the one you've written. Makes no difference. Now's the time to start promoting. I believe in the Five Ps. They are: Prior Planning Prevents Poor Performance.

My father quoted those five Ps, often in situations when the damage had already been done, always with a twinkle—make that a glint—in his eye. For emphasis he added another P. It's a four-letter P-word, so close your eyes for the next two lines if you're sensitive to them. It goes, "Prior Planning Prevents Piss-Poor Performance." Sometimes the unexpected, even the unacceptable, is the best teacher.

The Six-P maxim is the one that makes me a nag. The more organized you are, the more you know early on, the earlier you start to practice promotion and publicity magic, the more good it will do for your book. The more you learn the easier it is. And that leads me to the three most important Ps for marketing books. Platform, Publicity, Public Relations.

Chapter Five

The Three Ps and Your Writing Career

Publicity is a surprise package. We think we know what's in the box but don't. Surprise! Publicity, platforms, and the rest are not about book sales. They are about career building. ~ CHJ

If you decide to publish your own book, you must know how to market it. You also should know how to market if you hire someone to do most of your publicity for you or if your publisher assigns you a publicist armed with a decent budget. You *need* to know the basics early on for the good of your writing career.

Too often an author elects to write a book and then sits back and hopes—never turns a hand to market it, not before the book comes out, not at its release, not after. Here is what might happen to an author who dodges a publicity campaign:

- Unless the universe is truly smiling on him, he will neither sell many books, nor will his publisher be endeared to him.
- The author's book—perhaps years of work—will be out of print in very short order. He'll see it again, trashed on the remainder pile in discount book stores.
- If the author is self- or subsidy-published, the book will be available but will languish.

- If a talented author refuses to participate, he may have trouble retaining or finding an agent for his next book. Ditto if his book sales are dismal.

So, the first step to great marketing is to know the essentials, the parts that make you the little writing engine that could. Those are the Three Ps. When you work on the Publicity and Public Relations, the Platform comes chugging along as the caboose. You need only know it's there, that it's the backup container for all the marketing you do. When it comes time to show someone what you've been up to—in the writing of a résumé, book proposal, query or cover letter—your successes are waiting in the caboose for you to call on them.

You'll learn something of branding in this section, too. Branding is the track your marketing train runs on. Keep it always in mind and in good repair and your publicity train will run smoothly indeed.

When authors first start working on publicity they may get discouraged. Publicity is not a quantifiable or predictable science. Professional marketers may talk about statistics and try to convince us otherwise, but lots of times they're fooling themselves. If their tools are so perfect, why did the world's best marketer get in trouble with its "New Coke" introduction and have to backtrack with the "Classic" brand, the one they had (the one we loved!) all along. And there's no good reason to even bring up Ford's Edsel fiasco, now is there?

The practice of publicity requires a positive attitude and perseverance because it is difficult if not impossible to trace a direct line from your promotional efforts to the sale of a book. Of course it's possible for an author to snag an interview on "Today" and see his book sales bounce, but generally if he measures the success of his publicity efforts by the number of books he sells, he will soon consider his efforts unsuccessful.

On the other hand, if an author thinks of his efforts as a process toward branding—that is, long-term image-making for himself and his writing career—his efforts toward building relationships with publishing and media professionals will eventually be rewarded in significant ways. And he won't be tempted to give up just before his efforts start reaping benefits. Publicity, Public Relations, and your Platform are career builders. You're going to hate this. Forget the big S. Sales eventually come, but only if we stay focused on the essential Three Ps.

Chapter Six

Public Relations: The Granddaddy to Great Publicity

Without publicity there can be no public support.
~ Disraeli

The basics of public relations and publicity are much like the golden rule. Good PR, of course, is carefully targeted. But mostly PR is connecting with people in a way that makes them feel cared for, and those connections are made—with love and expertise—over and over again. Those are the essentials and they work. Done this way, great publicity becomes great public relations and vice versa.

Beyond the golden rule, I have some commandments—eighteen of them—for getting free ink. But they'll do lots more than get free exposure for you. They will build your career, starting now.

-∞-

EIGHTEEN PUBLICITY COMMANDMENTS

1. Thou Shalt Educate Thyself
Hooray for the Web. There are lots of freebie ways to learn more about book marketing. And books are an inexpensive way to learn more.

- Learn to write a great media release. A release is one of the best tools for getting the publicity you want. Use the instructions in this book and the samples in the Appendix. Find more samples at howtodoitfrugally.com/recent_releases.htm.

- Subscribe to writing-oriented e-letters from fellow authors like Krista Barrett at writergazette.com, the Self-Publishing Coach's letter at self-publishing-coach.com/newsletter.html, and my Sharing with Writers at howtodoitfrugally.com.
- Join groups of folks interested in the subject matter your book covers and organizations of like-minded authors.
- Find lots of free publicity on the Net. Dana Lynn Smith keeps her e-book guides for online promotion updated. Find them at SavvyBookMarketer.com.
- Check out *The Guerilla Marketing* series by Jay Conrad Levinson from Houghton Mifflin, budurl.com/GuerillaMarket. Levinson's advice is not specifically for the marketing of books, but you may pick up some radical ideas for your own marketing.
- Borrow ideas from other industries that suit your personality and titles. With that advice in mind, see my books for retailers at howtodoitfrugally.com/retailers_books.htm.
- For the concept of "free," including information specifically related to book marketing, get *Free: The Future of a Radical Price* by Chris Anderson at the library or buy it at budurl.com/FreeRadicalPrice.
- Read more than one book on publishing and marketing. You're reading this one. Try Patricia Fry's *Promote Your Book, Over 250 Proven,*

Low-Cost Tips and Techniques for the Enterprising Author. It's also an example of how a writer can network effectively with other writers.

2. Though Shalt Not Be Snooty

Read everything. Your newspaper, your e-zines (online magazines or newsletters), your rubbish (and that includes spam) can be geese that lay golden eggs. My daughter found a flier from the local library stuffed between grocery coupons in the Sunday paper. It mentioned a local merchant's display in a window at our city library. I asked the library personnel if I could do a window for my book, and they said yes. People who frequent libraries borrow books. Borrowers are readers and tend to recommend books to other readers.

3. Know Thyself, Know Thy Book

Reread your book. Pretend you didn't write it so it feels fresh. Look at its themes to find angles you can exploit when you're talking to editors. What's different about your book? How does its plot or subject matter fit with what's currently in the news? What different demographics does it appeal to? What's happening in the publishing industry that you can exploit with your queries? A romance Web site might like my novel, *This Is the Place*, but so would a literary one. That it is set in Salt Lake City where the Olympic Games were played in 2002 was an unexpected publicity bonus. I found sports and feature editors open to it as winter games fervor grew and even as it waned because they still needed news and had used all the closely related material they had access to.

4. Thou Shalt Cull Contacts

When you add a new file of media contacts to your computer's database, you will need to develop new habits. If you find the name of a new editor and wait to record it, that name may get lost forever. The Web site gebbieinc.com sells targeted lists of media contacts. Some partial directories on the Web are free (check John Kremer's bookmarket.com), and so are your yellow pages. Ask for help from your librarian. A good research librarian is like a shark. She'll keep biting until she's got exactly what she wants. But after all that, the best contacts of all are your own. You'll learn more about how to build lists and put them to good use later in this book.

5. Though Shalt Write Notes

Send thank-you notes and small gifts to contacts after they've featured you or your book. Editors will pay attention to the next idea you have because people they work with so rarely remember their manners. Once you've made a good impression on a gatekeeper, stay in contact. The more pleasant you make it for others to help you market, the more likely they'll be there for you.

6. Walk Not Alone

Partnering with others is essential, especially your publisher. Ask for help. Ask for anything you need like a sample media release or an image of your bookcover. Building a good relationship and showing your associates you are willing to work with them may spur them to do more. As an example, give your publisher or agent a good reason to feature your book more prominently on their Web sites. What will benefit their visitors? Suggest that you write a feature story for them, a poem on the joys of writing, or an article on how to query a publisher.

7. **Publicize Thyself**

You needn't be humble, just caring. Approach the gatekeepers who could use your ideas so it is evident you are concerned about their audience, not just about making a big splash for yourself.

Think about your own life and career. Hundreds of thousands of books are released each year so the release of a book is no longer newsworthy; what else about you will interest an audience? Utilize the fame you may have accrued in your day job. Several editors liked the idea that I wrote my first book at an age when most are thinking of retiring; they saw me as an example that it is never too late to follow a dream, an idea that might inspire the growing Boomer demographic.

My local newspaper publishes pictures of residents holding up a copy of their newspaper as they stand proudly before a tourist attraction during their travels to China or Key West. Maybe yours does, too. Your son gets engaged, married, has a baby. You're elected secretary of Kiwanis. You hit a hole in one. Some media don't use these kinds of things but some TV stations and small papers sure do, and the fact that you are also a published author makes you more newsworthy.

Here are five things that may interest your local newspaper:

- You are asked to teach at your local college.

- A publisher asks you to act as an advisor or ombudsman. Mine did, and I didn't think of it as something that might interest a business editor until later.
- You are asked to be a panelist at a book fair.
- A national journal publishes an excerpt from your book.
- You win an award. (See Chapter Eleven on the importance of awards and how to use them.)

You can see that what seems mundane to you may be newsworthy to local papers, and what seems like the biggest news of your life may not interest some media at all. It's all in who you present your news to—and how.

8. Use Thy Creativity

Develop new activities to publicize and manufacture reasons to send out releases.

- Utah novelist Marilyn Brown sponsors an annual writers' award in her name through a writers' organization. Nora Roberts' foundation funds a course in writing romance novels at McDaniel College in Westminster, MD. I do something similar. I offer the Noble (Not Nobel!) Prize in conjunction with MyShelf.com. It merely offers encouragement to emerging authors and gives them an opportunity to promote their book. You can see that a publicity-producing effort like this can cost a lot or be very nearly free.
- Some colleges and writers' organizations encourage people to sponsor scholarships in

their names. Giving to the community makes you feel good and you can tie the scholarship to writing in some way. The media will cover the story when you fund the scholarship, when you name judges, when you submit names and pictures of the contestants, and when you hold a gala to honor winners. Use your imagination for a spectacular inauguration for your award. Involve a local dignitary. Get a charity involved.

- Throw a party for reasons other than a book launch—perhaps a salon where artists of all kinds pool their lists to provide a stimulating day for their friends and for the press.

9. Thou Shalt Listen to Thy Readers

Did your book, poem, or story inspire a reader to start a new career? Suggest that story to an editor. Human interest angles like this make you a hero to your reader and to columnists looking for content. Your book's title may get mentioned in the story she writes.

10. Do Good Turns When They Are Needed Most

Do a good turn during a crisis. Donate your books for earthquake or tornado victims to read while they are waiting for permanent shelters or to those who are giving their time to help.

11. Thou Shalt Make Thyself Helpful

When you make a reporter's work easier, you become her preferred resource. When you give her a way to visualize your idea or event, she can imagine how to use your story more easily. When you supply contacts for opposing opinions, she's more likely to use your story idea. When you thank her, she's surprised and appreciative because so few do it.

12. Thou Shalt Make Thyself Evident

Frequency counts. The editor who ignores your first release may pay more attention to your second or twenty-fifth. She will come to view you as an expert and call you when she needs a quotation. Both nonfiction writers and novelists may qualify as experts.

13. Time Thy Contacts

Put yourself in editors' shoes. Time your contacts with them. Asking for exposure in a slick, print magazine's Christmas gift guide in November is futile. Magazine editors work four to six months in advance. Contacting editors of morning newspapers late in the afternoon as they are going to press is not a good idea. Nagging is also a no-no. Wait a decent amount of time to check on correspondence or offer a new idea. Don't wait too long before following up on a breaking news story related to your book.

14. Thou Shalt Follow Up

Follow-up calls boost the chances of a media release being published. Voice contact builds relationships better than other means of communication.

15. Thou Shalt Keep Clippings

Professional publicists keep clippings for their clients. Mindy P. Lawrence (freewebs.com/mplcreative) keeps a database of the clips she gets for hers. The clip file you maintain will be both a record of resources and a visual of how well you are doing.

16. Thou Shalt Evaluate

One year after your book's release, add up your column inches. Measure the number of free inches in any paper that published anything about you or your book. Include headlines and pictures. If the piece is three columns wide and each column of your story is six inches long, that is eighteen column inches. How much does that newspaper charge per inch for their ads? Multiply the column inches by that rate to know what the piece is worth in advertising dollars. Add fifty percent for the additional trust readers put in editorial material over paid advertising.

17. Thou Shalt Set Publicity Goals

You now have a total of what your year's efforts have reaped. New publicist/authors should set a goal to increase that amount by 100 percent the next year. If you already have a track record, aim for twenty percent.

18. Thou Shalt Observe Progress

Publicity is like planting bulbs. It proliferates even when you aren't trying very hard. By watching for unintended results, you learn how to make them happen again in the future. So don't stop working at it, even at your busiest, most creative times.

Chapter Seven

Free Publicity Isn't Really Free

There may be no free lunch, but publicity is better than a mere lunch and about as free as anything gets. ~ CHJ

I **don't** want to lead you astray with my frugal approach to marketing. "Free" publicity costs, whether you hire a publicist or do it yourself.

Rolf Gompertz, an author and thirty-year veteran of NBC's public relations department, once said, "If I had to pay me, I couldn't afford my services." That seems to be the ultimate reminder of how important it is for an author to know something about promotion, and it dispels the notion that getting publicity is scot-free. Time is money, too.

Gompertz reminded me that review copies add up in real dollars, too. So do supplies like media kit folders; postage; a new computer; and gas for runs he makes to the post office, Office Depot, and speaking engagements.

The skills you build for getting publicity are well worth your time in spite of these hidden expenses. Publicity—the art of interesting the media in ourselves or our books enough to result in no-cost ink or airtime—is economical compared to advertising. Never fear, later in this book I'll give you tons of ideas that truly cost you nothing but time.

> **Hint:** For more day-to-day publicity ideas, subscribe to Joan Stewart's e-letter, *The Publicity Hound*, publicityhound.com.

Chapter Eight

Branding: Publicity's Cornerstone

Branding is not advertising, nor publicity, not even general exposure. It is the result of all your efforts working together and how they coalesce into the public's perception of who you are, what you do. ~ CHJ

Back in 2003 when I was still laboring under the misconception that big presses give big marketing budgets to new writers, *Poets & Writers* reported writer ZZ Packer's publisher, Riverhead Press, "Bank[ed] on...name recognition" when they sent her on a ten-city tour, something that her publisher's publicist maintained was a rare occurrence for a first-time author. The implication is that if Packer hadn't already built a platform of her own, Riverhead wouldn't have bothered spending that kind of money on her.

We've talked about the importance of your platform before. But the idea that without one a publisher might not give you every opportunity possible to make money for them was astounding and still is! Unless you are already well known in a field and are writing a nonfiction book allied with it or you've been diligent about publicity for some time, it is unlikely you will have built the kind of brand Packer had. That is why *now* is better than later for beginning a publicity juggernaut firmly rooted in branding yourself. That's why your publicity efforts should *not* be aimed at your *book* early in the game, but rather at who you are, including your other writing.

Even with a general background in PR and journalism I fell into a pothole or two. For one, I put my book—my passion—first. One day I realized I should be branding me instead of my book. I was designing a business card on vistaprint.com. I wasn't very computer savvy and I couldn't get the cover of my first book to load. I had seen business cards for real estate professionals that used thumbnail photos, so I loaded my photo instead. Then I muttered to myself, "Well, it's okay because I won't have to do much redesigning when and if I complete another book." Another book! Of course! When we think of books, it is the author's name we think of first and, if she's written quite a few, we probably can't name them all.

Even after this burst of clarity, I continued to use the name of my book because "This Is the Place" is a metaphor at several levels. It is, of course, Utah, my beloved home where I was born and raised. "Place" also refers to the farm where my protagonist goes to learn about her history and to that singular spot inside each of us where we must go to find the courage to follow our passion. That's when I realized I wouldn't have to change the name of my Web site. It, too, was a place—*the* place in fact—for learning more about me and my books. Since the HowToDoItFrugally series for writers (the book you are holding is from that series) became popular, I was forced to change to

HowToDoItFrugally.com because the tail had begun to wag the dog and wasn't doing a very good job of it.

The world's savvy marketers like Coca-Cola use several related approaches to branding themselves (Coke is it! The real thing!—More than 50 of them since 1904.) Branding is not necessarily an all-or-nothing proposition. If I work fervently to promote tolerance, "The Place" will be like Coke's "It" or "Thing." The public will subconsciously assign a meaning to it—the spot inside each of us that is similar or identical to that place in every other person in the world regardless of race, religion, or gender.

It just worked out that my next book was a collection of creative nonfiction. I'm glad I didn't brand myself too narrowly because stationery or business cards that say "novelist" would no longer fit nor would they have fit the HowToDoItFrugally series. My next book was a chapbook of poetry. Again, "novelist" is wrong, and "writer" seems too broad because it encompasses everything from someone who pens letters to a journalist. Since then, I've been forced to do some sub-branding. Usually branding works better when different segments can be made to fit under one big umbrella.

That one big umbrella is almost always the author. One logo. One Web site. Related colors for each separate product or genre. In my case, my nonfiction for writers and retailers are one thing, my creative work another. And there are divisions even within these categories. Even horror guy Stephen King wrote *On Writing* and that had to make life lots harder on his publicist. From a marketing standpoint, you'll be lucky if your writing is more or less homogenous, but authors shouldn't usually let the marketing of their books determine their career paths unless their reason for writing is to further another profession or career. This may sound nitpicky, but one word can be important.

Some writers use *nom de plumes* to keep their branding efforts from mucking up one another, but using pseudonyms is usually counterproductive. The author misses crossover sales, however small that percentage may be.

Here are some aspects of branding to consider:
- Decide what you want your brand to say. What might you do in the future? If you choose a red hot image for your romance and decide to write a literary book, you will have chosen your brand unwisely.
- If your pre-book experience is associated with the subject of your book, consider ways to tie your branding to that expertise.
- Select color, style, font, and artwork for your Web site with branding in mind. Coke is always red and white. Its sub-brands like Sprite and orange juice have their own colors.
- Coordinate a look for your stationery, cards, invoices, Web site, and bookmarks. Do it for your voicemail greeting, your e-mail signature, the look of your instant messaging, and more.

   Hint: Once you or your publisher has firmed up your title, think about banners and a logo for your online efforts. If you are not graphics-savvy, try Chaz DeSimone, (ChazDeSimone.com). Know that bookcovers and logos require a different skill set than the illustrator of your children's books or your aunt who paints murals for your state capitol building.

Caveat: Wait until just before your book is released to print your media kits and other promotion material. You'll want to include your bookcover image in as many places as possible.

- Make yourself into an expert based on something related to your book. The author of a series of mysteries might be a forensics expert.
- When you're making these decisions, follow your star. It is easier to pursue a subject for which you are passionate.
- Don't be afraid to widen your path. A literary author's expertise could include grammar or communication. You are building a reputation. You wouldn't want to be known only as honest among dozens of other traits you aspire to.

   Hint: When your book is about to be published, marketing leans a bit from branding the author toward what's exciting about the book and how it will benefit its audience. Notice I said "a bit," not a 180 degree turn.

Dress the part when you are in public. So what if you hate cocktail dresses or tuxedoes! So what if you hate costume parties. What *do* you like? Use the parts of *you* that are real to forge a visual identity. Whatever that is will likely fit in with what you write, too, for what you write cannot fall very far from your essential self. One of my poetry mentors, Suzanne Lummis, wears berets. She often wears one when she teaches her poetry classes. A photograph of a bereted Suzanne appeared on the cover of a popular writers' magazine. That beret suits her Leslie Caron-type features as well as her poet-self. We love that Steve Jobs isn't an IBM type, and we sense that his jeans and turtlenecks are his own brand.

I mentioned Mark Twain earlier. People like Twain, Jobs, and Lummis are individuals. They would be wearing their Levi's, Panama hats, and berets in any case, because that's what they like. But their own look is affecting. They will be remembered both for their public presentation and for being exactly who they are.

Here's a final shot on branding. When corporations choose a brand too narrowly, we see them struggle to present a new image when they diversify. That is bad enough for corporations with big budgets. It can be deadly for writers on smaller or nonexistent budgets.

Chapter Nine

Advertising: The Weak Partner

Advertising works, we just don't know how, why, or where it works best. ~ Paraphrased from a quotation from the founder of a large chain of retail stores

Here's what we know for sure about marketing success: Advertising's less mysterious cousin, publicity, works better than advertising. It is the more reliable relative because it is judged on its merit alone and carries the cachet of an editor's approval. It also is surrounded by the ever-magic word "free." Advertising and publicity are easily identified as kin to other branches of marketing, too.

I don't advise an author use his or her budget—large or small—to advertise. It is nearly impossible for anything but the largest advertising expenditure to penetrate any given market. The word "market" here means the media most likely to reach the audience interested in a particular book and therefore the most likely to buy it.

Having said that, if the publisher of a book decides on an advertising campaign, the author should assume (or at least hope!) the publisher has allotted a sufficient budget to make those advertising dollars work. Even then, it wouldn't hurt for the author to ask about their advertising plans and their expectations for them.

Sometimes it is helpful (but certainly not necessary) to advertise. Occasionally the author or his publisher runs across what appears to be an especially fortuitous advertising opportunity for a particular title.

In that case, you should know that even though advertising and publicity often walk hand-in-hand, they can still be incompatible. The editors of good media outlets don't allow their advertising department to influence their editorial staff. Still (in an effort to be impartial) they reserve the right to use advertisers' stories editorially if they deem them newsworthy. If a particular media plays to the audience you would like to see standing in line for your book, paid-for exposure may then become an entrée to the editorial (another word for all that space or exposure that *isn't* paid-for advertising) decision-makers. Your contact in the advertising department may be willing to put your media release on the desk of his editors to look at. He should not promise you results, but his efforts might help.

If you decide to go the advertising route on your own, choose a small media outlet—perhaps a local weekly or an arty quarterly. That way the dollars you spend will be noticed. And don't run the ad only once. In both advertising and publicity, frequency is important.

Sometimes a magazine or newspaper runs a special promotion called advertorial. These are sections where you pay for space to cover the story you want told. This paid-for article may be "free" with the purchase of an ad or you may actually purchase the advertorial outright. Advertorials carry some of the prestige of editorial copy because its copycat character can lead the general reader to assume the article has been chosen only on its merits. The writer or editor you work with on a project like this can be more effectively approached when you have something exceptional you want to submit as honest-to-goodness news.

Advertorial is generally only a little more frugal than advertising. If "free" sounds as if it will serve your needs better than "paid," carve out time to do your own publicity. Follow the Eighteen Publicity Commandments in Chapter Six and learn the now-and-forever PR skills in the next chapter.

Chapter Ten

Your Now-and-Forever PR Skills

Marketing skills are essential to success in every business, every profession. They are so basic to most of the world's way of life they should be a compulsory subject in schools everywhere along with math and history . ~CHJ

The HowToDoItFrugally method of marketing includes using our time and skills well, er . . . frugally. It's about the proven essentials that worked in the past and will continue to work. It's about making everything we do build while we avoid reinventing the wheel.

In his run for the presidency, Bill Clinton had a Keep-It-Simple-Stupid (KISS) philosophy. The five p's (maybe six p's—but only if you prefer!) maxim I talked about in an earlier chapter is a keep-it-simple promotion philosophy. You'll see many ways to simplify in this book, from recycling articles to integrating your online presence. Yep, practical, frugal me. My brand. Along with, I hope, the words "accepting" and "caring."

As an example, I make building a media kit (which we discuss in Chapter Eleven) a double-process tool; you use a kit to plan and record your progress rather than merely as a marketing device. It is one of the now-and-forever PR skills that will stand you in good stead. When you collect information for your media kit from the first time the idea of a book enters that creative little brain of yours, the process of building it helps you get confident. A record of your progress is evidence of how well you're doing—in black and white—so you can't forget or deny it.

This build-a-kit-as-you-go also helps you remember all the stuff that needs to go into your kit before the next step in your writing career pushes it out of your memory banks. And your mock kit will make it easier (and faster!) to whip your real media kit into final shape when the time comes.

I call this method "The Great Book Promotion Planning Media Kit" and it has become one of my most popular seminar topics at writers' conferences.

> **Hint:** I store in my computer several iterations of my media kit. One focuses on my teaching and speaking, another on my retail books, another on my poetry. You will probably do something similar, depending on how your career grows.

So, now we are going to learn several other basic, multi-use PR skills. They will help you do just about everything you're doing in the world of business now (that includes publishing!), and everything you're going to do later.

-∞-

YOUR CREDITS, TAGLINES OR MINI BIOGRAPHIES, identify you as the person who wrote a certain piece. It gives the entire work credibility because it mentions your expertise, not least of which is that you are the author of a book on a related subject. One of these credits becomes the caboose on almost everything you publish. It is as important to you as a well-tied elk hair mayfly is to a fly fisherman. Without one he may have difficulty reeling in his limit.

You know which media use credits and what styles they prefer because you read their submission guidelines and pay attention to the styles of the magazines, newspapers, and Web sites you read. You save your editor the trouble of writing one (and maintain better control of your own branding) by submitting your material with your credit already attached.

> **Caveat:** Editors often ask you to put no identification on contest submissions, but they ask for credit information once you are a winner.

Your credit or tagline goes into your media kit, too, so gatekeepers can easily paste it at the end of the essays, op-ed pieces, stories, or articles they accept from you.

In your credit line, include at least your name, the URL or address of your Web site, the name of your book, and a little about you. It's a nice extra to include an e-mail address your readers can use to give you feedback.

> **Hint:** Rarely seen in taglines is some kind of a hook (perhaps that mayfly a fisherman uses?) to encourage the reader to visit your Web site. It might be an offer for a free e-book, a contest, or an intriguing bit of information that will pique the reader's curiosity enough to take action.

You may also need a longer biography. You'll need one for your media kit, for your Web site, and possibly for the flap of the dustcover for your hardcover book.

Here are two examples, the first a mini bio, the second a shorter tagline. The longer one might be a credit used with an article on a Web site where length is not as important. Note how this author tailors her tagline to fit the audience for one of her nonfiction articles. She could write a similar one for a different audience featuring only her literary achievements.

Example of a long tagline or mini bio: Leora Krygier is the author of *First the Raven* and *When She Sleeps*. She was a finalist in the Ernest Hemingway First Novel Competition, the James Fellowship, and the William Faulkner Writing Competition. Lauded for her "linguistic spell" and "poetic prose," Leora is also the author of *Juvenile Court: A Guide for Young Offenders and Their Parents*. She is a referee with the Superior Court of Los Angeles, and has been profiled in the *L.A. Times* for her innovative use of essay writing in juvenile dispositions. She lives in Los Angeles with her husband and her dog, Kobi. Her Web site is leorakrygier.com.

Example of a short tagline: Leora G. Krygier is a juvenile court referee and frequent contributor to magazines for young adults and parents. She blogs at starbuckled.blogspot.com.

Humor and a personal touch can work very well in your credits or biographies.

Caveat: Editors have style preferences and space limitations. They may edit your tagline or may not use it at all. If they publish content you have offered at no charge, they should include a tagline or mini bio as a courtesy and probably will if you've included it as part of the copy you submit. If not, politely request that they use one. If they refuse, offer your material elsewhere next time.

You'll add to your assortment of taglines and subtract from them as you accrue experience or as your focus changes. Keep examples in a special folder in your computer so you won't need to rewrite every time you use one.

I include several versions of my biography in my media kit—a two-line tagline, a mini bio, and a longer About the Author biography. Doing so gives me more control over my brand, and it makes it easy for an editor to use whatever version suits her needs.

-∞-

YOUR BYLINES are like mini credits. They can contain more than just your name. They might include an "author of . . ." or an "excerpted from . . ." addition to the usual attribution. When you submit your writing, it is a courtesy to include your byline just as you'd like to see it under the title. Your editor may use a different format, but having it there saves her time.

-∞-

ENDORSEMENTS, TESTIMONIALS, BLURBS–call them what you will, the business of blurbs has become nearly biblical, probably because the giver of such praise gets as much as he gives. They are a basic marketing tool because endorsements can be used across the board in every aspect of your marketing.

Well known book marketer, Penny C. Sansevieri, says, "As powerful a tool as a celebrity endorsement can be, it is the most overlooked marketing aspect of an author's campaign. In fact, most authors I work with—even those who have spent years in the business—never give any thought to celebrity endorsements."

Blurbs may be so neglected because no one knows quite what to call them. I've heard "endorsements," "testimonials," "praise," "quotes," "blurbs," and sometimes "bullets" because they are frequently printed on the back cover of books set off by little BB-sized dots. When my husband solicited blurbs from VIPs in the Asian community for his book *Everything Asians Need to Know About America From A to Z*, he came up with a few other . . . ahem! . . . choice words for blurbs because getting them from celebrities is so difficult.

I usually use "blurb" in this book because most publishers use that term. When you hang out at a bookstore, observe the behavior of book buyers and you'll see how important blurbs are. Readers unfamiliar with a work frequently look for these quotes on the back covers of books as they browse. They trust quotations from celebrities and even from readers whose names they don't recognize to tell them about the quality of writing or the author's expertise. Many books list quotations on the first page or two under the header "Praise for this Book," too.

When my Sharing with Writers newsletter subscribers ask me questions, I sometimes publish them in the style of the much-loved Dear Abby columns. A published author who was determined to promote her second book better than her first sent this one to me:

Author: Do you know how traditionally published books get the advanced blurbs from famous authors? Does the publisher go after them, or the author, or both? Do the famous get paid to read the manuscript and write a blurb? I have an idea for my book, but I don't know what the industry norm is.

My Answer: A distant relative of mine works as an editor for a fine literary press. To get blurbs for her authors' books, she calls in favors using her power-packed Rolodex. She is known as the pit bull in her office; few of her fellow editors take the time or have the tact and persistence to do this for their authors. Like just about everything else in the world of publishing, it is best if the author chases blurbs down for herself.

Though you may need to give a book or a manuscript to whomever you ask for a blurb, the famous don't get paid; that would invalidate the authenticity of the process. The famous do it because they are charity minded toward emerging authors, because they owe the publisher a favor, or because they feel the exposure will help their own cause in some way. Many of the most famous won't do it at all—it's too time-consuming to read an entire book, and they fear putting their names on something without thoroughly investigating it.

Try these resources to contact celebrities for the endorsements you covet:

- The Screen Actors Guild at sag.org.
- To find well-known authors, go to the list at Authors Guild at authorsregistry.org.
- Use a search engine to find writers' Web sites. Once found, use their guestbooks or the contact information you find there to submit your

request. You can also write to their publishers or agents who should pass on your appeal.

As difficult as it is to get endorsements from well-known authors or experts, it is not impossible. Here are the secrets:

- Ask for endorsements with a query letter. (See the Appendix in this book for sample query letters.) In that letter:
  o Let the recipient know why you value her endorsement.
  o Use the word "endorsement." People outside the publishing world may not understand the word "blurb."
  o Tell something about you and your book.
  o Spell out the benefits of providing an endorsement, like how being included in your publicity efforts could favorably expose an endorser's name, business, or pet charity.
  o For convenience and courtesy's sakes, enclose a sample of what you'd like the endorsement to say with the assurance that a blurb using the endorser's own words is welcome.
- Shoot for the stars, but shoot for the moon, too. In fact, go moon-shooting first. Ask for blurbs from teachers, from people in your field of expertise, and from fellow authors you know.
- Your contact may ask for more information than you sent in your query letter. They may want a synopsis, an outline, or a copy of the manuscript. Accommodate such a request

promptly before your celebrity forgets or has a change of heart.

- A written query will carry more clout than one sent by e-mail. Send it by USPS and include a self-addressed, stamped envelope (SASE) to make responding easy.

    Hint: Many organizations and institutions block mail with attachments. Many public figures won't open e-mail with attachments or won't open the attachments themselves for fear of viruses. If you *must* send your query by e-mail, *offer* additional materials upon request.

- If someone chooses one of your prewritten blurbs, remove it from the query letters you send to others in the future.
- Don't get discouraged.
  - When your request is ignored or denied, a phone call may be all it takes to clinch the deal.
  - You might try again once you have snagged another celebrity's endorsement. A good blurb is like honey. Spread the early ones you get around in your future requests and they may attract someone else who is impressed by the sweet stuff you're offering.
  - When you read, watch TV, and open your mail, watch for new blurb-getting possibilities.

    Hint: People who write endorsements tend to be more reserved with their tributes than those who spontaneously compliment your work. To collect passionate blurbs, watch for mini raves in your casual correspondence. Drop the person a note asking if you might use what they said in future promotions. Opportunities like these increase once your book is in print because you will receive congratulations, even fan mail. Yes, you will! And you can still collect endorsements after your book is published. For your next book, for your Web site, for your media kit.

Here's what to do with blurbs once you have them in hand:

- Those who endorse your book have done you a favor. Credit them, but choose what it is about their expertise that will most benefit *them—and* will most impress your reader. "Billie A. Williams, author," is nice. But is she an award-winning author? Could you include the title of her most famous book? Does she teach for a well-known writers' program?
- Once someone has complied with your request, you may use the whole statement or fragment from the quote. If you omit words, use ellipses to indicate the omission. If you substitute, say, a noun for a pronoun, or add a word to help understanding, put it in those little squared-off [] parentheses to indicate that those precise words were not part of the original quote.
- Send thank-you notes. Send copies of your newly-minted book when it is released.

Put your blurbs to good use:
- Put your new endorsement on the Praise page in your media kit.
- Use them in your e-mail signature lines.
- Some make good teasers in mini biographies.

- Garnish query letters (or the footer on your printed stationery) with a suitable blurb.
- Use a blurb on your promotional postcard, just above the bookcover art.
- Use blurbs on business cards.
- Use blurbs on your signs. (Kinko's/FedEx is a good place to get posters made and laminated. Research floor- and table-standing retractable canvas banners and other display goodies at american-image.com. Some are expensive but worth it if you choose book fairs and tradeshows as one of your major promotions.)

Ask for blurbs with confidence. You can see that the author who puts blurbs to good use is doing a marketing favor for those who contributed them.

> **Hint:** Once you are an established writer, remember what it was like to be a newbie. Try to accommodate requests for blurbs when you can. Being quoted as an expert will benefit your own branding, too.

-∞-

SOUNDBITES are the little sayings that set your promotion apart from the pack. They are clever metaphors, similes, or other groups of words that someone says on TV or radio that grab attention. They appear off-the-cuff, but someone probably wrote them before they ever came out of the mouths of celebrities, newscasters, or authors.

You're a writer. You can do it. Your soundbites should be about seven seconds long or twenty to twenty-five words. With practice you can toss these memorable and clever phrases into your interviews, your titles and headlines, and your pitches.

Often soundbites that fit your needs come to you as you do more marketing. Interviewers or hosts sometimes use great ones. Jot them down. Memorize them. Use them again. One might become your motto. The best soundbites become part of your brand. Someone may have tossed off "It's the real thing" in a conversation about Coke. Soundbites are marketing gold.

-∞-

YOUR PITCHES are tools you'll probably have to rethink. You've seen characters in films about the movie business. A screenwriter sits across the desk from a big producer and pitches his screenplay. He is scared and miserable. His job is to convince this gatekeeper that his script is the best thing since baked Alaska. We shudder. We think that pitches are pushy at best, desperate and seedy at worst. In our real world, authors need to know how to make pitches that don't feel like that.

Sales are the cogs that make our capitalist society work. Pitches are what make sales. Simply put, if you have a distaste for selling, you need to get over it fast. The best way to do that is to be so passionate about your book you know you aren't selling something to someone who doesn't want it, and certainly not to someone who won't benefit from it.

Pitches come in two flavors. Let's call them the "benefits" and the "beejeebees." First we'll talk about those two categories which are as different from one another as licorice ice cream is from French vanilla bean. Then we'll talk about how to write them and then how to use each of them when addressing different audiences—the publishing industry, the media, and your prospective readers.

Two kinds of pitches must be stowed in your bag of now-and-forever PR skills. Most of us are aware that our sales pitches make audiences aware of the benefits of the product we offer—in this case our books, our expertise, or our personal entertainment value. We know how to list what readers will get from our books. Entertainment. A thrill. A little romance in their lives. Important information. The trouble is, many times those things don't seem much different from what they would get by reading any other book of the same genre. So we may need to examine the advantages of pitching consequences (what will happen if a reader doesn't read your book).

Using consequences instead of benefits is espoused by Dan Seidman in *The Death of 20th Century Selling*. As unfortunate as it may sound to you, consequences can be more powerful arguments than benefits. Our politicians know this. They use consequences against the public all the time—quite effectively.

When I owned retail stores I told my new sales associates that people shop because they want to buy something. I was surprised that I had to give them this lecture, but past experience told me it was necessary. "Shopping makes them happy," I'd say. "When we shop, our friends may ask, 'How did you do?' They know you 'did well' if you found something to buy. If the shopper didn't find something she loves, she is disappointed. Her shopping companion is disappointed. And the sales associate who was trying to help her is disappointed, too."

We almost always sold the benefits of a product but sometimes consequences were implicit. As an example, when people bought gifts for their bosses, they were often reluctant to buy less prestigious brands.

It is no different when customers are thumbing through the books at a bookstore; your book's cover is a silent sales associate. Of course, if you happen to be a presenter or are signing at an event, you shouldn't be at all silent. Your pitch must jump from print to the spoken word. You will become a walking, talking pitch from what you say, to how you say it.

Seidman's book gives readers detailed instruction on how to turn benefits around to scare the beejeebees out of prospective readers and tell them the horrors that will befall them if they don't buy your book. You already hold *The Frugal Book Promoter* in your hands but, if I were trying to sell you using consequences, I would tell you:

- One-third of all books published traditionally each year get returned to publishers. Those publishers ship them off to be used on remainder (discounted) tables. When they're returned a second time, they're often shredded.
- If you don't promote yourself and your book early, the same thing (or something like it) could happen to your book.

- And that the best place to learn to promote yourself is with this book because it gives you marketing basics and ideas straight from someone who has used them herself.

The first two are "beejeebees bullets." The third bullet gives a benefit. You can see how they may be used in conjunction with one another for greater effectiveness and to soften the beejeebees part.

Paul Hartunian, the author of *How To Find the Love of Your Life in 90 Days or Less*, used a twist on the consequence approach in one of his media releases. He used a short list of "Don'ts" and included: "The worst place to go on a first date—go here and you'll probably never get a second date." He tormented the editors by not giving them the answer to the question he posed in his query letters. The recipient of such a release is not only curious but also aware that his audience will be, too. It's a sure bet that Hartunian's release was effective.

Though it is easier for writers of nonfiction to use consequences, fiction writers should try to use them, too. In 2002, I might have told prospective readers that their enjoyment of the Olympics would be severely impaired if they didn't read *This Is the Place* so they would understand the history and culture of the city in which the games were set or why they would have difficulty getting a Rum Bacardi with their dinner in that state.

> **Hint:** Select benefit, consequence, or both when they fit the occasion, not when they feel forced.

Crafting a pitch may be easier if you reread your book to find possibilities for pitches within it. As you read:

- Identify the aspects of your book that will most interest a reader in a given market or at a given time.
- Write them down.
- Turn these features into statements that show how readers or audiences will benefit.
- Here's an example of one I might use for this book: "*The Frugal Book Promoter* is a super coach for your book's marketing campaign." On the back cover of my book *Your Blog, Your Business: A retailer's guide to garnering customer loyalty and sales online and in-store* (budurl.com/Blogging4Retailers), I tease future readers with practical ways to:
  - Build a blog in five easy steps.
  - Minimize the time it takes to run a blog.
  - Find material to blog about.
  - Integrate your blog with other social networks.
  - Manage a blog frugally or free.

- A frequently-used fiction example is: "This book keeps readers turning pages late into the night." I'm sure you can do better than this because you have the details of your plot stowed in your head. Working with and learning from the screenwriters' loglines we discuss later in this chapter will help you with this project.

You *can* find possibilities in your book of fiction. My first novel, *This Is the Place*, is one of the most difficult genres to promote. I thought of it as a literary novel but found that it also fit into little bitty categories: a little bit historical, a little bit saga, a little bit romance, a little bit feminist, a little bit women's, a little bit western. I also found that, by virtue of my age, there were lots of aspects of my past life and former careers that interested editors and could be worked into pitches for feature articles.

To avoid missing the obvious pitch for your book, set up a brainstorming session with three or more who have read it. Assure them no idea is too silly. No idea will be booed. Nothing is to be repressed. You may be surprised at how many angles come from such a group effort.

Because we are so immersed in our own writing we don't see it clearly, writing a pitch for someone else's book is easier than writing one for our own. Practice writing pitches for books you've read and movies you've seen.

Once you have an idea for a pitch, add a little cayenne.
- Boil down your plot or nonfiction premise into three sentences or less.
- Maintain the passion you feel for your story.
- Use present tense. "Is" instead of "was."
- Use punchy, specific verbs. "Lobs" instead of "throws."
- Avoid adjectives and adverbs. (If your verbs are strong enough, you probably won't need them!) Find more on getting rid of unhelpful adverbs and adjectives (and turning them into metaphorical gold!) when you read my *The Frugal Editor* (budurl.com/TheFrugalEditor).

103

To learn more about writing pitches in all its forms, take a lesson from screenwriters:

- Join a screenwriters' forum. Throw out the topic of loglines (very short, catchy plot synopses) and watch members of the group go to town. Offer up one of your own and let them tear it apart and rebuild a thing of beauty. Search for these groups at YahooGroups.com and GoogleGroups.com. With any such group it is only right for you to contribute as well as learn from others.
- Study Jonathan Treisman's article at writersstore.com/article.php?articles_id=231. He is President of Flatiron Films and produced Warner Brothers' film *Pay It Forward*.

> **Hint:** The screenwriter's craft is a fertile ground for learning both marketing and writing skills that may be adapted to any kind of writing, from poetry to science fiction.

Now you have a picture-perfect pitch or two, find a place for one or more of them:

- In your media releases.
- In your fliers.
- On your business cards and other stationery.
- On your posters—the ones you use for events like fairs and book signings.
- In taglines and credits.
- In your e-mail signature.
- On the back cover of your book.
- In your advertisements.

Stockpile your pitches in a special file in your computer so you can pick, choose, and perfect them as needed.

Now you can write pitches, let's put them to work. Pitch an agent or publisher. Pitch the media. Pitch that all-important group we call readers.

Note: Your pitches to the media are indirect pitches to your readers. Their audiences will be the folks who read your book.

Pitching the publishing industry is like offering a taste of perfectly chilled spring water to the publisher or agent most suited to selling your book. You proffer your book's essence so that whoever drinks of it is sure to want more.

When authors offer their book, they generally don't use the term "pitch." They say "shopping a book." Many are averse to the term "sales." In reality, they are pitching, and their efforts will be more effective if they admit they are . . . mmmm . . . selling.

Even if authors don't know or won't confess to what they are doing, most already have experience as pitch writers. That's because they have been writing query letters, a basic skill we discuss in Chapter Fourteen. Some of you have already used pitches to get an agent, to get published, to get reviews. You may have embedded pitches into media releases and book proposals.

A book proposal is, in fact, a very long pitch. Some fiction writers need to know how to write them but proposal writing is essential for writers of nonfiction. Learn more about when to write a proposal and how to write one with my booklet *The Great First Impression*

Book Proposal: Everything you need to know to sell your book in 20 minutes or less (budurl.com/BookProposals).

Pitching your readers is like sending them a love letter. It may be commercially packaged, but it must be delivered with passion for your book and the needs of your reader.

Early on you pitch readers in writing; later you'll pitch both friends and strangers verbally. In an elevator or a restaurant, at a book signing, and when you're being interviewed by an editor or radio or TV host.

When a reader (anyone really) says, "What is your book about?" you need to tell her quickly (in the time it takes her to get to her floor in an elevator) why she will benefit from reading your book or give her a synopsis of your fiction that will make her want to read it.

When you see a tease like this on a movie poster, they call it a logline but it's also a mini pitch. It goes something like this: "When . . . (fill in the blanks here), then . . . (fill in the blanks here)." Here's an example:

> "When an earthquake rocks Carrie's world, she faces the consequences with a pickax, stored water, and the talents of her two young sons."

Notice that a good pitch or logline for fiction focuses on conflict just as all great fiction does. Nonfiction authors can find conflict in their books, too.

Pitching the media requires courage. And knowledge. It helps to know that the likes of journalists, hosts, and bloggers need you as much as you need them. Without content (that's where you come in!) they have no reviews, no stories, no interviews.

Think of yourself as building relationships when you approach the media. You present yourself as someone who can help them do their job. You present your book or expertise as something that will interest their audience. To do that, your pitch might include:

- Information that is brand new to a gatekeeper's audience.
- Something that will solve a problem for him or for his audience.
- Something that will entertain his audience.
- Something that will involve the audience emotionally (a human interest story).
- An idea how he might use your message or skills in a regular feature that appears in his magazine or an idea for an article for his blog.

The time or space you have to catch a prospect's attention is limited. The journalist/editor/host/producer needs to know what you can offer that will make his job easier. In the sample Tip Sheet I give you in the Appendix of this book are twelve publicity "No-Nos," one of which tells you that editors you are pitching do not exist to give you free publicity because you want or need it. They are on deadlines and overworked. It is your job to make this editor's job really, really, *really* easy for him. Make it clear that you are there to help and that you have all your ducks quacking in unison.

Start your pitch quickly. Make the media person aware of a problem that you can solve for him, then—just as rapidly—outline how information about you or your book is the solution to that problem. He won't want your life's story or a synopsis of your book until he's convinced that he *needs* you.

Here are some ways *you*—not necessarily your book— might be interesting to the media gatekeepers:

- Hometown reporters want to know they have a published author living in their town.
- Journals for seniors are interested if you are over fifty-five, but almost all publications will be interested if you are very young.
- Perhaps you've changed careers midstream. That might interest editors of newspaper business sections or business magazines.
- You might have a women's or men's angle that will work for gender-related periodicals.
- You are a vegetarian or practice yoga and that affects your creative process.
- You can be controversial. Some say there is no such thing as bad publicity. The exposure and sales of Richard Clarke's book, *Against All Enemies*: *Inside America's War on Terror* was helped considerably by controversy *and* its well-timed release.

Here's how your *book* might fill a reporter's need:

- Some editors like the idea that a novel is set in their locale.
- Are there any premises or themes in your fiction that shed light on what is happening in the news? A book that exposes the corrosive nature of intolerance after 9/11, as an example.

- Is there a literary interest? You might have written in a cross-genre or experimented in some other way. If your concept is unusual enough, that will be news for periodicals marketed to authors.
- Is there a strong similarity in your work to a film or book that everyone is talking about? Sometimes reporters tie one book to another, and some reviewers pack reviews of two or more similar books into one commentary.

When we are squeamish about meeting the media face-to-face or by phone, we often rely on mail, e-mail, and faxes. We shouldn't. In-person contacts bring a caring attitude to your association with editors. Aesop said, "Do you, while receiving benefits from me and resting under my shade, dare to describe me as useless and unprofitable?" He knew that those with whom you've built a relationship are more likely to do you a favor and more reluctant to be negative about you to others.

> **Hint:** Scripting a pitch can help. In fact, when you make contact by phone, you can use your script as crib notes to guide the conversation. Well-known publicist and author Raleigh Pinskey graciously allowed me to use her scripted pitch in Appendix Five of this book. I encourage you to learn from her example.

Why do publishers put the pictures of authors on the flaps of dustcovers? Because human beings relate to faces. Although editors try to be impartial, they are human; they relate best on a one-to-one basis just like readers or anyone else. You will have more success if you get to know your media contacts at close range. When that's impossible, include your photograph in your media kit or add a link to a video of you on the Web or, second best, a podcast of your voice.

If this feels scary to you, make your first contact a fact-finding mission so the editor is aware you want to make her job easier. You might even arrange to see her in her office. Let's pretend you're working on your first, big event—your book launch. This contact will require your short pitch to be as close to letter perfect as you can make it. It will include one or two sentences about your book and then a sentence about the launch you are planning. Then ask her questions like these:

- "How can I help with pre-event coverage?" Word this so that the benefits of covering your event before it occurs rather than after are visible to her.
- "May I give you photos to accompany your stories or would you prefer to have your photographers cover them?" I wrote to ask for a copy of a picture the head photographer of my local paper had taken of me, complimented her on it, and copied that praise to her superior. All sincere. They didn't charge me for a copy of the photo.
- "How are photos best submitted? Electronically? By mailing slick copies? Color or black or white?"
- "Would you be interested in learning about (you fill in the blank about one of the remarkable people associated with your launch) as the subject of a feature article?" In case she shows an interest, be prepared with specifics about your story idea. When an editor uses your idea, she usually mentions you and your event.

- "I would love to have you attend as an honored guest. May I send you a map? A parking pass?" If the editor accepts, formally introduce her to the audience during your presentation.

> **Caveat:** Match the editor to the kind of coverage you're seeking. Study the newspaper's roster to learn what each editor covers. Call TV and radio stations and ask the receptionist to direct you to editors interested in different kinds of stories. Check Web sites. Pronounce names correctly. You may want to contact more than one editor for a given event. Here are some possibilities for newspaper editors who specialize:
> - Calendar Editor.
> - Feature Editor.
> - Weekend Editor.
> - Book Review Editor.
> - Assignment Editor (usually TV).
> - City Editor.
> - Beat Reporters. (These can range from business to arts and entertainment.)

When you work with the media, you may need more than one pitch. You'll need one for what your book is about. That can be wrapped in a pitch about how your story can benefit a specific audience. And you'll need a pitch about *you*!

-∞-

YOUR PHOTO is another element of your marketing campaign that gets used so often it defines your brand (who you are as a writer). Because it is so ubiquitous, it is important you get it right.

The photo that most authors get wrong is the headshot or what the trade calls a "glossy," a term left over from the days when pictures were printed on shiny black and white Kodak stock. Today they can be transmitted digitally. Your headshot appears on the dustcover, cover, or last page of your book. It appears on your Web site, your blog, your business card, and your media kit. It gets sent to about anyone in the media you work with. You need not be picture-perfect, but your glossy must be.

"The best" is *not* the studio photographer in town who does prom portraits—no matter how expensive and artistic he is. It is not your Aunt Minnie who just took a photography class and needs a confidence boost. "The best" for your book and your marketing campaign is a photographer skilled in taking photos for models' and actors' portfolios and casting Web sites. He captures not only your features, but also your personality. He understands lighting and has the proper equipment to achieve it. He knows where your eyes should be focused, how your head should be tilted. Though it is hard for the novice to tell exactly why, the finished photo tells the whole world it was done by a professional

I used John Gibson (gibsonphotopro.com), photographer to the stars. He captured something that no photographer ever had, even when I was younger and had fewer flaws to conceal. John's in Hollywood, but you can find the best available in your nearest metropolitan area. Discuss with him your branding goals, something about your book, and where your photo will be used.

After John took shots of me, some with my Great Dane, he provided glossies and permission to have my choices reproduced by editors who choose to use it. He also supplied .jpg files of these photos. If you're not techie, don't even ask what a "jpg" is—just know that pictures coded this way are the ones most editors want or need. I keep mine in my computer's "My Pictures" file to send electronically to editors and others.

Order five-by-seven color prints from a commercial graphics company that can put your full name or *nom de plume* in the white margin beneath the image. Order only a few more of them than the number of media kits you plan to send out via post.

-∞-

CROSS-PROMOTION helps authors reach more people in less time. Unfortunately, authors seem to be as confused as Hamlet: Ahh, to cross promote or not to cross promote, that is the question. If we reword this so it becomes "to share or not to share" we can see the folly in questioning its usefulness.

Sharing resources, contributing time and skills to a common cause, and sharing information can only help authors do what they need to do for the welfare of their careers and books. This is not a competition. We are all in this together.

Cross promotion can even work for your book launch. We think of launches as a time to shine on our own, but what would happen if you asked another author to read from his work at your launch? That someone would invite his readers to your party. They might become your readers. Your guests would be introduced to your partner. You both sell books. You both increase the size of your contact lists. You provide your guests with an even more festive event. Your spotlight doesn't fade because it is trained on your cross-promotion partner for ten minutes.

Because you've been promoting you know other authors. The benefits of sharing projects are:

- Sharing allows you to participate when costs would otherwise be prohibitive.
- The support offered by others will give you confidence to try new things.
- Cross promotion can result in better trafficked events because authors share their contact lists.
- When cross promotion draws crowds to these public events, that cluster of interested people attracts even bigger crowds.

> **Caveat:** Do not assume authors who write in your genre are competition. Authors who write cozy mysteries may be ideal cross-promotion partners for you if your book is a cozy mystery, because fans of cozy mysteries probably read many more than one book in that category each year. It is more reasonable to be concerned (and selective!) when it comes to your partner's reliability in terms of shared costs and shared promotional efforts.

Magdalena Ball and I have a special collaborative and cross-promotional effort going. Our Celebration Series of chapbooks (howtodoitfrugally.com/poetry_books.htm) started when we both decided to contribute to a chapbook of poetry for Mother's Day. She's an Aussie, I'm from Los Angeles. Improbable, I know. But there we were sharing skills: She publishes the e-books and paperbacks; I supply resources for covers and editing skills. She writes half the poems and I write the other half. We critique one another's work. She found us an online florist to sell our Valentine chapbook *Cherished Pulse* as an add-on to the traditional bouquet. I got some of our individual poems published on the Web with credits and links to our Amazon sales page (budurl.com/CherishedPulse). You get the idea.

Here are a few other times cross promotion works especially well for you:

- Book signings.
- Workshops and teaching gigs. University program directors may judge your effectiveness in part on the visiting lecturer you invite to address your students.
- Book fair booths.
- Anthologies and other writing projects.
- Blogs and your newsletter. When you extend the planks of your platform to others, they tell others about your services.
- Partnering at tradeshows (like Book Expo America, bookexpoamerica.com) and writers' conferences. One person can't be at every seminar or cover every booth on a tradeshow floor. Your partner pitches your book over dinner. You talk up hers. You share notes, ideas, maybe even hotel room expenses.

–∞–

TUNING IN is how we know what's going on the world so that when something comes up that cries out for our expertise, we can be there! In a flash!

Tuning in is how you know where your book fits into the daily grind of news, what editors or hosts will be interested in it, and when the time is right. Spam is not the danger; censorship is. A good publicist knows that if she has a dearth of information, she and her clients will wither and die. It is your job to be a good publicist, or at least a great partner for her.

If you are lucky enough to be assigned a great publicist, she will need (want!) your help. She knows that you know your book better than anyone. She hopes you will voraciously read everything that comes your way, analyze it, and apply that new knowledge to your publicity campaign.

When I was studying at the University of Southern California (USC), the head of the public relations department insisted on teaching all the beginning PR classes. He wanted to lobby the best and brightest students to major in public relations, students like Steelers' pro-bowl star Lynn Swan who was then a USC shining light and a student in my class. Our professor's example showed us how being involved with the universe is crucial for success.

Each day Mr. PR gave us a quiz on the entire contents of the *LA Times*. He would cut me no slack and let me avoid the sports section. Years later when I had retail shops I was still no sports fan, but the habit he enforced helped me put our stores ahead of our competitors by timing our shipments of great-selling Christmas ornaments emblazoned with the colors and logos of our Lakers, Dodgers, and Pac10 winning teams.

Use a search engine to find e-groups and chat rooms to discuss writing and book promotion. Use alert services like Google Alerts to learn what your competition is doing—not to sabotage them but as resources.

Subscribe to e-zines (online magazines and newsletters). You don't even have to tear open an envelope to learn from them. Submit releases and articles to them, too.

> **Hint:** Include a short thank you in your subscription request. In the world of public relations, blank e-mails to individuals aren't acceptable.

Here are some newsletter starters:

- Radio expert Fran Silverman's *Book Promotion* newsletter is both a place to learn and a place to brag about your successes. Subscribe at bookpromotionnewsletter.com.
- Marketing sage John Kremer puts out *Book Marketing Tip of the Week*. Send an e-mail to JohnKremer@bookmarket.com to subscribe.
- Publishing expert Dan Poynter's newsletter: parapublishing.com/sites/para/resources/newsletter.cfm.
- My *Sharing with Writers* newsletter is loaded with writers' resources. Subscribers may submit articles, writing tips, and announcements of successes, along with their book's title and sales link. Send an e-mail with SUBSCRIBE in the subject line to HoJoNews@aol.com.

When you put your tuned-in antennae on, you become aware that even unlikely messages lead to new contacts, new promotion opportunities.

-∞-

THANK-YOU NOTES are not duties but gifts. Throw in notes of congratulations, sympathy, and those others your mother made you write, and you have an important component of your book's marketing campaign. Carolyn See, author of *Making a Literary Life*, suggests writing thank-you notes and one "generous, lovely letter a day."

Notes create goodwill. Goodwill creates opportunity. Use your writing skill to make the recipient feel valued rather than a cursory note like the ones you tried to get away with when you were in the third grade.

Here are ways to let gratitude boost your promotion efforts and leave a little happiness in your wake:

- Write a sincere thank you after every promotion you do. The list of promotions is as long as this book: When your book is reviewed, online or in print. When you are interviewed. When you are mentioned or quoted in a newsletter or article.

    Hint: Your most memorable note may be the one you send to a reviewer who was critical of your book. One of my least favorite reviews was written by Rebecca Brown at RebeccasReads.com. I told her—sincerely—that I learned much from her critique and soon my essays and rants appeared regularly on her site.

- Collect the addresses of these people in a special contact file. It's your Top Fifty (or Top Hundred) list. Stay in touch with them. Send them postcards when you travel, cards during the holidays—communications both personal and book-related.
- Follow up. Send an e-mail to see how that person is doing when it's appropriate. Friend them on Facebook.

Closely aligned with thank yous are other niceties like asking editors if this is a convenient time to talk, offering collateral material to make their job easier, including alternate contact information, and anything else that brands you as caring.

Hint #1: A snapshot taken at an event that includes poses of the person you're thanking is a thoughtful addition to your note. Something too costly may smack of bribery.

Hint #2: Send congratulatory notes when media friends receive awards, redesign their Web pages, write a great feature story, or are assigned a new column.

Personal notes build relationships. When we have relationships, we don't have to *sell* ourselves or our books. Friends want to be there for their friends.

SECTION III
Do-It-Yourself and Partner Publicity

A good contractor builds a home with a strong foundation and sturdy studs. They support his vision no matter what else he takes on. ~ CHJ

You want to boot your book up to the bestseller lists and keep it there. You want to earn back your advance and draw down even more in royalties. You can't count on your publisher. Publishers must focus on their next big profit maker when the sales of your book dwindles. Besides, no one knows your book as well as you do. No one can be the passionate advocate for it that you can.

When it comes to marketing, your book advance only goes so far. And you'd like to keep some of it. You need a budget. If you've hired a publicist, your schedule will limit the time you can spend with her, and your budget will limit the time you can afford to have her spend on your book. The answer is forging a money- and time-saving partnership. Or going the do-it-yourself route. You can see it is smart to learn to do for yourself what you can do better than anyone else, anyway.

This will be easy for you. You *are* a writer. Lots of publicity *is* writing. This section is where you learn the skills you need to advance your entire writing career.

Chapter Eleven

Media Kit Preparation Now

An author's media kit is a tool box for any editor or producer who opens it. It should provide any gizmo they need to get a story out fast and easy.
~ CHJ

A well designed media kit assures your contact that you are qualified. It is a resource and a sales tool that makes it easy for a gatekeeper to write the news, review your book, conduct an interview, or write a feature story. Today's editors have more responsibility than they ever had. It is only natural that they favor news that is supported so well it nearly writes itself. Your kit serves you in many ways. Mostly it lets you be the go-to resource for gatekeepers who can make a difference for your writing career.

We'll build the skeleton of your media kit so you can begin to construct it right now. As you add tendons and muscles to your credentials, you'll have a place to store the information so you don't forget it and don't have to build the whole kit from scratch. This structure will then require only a little grooming before your publicity campaign starts in earnest. Having the bones in place early on helps you visualize the progress of your career and helps you select the promotions that best suit your needs.

Make a new major folder in your computer titled MEDIA KIT GENERAL. In caps. It will contain subfolders labeled in lower case for different sections in the kit. The word "general" lets you identify it later when you have several kits focused on different aspects of your career.

We'll talk about those subfolders for each section of your kit later in this chapter. Right now you need to know that "immediacy" is a keyword. Whenever you have new information for your kit, drop it into the proper subfolder. You can format and edit as you go or just throw stuff in as it comes to you. Your mess quotient is not a consideration. What we're working on is the Prior-Planning-Prevents-Poor-Performance issue.

-∞-

YOUR CONTACT LIST is not part of your media kit, but without it your kit is nearly useless. Contact lists are essential to almost all your book promotion. In fact, your contact list is not one list. It's many. The idea is to send your query, media release, or kit only to those who might benefit from the information you are disseminating.

There are three ways to build your list. Buy a list, assemble a list from online and library resources, and build your own list as you personally come in contact with folks—everyone from readers to editors to new media outlets. Of course, you can always combine these methods, but the list you build yourself will reap the most rewards—by far.

We'll work on your media list first. A good portion of it should be focused on media you know well. The better you know a medium, the better you'll understand how to pitch ideas to them.

So, you are on the lookout for media when you're out and about. You run across a newspaper, a magazine, or even a throwaway (remember what we said about finding important information where we least expect it?). You put your thinking bonnet on. "Aha!" you say. "This little community weekly may be interested in my story because it's just for women . . . or about men's health issues . . . or about natural food." The roster that lists editors and other contact information is usually on page two. Enter that information into your contact data base as soon as you can.

You get those separate lists by assigning codes to your entries. My codes include NAT for national, LOC for local, LIB for libraries, BKST for bookstores, CAT for catalogs, and several other codes that work for the kinds of books I write including WRT for media with an audience of writers. I also make notes that will help me address an editor in a more personal way. The note might give me the name of a humor column or section of the newspaper that would be an especially suitable target for the topic of my book.

A properly coded list lets you use your filter function and e-mail-merge function to target your kit, invitation, or media release to editors who might have an interest in the information you are sending out or to readers interested in the different genres you write in. (Stay tuned. How to write a media release—which is the new term for press release—is coming up!)

> **Hint:** New authors may have trouble accepting the idea that information they disseminate won't always be about their books. That's part of the tuning-in process we discussed in Chapter Ten.

When editors get information that fits their needs, you build credibility. When you send what appears to them to be unrelated to their audience, you lose it. Editors open mail they are certain will benefit them.

The tuning-in process works when you're watching TV, listening to radio, or whatever. Make notes. Google that medium as soon as you can, and keep building that database.

There are 350 million magazines published in the U. S. each year. Some of them are bound to be interested in what you write. You can find newspapers—dailies and weeklies as well as TV and radio stations—at newslink.org and usnpl.com.

One of my favorite resources is *Bacon's Directories*. Find them online and in your library. When I am promoting at an out-of-town venue, I use it to find resources that may help me get publicity for the event.

Let's talk about your personal or general contact list, (think "reader" when you see these terms). Your contact-list thinking cap should be on at all times. Your goal is not to lose anyone. When I forget to make an entry, I'm sure to regret it later.

126

You want the names, e-mails, and addresses of anyone you meet who might be interested in your book or your expertise. Don't overlook your holiday card list, lists from club rosters, social groups, and your mother's bridge club list. You'll use them for your book launch and forever after.

Chapter Twelve

The Media Release

A compelling media release is like a good quarterback; even if he can make a perfect pass, he needs his team to be consistently effective.
~ CHJ

Now you have a media list, you need a media release. A media release is often effective all by itself, but when you want to supply the kind of support that makes it hard for gatekeepers to ignore your story, your release needs backup. That's when the release becomes part—albeit one of the most important parts—of your media kit.

To clarify, press releases *are* media releases. We wouldn't want to offend those TV producers, radio hosts, or online folks by using a term that neglects their existence, now would we!

Media releases come in all shapes, sizes, and formats but you still need to be familiar with what is accepted or expected by the gatekeepers. You can drive yourself crazy finding and imitating different media release formats, but the step-by-step instructions I give you in this chapter are basic, generally accepted, and will save you time and keep a headache at bay.

-∞-

BUILDING YOUR MEDIA RELEASE is easy if you do it one step at a time. Writing a media release is less like manipulating a Rubric cube and more like putting together a puzzle—the kind of puzzle with big, easy pieces that you could do when you were three.

If your release is assembled before you actually need it or before a publicist's fee-clock starts ticking, you'll save a lot of money and time. Start now. Leave blanks where you don't have the information you need. Save it in a special MEDIA RELEASE folder in your computer.

When we put a puzzle together we spread out the parts on a tabletop. I'm providing the parts for assembling your release below. Before you read it, find the sample release in the Appendix of this book. Like the cover of a puzzle's box, an example serves as a visual aid for the work you're doing.

Here are ten puzzle parts to fit together for a basic news-style release that won't appear unprofessional because you don't know the rules or because you're trying too hard.

Puzzle Piece One: The header consists of five lines below your stationery's letterhead.
- The first line says
  MEDIA RELEASE.
  Use caps, large type, boldface, 18 point Arial typeface with a space between each letter and three spaces between the words. Justify it on the left of your page.

- Double space. Enter **CONTACT:** in 12 point, Arial caps, left justified. If you hire a publicist, this is her contact information; use your own if you send the release yourself. Include a name, phone, fax, and e-mail address, each on its own line. Revert back to upper and lower case for the details. Include all this information even if it is in your letterhead.

> **Warning:** Authors often hear that they should rig their do-it-yourself media kits and releases to appear as if they are being sent from a professional publicist's office. I hope you won't be tempted to do that. Of course, you'll want your publicity material to look absolutely professional, but any pretense beyond that will only make you look foolish when you're found out once an editor begins to work with you. See Chapter Four on ethics.

Puzzle Piece Two: Release information goes one space beneath the contact information. Type in **For Immediate Release** in 12 point bold **Times New Roman**, left justified. Change this to a specific date only if there is a very good reason for doing so. Both available space and timeliness is an issue for editors. Don't limit them with a specific date unless you must. In that case this line would read: **For Release After Month/Day/Year**.

Puzzle Piece Three: Your headline is centered in sixteen point **Arial** bold. Your headline should seize an editor or producer's attention so she doesn't scrunch the release into a ball and toss it. Feature the most newsworthy (original, unique, or charity-driven) element of your release for your headline. Study newspaper headlines. Use active, strong verbs. Omit as many little words like "a," "the," "and," "but," and other articles and conjunctions as possible.

Puzzle Piece Four: Your dateline can be omitted if it seems irrelevant, but most print media appreciate it. It is simply the place—*not* the date—of the city from which the news originates. Usually that is where your office is located. These days some are using World Wide Web as a dateline.

Puzzle Piece Five: The lead is simple and brief. It is the first sentence in the body of your release. State who, how, where, when, and what. You will later learn how to make this line more appealing to editors, but until that can be mastered, a straightforward, old-fashioned journalist's lead is better than one that screams inexperience. Check to be sure that the "when" includes the date, not just the day of the week. Here's an example:

> "*Shades of Iris,* a novel by Marlena Reingold, was released by Schuster Arrow Press on August 1."

A year is not necessary. By definition, media releases are recent news.

Puzzle Piece Six: The body of the release follows, single spaced.
- Leave a space between paragraphs.
- Do not indent paragraphs.
- Mention the single most newsworthy aspect of your event in the paragraph after the lead.

- The next paragraph lists the author's most important credentials, including the author's hometown if the release is being sent to the local press.

Puzzle Piece Seven: Your logline or pitch for your book comes next. You may have already written your first pitch. It's that mini synopsis of your book meant to snare an editor's attention that was explained earlier in Chapter Ten. Something like, "Just as Sky Eccles is about to make the biggest mistake of her life, she returns to her family's farm and the example set by her feisty red-haired grandmother."

Puzzle Piece Eight: A paragraph about you comes next. It may be the mini biography we talked about in Chapter Ten. "Reingold has been writing ad copy and promotional pieces since she started her own party-planning business in 1988. . . ."

Don't worry if you don't have much writing-oriented information to include here. Use professional information that relates to your book or leave it blank. By the time you've finished reading this book, you'll be an expert on how to build your credentials.

- Do not include your hobbies unless they have something to do with the subject of the book.
- Use this paragraph in every release you write. We want to use our time frugally, too!
- Update this paragraph for subsequent releases as your credentials build. Eliminate the older or less impressive ones or those that don't support the information you are presenting in the release as well as the new ones you've accrued.

Puzzle Piece Nine: Your close is easy.

- Key in a line where gatekeepers can find more information: "This Is the Place is available in bookstores or online at budurl.com/ThisIsthePlace."
- On another line type, "Learn more at: www.xxx.com." Use your Web site address, the site you use as a sales tool for both readers and the press.
- Leave a space and type in and center three pound signs, "###" to signify the end of the release.

Puzzle Piece Ten: Mention your media kit, photos, and other support material.

- This is not part of the body of your release, so center it in eight-point bold, Times New Roman. Type "A media kit and photos are available on request." on a line of its own. Adapt this line to the situation. You may only need "Support materials available on request."

Puzzle Piece Eleven: Save what you have done as a sample or template for your media kit. That way you don't have to write every release from scratch.

Tweak this format each time you send out a new release. I save and categorize my releases in special folders with titles like Book Signings, Teaching, and Library Appearances. They serve as a record of my promotional activities. When your distributor, agent, or publisher asks for this information, you have it nearly ready to go except for an edit.

-∞-

WRITING RELEASES is part editing and part using the creative part of your brain.

Let's tackle the polishing and editing first. Here are techniques to make your media release professional:

- Your release should be one page or less. (Don't cheat by using a smaller typeface.)
- Give the media what they need to complete their jobs. If you are sending out a release to a host who uses several guests on a panel, include other resources or other authors who could give opposing views or flesh out the topic you are proposing. Include their contact information. To decide what resources editors might need, put yourself in their shoes.
- Verify the accuracy of the contact information you provide. Include as much information as you can and still maintain security. Incorrect information obviously renders a release useless.
- Introduce your release with the most powerful headline you can come up with such as "Sex Disappears from America's Bedrooms." Use large, bold type face.
- The subject line of your e-mail should not be vague or misleading. Remember the ad, "It isn't nice to fool Mother Nature?" In their own realm, editors are as powerful as Mother Nature. You don't want to tick them off. Your subject line reads, "Media Release," followed by a colon and punchy headline. Don't use anything intentionally vague or anything that might be interpreted as spam, like "Hello," "From a friend," or "Important information."

Example: Walter Brasch, a journalism professor and author of several books on politics, sent a release with this subject line: **NEWS: Brasch Allowed Out in Public Again.** Believe me, as editor of the *Sharing with Writers* newsletter I opened that e-mailed release to see what he was up to.

Hint: I sent out a release on a book fair booth I was coordinating. My response rate doubled compared to many similar releases I had sent out because I lead the release with a personal note suggesting that editors feel free to edit, cut, or otherwise utilize the release any way they wanted (many online newsletter editors don't have journalism backgrounds and seem to think releases must be used in the form sent to them). I also told them I had free articles on book fairs available for their use if they would prefer.

- Edit. Remove all the high-falutin' adjectives. In media releases, "Awesome" and "magnificent" are four-letter words. Your book is not "superb" until it has won the Pulitzer (Pulitzer.org), and even then you show how "superb" it is with facts or quotes from credible sources.
- If it's appropriate, bullet your information. Bullets leave lots of white space and that lets your recipients glean what they need easily.
- Include a link for a YouTube video or trailer featuring you or your book. (See Chapter Nineteen on New and Old Radio and TV or check this book's Index under "videos.")

- Punch up the headline with active verbs. Use image-laden nouns when you can. Rather than "cookies," use "marzipan." Rather than "bike," use "Schwinn."

  Example: "Local Woman Writes Book," is humdrum. How about "Mystery Writer Stages Murder on Will Rogers Beach."

- No opinions allowed unless you have a blurb (endorsement) from an expert who might convince an editor of your stature. If you do, by all means slice it into the release format.

  Example: "Dale Barton, President of Armand, Busch and Co., says, "This is the year's definitive book on world demographics."

- If someone is available to proofread your release for typos, use that second pair of eyes. Microsoft Word's spell and grammar checker is helpful, not perfect. Everyone must edit themselves—at least on occasion. Usually things like query letters, and media releases. For help with that and lots more, read *The Frugal Editor*, second in this HowToDoItFrugally series of books for writers (budurl.com/TheFrugalEditor).

- For dozens of sample media releases covering everything from book launches to winning contests, go to my site (howtodoitfrugally.com) and click on the Media Room rectangle at the top of the page. From there you'll find a Recent Releases link.

Dolling up a release is like writing in general; you need to know the basics so you'll know when to break the rules and when you've gone too far. Most releases don't lend themselves to mascara and lipstick.

There is nothing wrong with keeping a media release simple. However, if the subject matter calls for a more enticing lead than the usual how, where, when, and why lead used by journalists, here are a couple of approaches that might work. If your generic release reads:

> "Palm Springs—Peter Morton, CEO of Tyr Publishing, Los Angeles, signed a contract for *Christmas Cookies Are for Giving* with longtime Palm Springs resident, Kristin J. Johnson. This book, a combination of cookbook and book of inspiration, will be released in August of this year."

That *Christmas Cookies* is a combination cookbook and book of inspiration is the most interesting part of this lead. That's what makes this news—not that it's a book that's just been released. So, this might be better:

> "Palm Springs—A concept especially suited to a Christmas release is Kristin J. Johnson's *Christmas Cookies Are for Giving*, a combination of inspirational essays and recipes that will have you licking the mixing bowl. It will be released by Tyr Publishing in August in plenty of time for people to put it on their gift lists for sweet tooths and those who love to bake."

You could skip poor old Peter the Publisher altogether unless he is local, too, or you could work him into a later paragraph.

To tackle something more daring and probably more effective, write a lead that points out the benefits of your book or warns of the dangers inherent in ignoring it. We discussed benefits and consequences in Chapter Ten under "Your Pitches." Here's an example of a lead that uses a little scare along with a bit of benefit.

> Carolyn Howard-Johnson, author of the multi award-winning HowToDoItFrugally series of books, spent the first four years of her career stepping into dangerous publicity potholes. She shares her hard-won expertise with the release of *The Frugal Book Promoter* to help other authors avoid her booboos.

When a lead like this is used, some of the essential details need to be moved down to the next paragraph. This may misalign that puzzle you are building but you're a writer. You will figure it out.

Another variation that works well for novels, poetry, and nonfiction is the use of a memorable quote from your book, an endorsement for your book from a celebrity, or a fact that sets up the reason why your book is important. Indent it, and place it just above your lead. I chose this one for the release from my book of creative nonfiction because it reflects the book's voice and gives the reader an immediate idea of its setting:

> *My city is like a saltwater pearl, gently, gently cradled by the Wasatch Mountains. The crescent of the foothills tenderly curves around the city like the palm of a mother's hand. It is a city one cannot lose one's way in, for the range of shale and . . . ."*

Notice that I didn't use quotation marks (though I could have), but instead chose to use a very small italicized font. There is some leeway for style choice in most everything we do.

A subhead (sometimes called a deck) under the headline is another approach that lends a little spice to a release. A deck marks you as someone familiar with publicity or journalism. It appears indented in a slightly smaller size font than the body of the release. It needs nothing more to separate it from the rest of the release. It may focus on conflict or a benefit, and it can be quite a bit longer than a headline. This is an example of a short one:

> Academics are looking to the new erotic politics in a search for trends.

The word "erotic" will hook your gatekeepers, but editors are also intrigued by "trends."

-∞-

DISTRIBUTION OF YOUR RELEASE may be done several ways. It may accompany your media kit, either inside the folder or attached with a paperclip to the outside. You may mail, fax, or e-mail your release or use a combination of two or more methods.

- If you don't use your release as part of your media kit, send it first by e-mail rather than snail mail. Editors prefer e-mail because they can save time by copying and pasting. They must scan or retype something that comes by post. Have I told you before how busy editors are? You can follow up with another release—one that is slightly different—by snail mail or fax.

- To give snail-mail envelopes a more professional look, send them through the feeder on your printer rather than handwriting them.
- If you fax your release, direct it to the proper editor with a separate cover sheet. This will usually be the feature or managing editor. For radio and TV, it will be the producer (or sometimes the host) of each show.
- Use the current editor's name and spell it correctly.
- If you have a photo that will convince an editor your story is visual, send it by USPS, FedEx, or UPS along with the release and a query letter. Attach the photo with a paperclip to the query letter. Offering the image at the bottom of your e-mailed release will not be as effective.

> **Hint:** I know. I know. But this bears repeating: Don't attach your release, photo, or anything else to your e-mails. Many media outlets don't let e-mail with attachments through their servers and many editors won't open them if they do make it through.

Avoid letting your release die a slow death on a gatekeeper's desktop. Remember that relationship thing. This is your chance to build on it. Followup is as important to clinching a publicity deal as a homerun at the bottom of the ninth inning is to the World Series. After a reasonable wait, phone your contact. Ask if your editor received your release. Be prepared to pitch a new angle on the story if he tells you your first idea isn't quite right. It wouldn't hurt to guarantee exclusivity on any new idea you present to him.

Media announcements or a different version of your release might be faxed or e-mailed a few days after that.

Media *announcements* are shorter and sometimes, to the eyes of an editor, sweeter than media *releases*. They are especially useful as followups, as introductions to a planned media blitz of well-spaced releases (each touting a different angle), or to notify editors of an upcoming event.

Media announcements read like barebones invitations. They include:
- The term "Media Announcement" as a header.
- Contact information.
- A captivating headline.
- A pithy lead.
- Follow up with the place, time, date, and a resource for gleaning more information.

Media announcements are quickies. Don't put much more than what's on this list into yours.

Chapter Thirteen
The Rest of Your Media Kit

Media kits are the body and soul of your writing career. They are record keepers, confidence boosters, and organization wizards. ~ CHJ

You will save eons of time if you have all the subfolders of your media kit ready to plop information into as your writing career grows. Your additions needn't be polished. Think of them as first-draft folders. You'll reorganize, edit, and polish them when you need your media kit or its bits and pieces.

In this chapter, I give you a list of folders. The list is not engraved on sterling. With each kit you send, you may eliminate some segments or subfolders and add others.

If you are familiar with media kits, you may notice that I suggest more sections (or subfolders) than you might see in kits for other industries. The publishing industry is different from others and, because I have been on the receiving end of media kits as a staff writer for a newspaper, I know how important it is for you to both have what the editor needs in the kit *and* make it easy— v-e-r-r-r-y easy!—for editors to find what they need. Without making a phone call. Without online research. And without shuffling through too many papers. When a contents page is included, it is more likely your kit will do what it is intended to do. That is, get you free exposure. Here is a list of the subfolders you need for your kit:

- Contents page.
- About-the-Author page.
- Awards and Publications pages.
- List of Appearances.
- Praise-for-the-Author's-Work page.
- Sample Review.
- Sample Interview.
- First-Person Essay.
- List of Available Seminars.
- List of Fellow Experts.
- Tip Sheet.
- Other media kit items.

You pick and choose from among these subfolders depending on how your kit is being used. If you are sending it to a feature editor with a query about a story, you will include your tip sheet. If you are sending it with a pitch to a radio host, you might not include it.

Next, let's learn what each of these subfolders (or segments of you media kit) contain and what they do for the gatekeeper who receives your kit.

-∞-

YOUR CONTENTS PAGE is rarely seen in media kits used in other industries or even in the publishing industry. Having one, however, makes it easier for the gatekeepers who receive your kit to find what they need. And you already know how important that is!

Go to your word processor's manual and learn how to format titles and chapters. Knowing how to let Word do it for you is a skill you will use many times over the life of your writing career. Of course, if that sounds like too much work, you can do it manually.

Divide your Contents (call it "Contents," not "Table of Contents," which is redundant and unprofessional) into two parts. One part shows the gatekeeper what she will find in the left pocket of your media kit folder. The other part lists what she will find in the right. You decide the order depending on what is most important for the title of your book or the pitch you are making.

-∞-

YOUR ABOUT-THE-AUTHOR PAGE is a third-person piece about you. Call it a biography if you prefer, but it is focused on aspects of your life that pertain to your writing life. It contains information similar to what publishers use on the flyleaf of your book's dustcover or on the back cover of your book. However, it includes more information than you usually see there. It's a place where editors go to glean both personal and professional information about you and to get a feel for your voice or ideas for a story angle.

Your About-the-Author page should be written by you rather than by your publicist or publisher. If you must give them the information to write it for you, the work is being done twice. You pay for it in time when you write it. You pay them in real money when they take that information and rewrite it. Further, you know yourself better than they do. You have more passion about your life and how it relates to your book than anyone else. This is a place where you can let your voice, even some humor, come through.

Until your relevant credentials grow, you may prefer to title this page "Mini Biography" when you put it in your media kit. Later you can add a longer Author page but keep your Mini Biography as part of your kit. An editor may find it convenient to have a choice. The idea is to provide editors with the information they need and in the format that will be most helpful to them. Here are some tips:

- Set your margins at 1 ½ inches. Use a twelve point font like **Verdana** or Times New Roman, single spaced. It should be one page or less. If you don't have much information yet, widen the margins a little.
- Avoid clichés. One of the most common errors new writers make is saying that they "always" wanted to write. I made this mistake myself and cringe every time I see printed matter that used this old version of my Author page.
- Carefully select what you tell about yourself. Readers of a novel set on Wall Street would find it relevant if the author is a financial advisor. If the author's book has no relationship to the world of money, that author would highlight other achievements.

You might include a twenty-five word mini biography or quickie credit line on this page in case that's all an editor needs. The editor may use different information, but it's worth a stab to point your branding in the direction you want it to go. (See Chapter Ten for more information on writing biographies and credit lines.)

-∞-

YOUR AWARDS AND PUBLICATIONS is one of the most important pages in your kit. On slow news days, editors see words like "prize" and "award" as unset jewels. They will not care if they are semiprecious stones or the finest cut diamonds because they know either will add luster to a story.

At first—until you have a long list of awards or places your work has been published—you may include them on the same page. In some ways, a published article is an award, a kind of affirmation of the quality of your work. When your lists become longer, use two pages or prune the less influential entries.

Organize your lists of awards and publications the way you would organize them for a résumé. Place the "Awards" first on the page, "Publications" next. List your most recent achievements first because, as your career progresses, the more current ones tend to be more pertinent and prominent. Occasionally you'll have a really important award or publishing credit that should be featured. Put it first or make it stand out with special formatting.

-∞-

YOUR LIST OF APPEARANCES is designed to impress gatekeepers. Oscar Wilde's satirical nature showed when he said, "It is only shallow people who do not judge by appearances. The true mystery of the world is the visible, not the invisible." His observation is funny because it reflects the way so many of us see things.

We *are* judged by the kits we present to the media. Our Appearances page is probably right up there in importance with Awards and Publications because radio and TV producers and other gatekeepers look for authors with enough *presence* to make them proud. After all, when they invite you as a guest, their reputation is at stake. So, like it or not, you want to include this page—at least until your name is a household word.

Because this page is so important, try to find something in your background that convinces folks that you are capable of handling exposure, that you will be comfortable before a camera or mike. Here are some possibilities:

- Did you study drama in college? High school? Been in a play?
- Have you taken a Dale Carnegie course? Or joined Toastmasters? Done any modeling?
- Have you been on a debate team?
- Have you led seminars or been a panelist as part of your business experience?
- Have you been an instructor in the education or business worlds?
- Do you sing? Been a member of a choir that performed?
- Have you read an excerpt from your book at a signing?

Stellar credentials are not essential. Nor is quantity. As you can see, this page may not be a list at first, but rather a little pitch that will give gatekeepers a sense that you can present yourself well. Something like, "References on request," will do nicely as a start. It's a trick used by beginning actors on their résumés.

If you have nothing for this Appearance page, make a subfolder for it anyway. The universe has a very nice way of filling empty spaces and meeting positive demands. In the meantime, take a speech class. Now you're an author, you'll find a thousand reasons to be grateful you did.

-∞-

YOUR PRAISE AND ENDORSEMENT PAGE includes what our industry usually calls blurbs. My favorite way to accumulate these is to ask if I can use nice comments I get from readers and other associates in my e-mail. Learn other ways to get them and other uses for them by looking up "blurbs" in the Index of this book.

This blurb-collecting process is fun. Each great blurb is like a positive affirmation that helps your confidence grow. Put your blurbs in this folder as they come to you. You'll eventually separate them into categories for different books or the different kinds of marketing you're doing.

-∞-

YOUR BOOK REVIEW is used by a gatekeeper as an indicator of the quality of your work. Occasionally, an editor may want to reprint a review just as they find it in your kit.

As soon as you have a positive review, add it to this Review subfolder in you media kit file. Here is how to do that:

- Ask permission from the reviewer to add it to your media kit.
- Ask if you have permission to reprint it or allow others to do so. If permission is granted, mention that in the header of the media kit review page. Include a request that editors print the review in full using the reviewer's byline and tagline.

> **Hint:** If permission is granted, use the review on your Web site and submit it to TheNewBookReview.blogspot.com and other review blogs and sites. The guidelines for submission are in the left column of that blog.

- State where the review originally appeared and give the reviewer a byline.
- When you have many reviews to choose from, select the one written by the most prestigious reviewer or the one that appeared in the most esteemed review journal. Very high praise is good, but review credibility is better.
- If the original review does not include a headline, provide one that is true to the reviewer's intent.

If you have a review that isn't as good as you'd like, resist the temptation to extract only a positive excerpt.

Media people know a review that is critical of one aspect of your book is more credible than one that praises a book excessively. Editors suspect that a pie-in-the-sky review was probably written by your mother.

If you have a short review and a longer one that includes a synopsis of your book, increase your chances of getting some free ink by using them both. An editor may find one suits her style or space requirements better than the other. Label them "Sample Short Review" and "Sample Longer Review."

> **Hint #1:** If you don't yet have a review, substitute a mini synopsis you wrote yourself. Use active verbs and third person. Don't give away the ending. Make your synopsis a tease that will entice even a jaded reviewer or editor to want to know more about your book. Don't attribute it to anyone.

> **Hint #2**: If you want to extract little phrases that rave about your book from a review, they go on your Praise page where gleaning the best of the best from reviews and elsewhere is acceptable.

-∞-

YOUR SAMPLE INTERVIEW is the text of an interview, imagined or real, that a reporter, blogger, or radio host might use to glean questions to use when he interviews you. You have seen interview formats in *People* and *Time* magazines. They look like transcripts of—usually very short—questions and answers.

Some reporters use the Sample Interview that you supply verbatim. Others adapt the questions to their needs, and others may not use them all. Bloggers and radio and TV hosts often ask for talking points. To save time, give them select questions from your Sample Interview. You'll be familiar with the questions and therefore better prepared with your answers.

The Sample Interview in your media kit is your chance to combat the inferior quality of interviews—both the questions and answers—that James Thurber described when he said, "My opposition [to interviews] lies in the fact that offhand answers have little value or grace of expression, and that such oral give and take helps to perpetuate the decline of the English language."

A little name-dropping in a media kit is essential, not a social *faux pas*. When the name of the journal or the interviewer will lend an air of prestige to your kit, that's the one you select.

Having said that, if the interviews available to you do not focus on content you consider essential, write your own. That gives you as much control over the interview process as possible. Of course, your answers (also written by you) will be witty, entertaining, and . . . I did mention short, didn't I?

If you can't get permission from a host to reprint an interview, there are no media-kit cops who will cite you if you list those same esteemed reporters at the bottom of your Sample Interview page, complete with links to the original review.

You could also mention influential reviews as one of the answers in your self-written interview or include them with links on your Appearances page. A media kit should follow guidelines closely, but the content is indeed more flexible than the inscription on your great grandfather's headstone.

> **Hint:** You might substitute a Frequently Asked Questions (FAQ) page for a sample interview, perhaps the same one you will eventually use for your Web site.

-∞-

YOUR FIRST-PERSON ESSAY is often ignored by authors. What a missed opportunity! These essays bring people (in this case, gatekeepers) into your circle—up close and intimate. In *On Writing Well*, William Zinsser said, "I almost always urge people to write in the first person . . . . Writing is an act of ego and you might as well admit it."

Zinsser might be alluding to the fact that it is disingenuousness to remove the author from the telling of her own story by using third person. After all, the author is the ultimate expert on herself and the pronoun "I" is not a dirty word.

> **Hint:** A first-person essay is a narrative. The one you use in your media kit is a little story with you and your writing as central characters. It is quite different from the About the Author piece (or biography) you wrote for your media kit's About-the-Author page. Editors use it differently, too.

Because you're a writer you are probably aware of how frequently the press uses first-person essays. Some newspapers label a column "First-Person Essay."

Others vary the titles. The *Los Angeles Times* uses "First Column." You usually find them in the left column of the front page and in the same location on the front pages of their other sections. A widely distributed magazine called *Guideposts* (guideposts.com) is dedicated to this kind of writing. First-person essays are often used in anthologies and collections of essays, too.

When authors write about themselves, their style sometimes becomes so stilted it reads like a college text. A first-person essay should be lively and full of anecdotes and dialogue, even if you write nonfiction.

Eventually you may want to have several different essays or versions of your essay stowed away in your computer because different publications target different audiences. One of my essays talks about my bout with cancer and how my search for health brought me back to writing after a long hiatus. Another is about my struggle with repression of women in an earlier decade and how that affected my early writing career. One tells of my love of yoga, and—you guessed it—how it helps my writing. Another, how travel informs my writing. One relates to how writing has affected my life as a senior. I switch out the essay I include in my media kit depending on where I am sending it. It doesn't take me long to rewrite one of these (dare I say "canned" essays?) when a new opportunity presents itself. For me it's a bigger trick to remember to save each version under a different name.

Here are some pointers for the first-person section in your media kit:

- Label this page "First-Person Story."
- It should run from 700 to 1000 words. Number these pages separately from the rest of the kit and staple them together when you are submitting a hardcopy of your kit.
- Use an attention-getting title.
- Include a free-use permission statement.
- Include your byline and tagline (see Chapter Ten under Credits).
- Try to include the title of your book in the body of the piece, but only if it is an integral part of the story, not an obvious add-on.

A well-written first-person essay might be reprinted by an editor exactly as it is presented. Sometimes you will be asked for more information or for permission to rewrite it under another byline (the answer is always "Yes!"). Other times this essay may trigger interest in featuring you in a different story.

> **Caveat:** If you hire a publicist, she may not use first-person essays in her kits. It may be up to you to convince her to use yours. You, after all, are the client. She should accommodate your suggestion.

-∞-

YOUR AVAILABLE SEMINARS LIST is an essential part of your kit, especially when you send your kit to bookstore event directors, to program directors of tradeshows or conferences, to schools and universities where you may want to teach, to library program directors, and even to TV and radio producers who will get an idea of the variety of topics that you can address if you should become a guest.

Excellent speakers tend to be successful in the business world. That is especially true for authors. If fear keeps you from sharing your expertise, take a baby step toward overcoming it for the sake of your personal growth and the success of your publicity campaign, not to mention the sales of your books that occur when you are lecturing or speaking.

Settling on your seminar topics is similar to searching for angles that will interest editors. Examine every aspect of your book. Rediscover the passion that inspired you to write it. Come up with at least two topics that appeal to audiences with diverse tastes. These might include a writing workshop, a moderated panel on publishing, or a seminar on the premise of your book. Keep adding ideas to this subfolder as they occur to you.

You needn't write the presentations that go with each of your ideas, but do consider whether you will have (or can research) enough material to make the seminars or workshops you offer successful if you should get speaking gigs. Write a catchy title and an intriguing pitch for each topic. Use the skills you learned in Chapter Ten for writing loglines, pitches, and beguiling synopses of your book. Study university extension catalogs for ideas on writing seminar descriptions and then spice yours up a bit.

> **Hint:** The Seminars page in your media kit indicates that you have presentation skills many gatekeepers need even if you choose not to pursue speaking as an essential part of your campaign.

-∞-

YOUR FELLOW EXPERTS LIST is a companion to your Seminar page. When you include a list of experts who complement your expertise—ones who are charismatic and know how to work as a team—you mark yourself as a professional and make it oh, so easy for an editor or producer to style a story or segment in which you are an integral part.

Here are some quick tips for your expert list:
- Get permission from your fellow experts to list them in your kit.
- Your Expert list should be on a page by itself, very brief, just the facts, ma'am.
- Include at least one expert who holds an opinion different from yours. Include another whose expertise adds a different dimension to the topic.
- Include contact information and one-sentence descriptions of what makes them experts and what they can add to the conversation.

-∞-

OTHER MEDIA KIT ITEMS isn't a page in your media kit per se, but a list of ideas, reminders, or stuff you will need. Each entry is like a string around your finger.

You put items you *need* reminders for in this subfolder:
- Your picture. (See Chapter Ten under "Your Photo.") You'll need hard copies and a digital file.
- Your business card.

- Your galley or Advanced Reader Copy, both a hardcopy and an e-copy. (See Chapter Fifteen on how to use ARCs to get reviews.)
- A color image of your bookcover.
- Get a logo and Web site banner designed. Banner Fan (bannerfan.com) is good for do-it-yourselfers.

You'll randomly toss other items into this folder like bookmarks and ideas for your promotional gifts (if you insist on buying them). But keep reading before you spend any money on these doodads.

As you complete each task, delete the reminder from this subfolder. It is different from your other subfolders in which you hoard entries as a record and resource.

I once added an idea for writing a tip sheet for my kit into this memory jogger. It was to be called "Ten Weird and Wonderful Facts about Utah." It helped me design a line of questioning for a late-night radio host, so it didn't go completely to waste. I never got around to writing this tip sheet for my kit. This note remains there to silently nag me. It is my prerogative to ignore it, just as it will be yours.

Souvenir and promotional gifts for media kits are not what they are cracked up to be. With the exception of quality thank-you gifts, authors will do fine without gizmos, especially the kind that all too soon get tossed into gatekeepers' clutter drawers.

I've rarely seen cutsie giveaways for media kits used effectively, except when they are used to attract editors to take a kit from the pressroom at a tradeshow. To work that way, they'd better be suited to the theme of your book, awfully cute, and have a high perceived value!

I viewed my first promotional item more as a thank-you gift than as advertising. I wanted something that suited the material in my book, but I hadn't yet learned that most of the stuff authors were spending money on was not effective. I bought miniature thimbles with "Utah" printed on them for my book's launch because it is set in that state. My mother made little felt slipcases for them and my husband tied tiny gift tags with a quote from the book to each pouch with thin grosgrain ribbon. Mom refused to make more than the original 100 or so pleading poor eyesight. My next promotion gifts were miniature hand-crocheted doilies made in China, presumably by women with no such excuses. We used similar tie-on tags. These worked better than thimbles because they more easily lay flat in books, envelopes, or thank-you cards. But think of the expense. Think of the time. Think of the guilt I felt about those poor Chinese women once I had time to think about it!

I made these choices because each had something to do with the sewing imagery I used in both *This Is the Place* and *Harkening*. Linda Morelli makes artistic blank journals and notebooks by hand for prizes and contests and tucks them into gift baskets.

If you must use items like this, your serenity quotient will go up if you forget about measuring their effectiveness in terms of book sales and think of them as means to promote goodwill. Here are guidelines to help make a decision about promotional items when you think you absolutely must have them:

- Shun the politically incorrect unless your book is a steaming gossip sheet. Avoid smoking accoutrements unless the title of your book is *Up in Smoke.*
- Hand or homemade items are appropriate only if those qualities are integral to the image you want to project. Unless you are a graphics and computer production whiz, handmade bookmarks—unlike some homemade gifts—might as well be printed with "Don't buy my book. I'm an amateur."
- Most gatekeepers appreciate food, but your edible should tie into the theme of your book unless the food is a thank you after the fact.
- Buy in bulk to keep costs down but don't be overly optimistic. Your needs will change.
- Flat is best. Lightweight is a plus. Green, these days, is a plus-plus.
- Consider cost and distribution. You can easily give away thousands of promotional gifts and if you restrict distribution because of the expense, you may defeat your purpose.

Bookmarks are often used instead of business cards. They are given away at book signings, tucked into books sent to reviewers, and even left in public bathrooms or at coffeehouses. I have never used them; my budget got in the way and they didn't make the cut. However, they are often keepers (some readers collect them!) and when they are printed with a great endorsement, bookcover art, and complete information for buying your book, they are effective because:

- They mail flat.
- They target the audience you want to reach.
- Readers don't discard them as readily as some promotional material.
- They may be produced relatively inexpensively. Let your printer duplicate an image on postcard-size, heavy-weight paper and then cut the card lengthwise.
- They are two-sided so they can feature effective marketing techniques like endorsements, free gifts to drive traffic to a Web site, and contests.

Logo- or bookcover-printed items like mugs, shirts, bags, and even baby clothes from local printers or Web sites like CafePress.com may be used for a variety of events:

- Authors and their helpers might wear T-shirts to book fairs if that casual look fits their branding goals. Use both a headshot and your bookcover on your shirts for best results. Use a book-oriented quotation to broaden the appeal. I once saw one that said "I was a lousy mother!" that had people stopping the author in the aisles of Book Expo.
- Carry necessities to book signings with a logo tote bag. Author Epstein LaRue says she sometimes sells books right out of the bag she carries with her when she runs her errands.
- Items that might get used on someone's desk like mugs or coasters remind editors, reviewers,

and producers of you after the fact. Other media people may see them there, too.

- Use them for prizes and drawings.

Online businesses that specialize in printing and shipping these items sometimes promise authors they can sell logo items to their readers for a profit. Readers can go online to order a mug or shirt for themselves or the author may stock a few to sell at book events. You know, like the concert promoters do for Madonna? Don't you believe it. Your mother probably won't buy one. How many coffee mugs that celebrate your favorite authors do *you* own? Rock stars, we're not.

Buy wholesale when you need large quantities of a promotional item. When you see something in a store that shouts, "Zinngg! This fits my book better than latex gloves," buy one as a sample (it seems only fair to the retailer!). Ask the merchant to put in its original box and, when you get home, check for the manufacturer's name. Sometimes the tag or box will carry a Web site address or phone number. You might get the manufacturer or their distributor to sell directly to you.

You can also find gift and souvenir items at tradeshows and stationary to-the-trade markets. Check with your city's convention center to see if they host these kinds of tradeshows.

If you have no luck buying the item of your dreams from the manufacturer, ask your retail owner or manager for a quantity discount. Expect greater cooperation and a bigger discount for very large orders.

-∞-

ASSEMBLING YOUR MEDIA KIT is the last step before you send your kit off to gatekeepers. It is a little like designing floral art. Floral designers place the healthiest, most impressive flowers up front where they show.

You've seen that you might assemble your kit differently from one mailing occasion to the next. You've seen that you may end up with several kits, each with a distinct focus. The basics may or may not remain the same regardless of what you do.

You've learned that your kit must make it easy for editors to do their jobs. And it is only reasonable that we also make ourselves look as good as we can. It's a lot to keep in mind, so you do it one step at a time and make decisions as you go.

To save stress and time, shop stationers, office supply businesses and online suppliers in advance. Your ideas and needs will change as you encounter new possibilities (and prices!) and you'll want to have samples of the stationery supplies you might use in your kit on hand to help you visualize your overall presentation. They might include:

- A few two-pocket folders, the kind with tiny diagonal slits in the fold-up pocket portion to accommodate business cards.

    Hint: It's seldom necessary to buy four-color, professionally designed, slick, heavy-weight folders. Not when you can order printed professional-looking labels that sport your book's cover art.

- A variety of possible paper choices.
- A printout of your assembled and formatted kit.
- Samples or mockups of your business cards and professional photo.
- A few media kits borrowed from other industries. I often pass kits from other industries around the room when I talk about marketing at writers' conferences. Use a couple of mine as examples. Go to howtodoitfrugally.com/media_room.htm and download one or more of the kits I offer as .pdfs.

Play with these materials and the pages in your kit. Pretend they're playing cards. You shuffle and arrange them to their best advantage depending upon the branch of the media you are sending your kit to and the aspect of your writing career you want to emphasize. Which pages should come first? Which should go in the left pocket? The right? Once decided you can format your Contents page.

Usually you assemble your material so the media release comes first in the left-hand pocket. Place your headshot (See Chapter Ten), your promotion gift (if any), a copy of your bookcover, and your book—if you are including one—on the left. Anything that is not in the realm of the usual media kit fare goes on the left, too.

On the right, put your About-the-Author page on top, your Awards page and then . . . well, you decide this order by determining which pages will most effectively convince an editor of your newsworthiness.

As a courtesy, attach a query or cover letter to the outside of the kit with a paperclip—maybe one that contributes to the design either by shape or color. Your letter should be a brief (and not necessarily formal) introduction that will pique an editor's interest.

The headers or footers of each page in your kit include simple contact information like those you find on thesis papers or at the top of pages in books. Use a gray tone to keep them from competing with the rest of the page. Don't use page numbers because you will rearrange the page order as the need arises.

Here are some quick don'ts:
- Don't print and assemble kits to use in the future. Your needs will change quickly. It's sad to see a gross of folders and pre-printed interiors you can't use sitting in your garage.
- Don't use a designed letterhead on each page. It clutters and increases the time it takes your computer to print your kit.
- Don't use four-color printing on your folder or in the interior of your kit. Color adds to the cost of any print job. Instead, design your folder and contents using one-color ink on contrasting paper. Make your statement with quality paper instead.
- Don't attach your digital kit to e-mails unless an editor requests it. Instead, explain that it is available on request in your media release.

- As your kit grows, don't squash everything you've done into it. Pick the recent or most prestigious entries.
- Don't trick up your kit with gifts. Since the payola scandal of the 60s, many editors refuse gifts, anyway. Instead, send a modest thank-you gift a few days after the reporter or producer's work has been printed or aired.

> **Caveat:** A kit displayed in an expo or tradeshow pressroom competes with dozens of others. On these occasions, your kit attracts attention by sheer force of its design or because it includes a freebie. To coax editors to pick it up and tote it around the show, use a value-added gift like a signed copy of your book. Some authors worry that an editor who can't possibly use the information in their kit will take a kit just to get a copy of their book, but editors are VIPs in the publishing industry—they may pass their knowledge and interest on to others. They're also readers. And readers recommend books.

- Don't be too uptight about trying something different. As an example, there is not a right or wrong kind of presentation folder as long as it fits your brand. Some brands may call for something with a handmade look. I cut corners with my HowToDoItFrugally kits because "frugal" is the brand. A kit for a children's book made with Kraft paper and colored with Crayons and reverse-image letters may be more effective than an expensive printer-produced kit.

Next we'll talk about your query or cover letters. They aren't enclosed within the kit but that doesn't mean they aren't an essential part of your presentation. The recipient needs to know why you are sending a kit and what you would like them to do for you. Queries and cover letters do that for you. They are like introductions.

When you network at a cocktail party, you make eye contact, extend your hand, make a little small talk (my son calls it schmoozing) before you get down to serious business. Query and cover letters are a lot like that process, but they tend to be more efficient.

Chapter Fourteen

Your Query and Cover Letters

Query letters are the ultimate assertiveness-training tool at far less cost than a therapist with a half dozen initials behind his name. ~ CHJ

You just about have this publicity thing ready to roll. Your contact list is growing by the day. You've prepared your media release and kit using time-honored basics of branding and pitching. You're almost done except for the important cover or query letter.

Gatekeepers—folks like agents, editors, publishers, and bloggers—usually first learn about you when they open a letter or e-mail with your query or cover letter in it. Sometimes you send it to them with only an offer to provide the kit you've prepared. Sometimes you use one when you submit your book, articles—even poems—for their consideration or for contests. When that happens, your query must do most of the work of a media kit because the only thing accompanying it will be your manuscript.

You can see, we've saved this most important part of your presentation until last. Many of the skills you used developing your kit and release will help you write a great query or cover letter. It is easier than you think.

For an author, there is little difference between a cover letter and a query letter. A *query* letter asks or tells the person it addresses what the author of the letter needs. A *cover* is an introduction to what is being presented. It may not ask for something specific, though it, too, benefits if you indicate your reasons for sending it.

You might be surprised at how many gatekeepers out there wear more than one hat. Without information about what you expect, they won't know what to do with your letter and it may get deleted or deep-sixed.

So, what *do* you want? A spot on a radio show? A featured article in a newsletter? To present at a conference or tradeshow? To be published? Do you want representation? The list goes on and on.

Of course you want to ask diplomatically. Making gatekeepers' jobs easier is considerate. It is tactful (and smart) to make them aware that you know who they are and what they do by naming their business, their TV show, or someone they represent. Or by letting them know where you met them or who recommended them. In fact, that information is a very good opener for a query or cover letter.

Your query or cover needs:
- An opener. Politely introduce yourself or start with a quotation from your book or an amazing fact that illustrates how important what you have to offer is.
- Next comes a bit about the idea you have for them (your pitch). That may require you to

include a logline (a very short synopsis). See "loglines" and "pitches" in this book's Index.

- Your letter should be one page or less, but occasionally when you're pitching a story idea to an editor, your letter may be longer because it doesn't have an accompanying document. However, the format stays about the same.
- Then comes a short paragraph on your credentials.
- A simple thank you and close follows. This may include the query or an indication of what you need from them, though you may want to work it into your letter earlier. It goes something like this: "I hope you will consider representing my (your title here). Please let me know if you need more information. Sincerely, (your name here)."

Here are a few don'ts for your query or cover letter:
- Don't make your letter into the driest business letter this side of the Sahara. It helps if your contact has a sense of your voice. Avoid words that are too formal or longer than three syllables.
- Avoid adjectives. Your contact—not you—should decide if your story idea is "amazing."
- Don't use the term "fictional novel." A novel by definition is fiction.
- Avoid saying "I think" or "I believe." The letter is written by you. Those words weaken your position.
- Avoid exclamation points.
- Don't say your book is "entitled." That's the wrong word. It is "titled."

- Don't include a chapter of your manuscript that relies on italics to indicate internal thought.

  > **Hint:** When you e-mail a query, use the word "query" in the subject line. Follow it with a teaser or headline: "Query: Local Story to Build on Yesterday's *News-Press* Headline."

There are sample query letters in the Appendix of this book and a couple more in *The Frugal Editor* (budurl.com/TheFrugalEditor) where you'll also find more on editing query letters and pet query-letter peeves straight from some of our industry's most powerful literary agents who shared their thoughts with me.

Chapter Fifteen

Your Reviews

. . . newspapers and magazines are trimming back their review coverage ~ Christopher Dreyer for Salon

Many authors think it's worth it to learn all this marketing business—especially the writing of query letters—just to get reviews even though they're scared spitless of what those reviews might say. Byron once asked his publisher to "send me no more reviews of any kind." He thought Keats had been killed by one bad review (which, we know in retrospect, was not true).

Some writers—particularly those who have made it to bestseller lists—believe that reviews were responsible for their success; many others have been successful without them or in spite of them.

What can't be argued is that librarians and bookstore buyers peruse *The Library Journal* and other major review journals, book review sections, as well as media material the major publishers send to them. Most authors would like to see their books in libraries and on bookstore shelves and good reviews are the fast lanes to those shelves—sometimes the only lanes.

Reviews—particularly rave reviews—are something you, as a promotion-minded author, would like to have.

However, here is an idea that should be inscribed in that author-brain of yours, and I want you to post this where you see it every day when you sit down to write:

Authors are no longer at the mercy of reviews.

The publishing world has changed, in good part because of the Web. Reviews are but one form of free ink. An author who has difficulty getting reviews can use other means of promotion including interviews, feature articles, book clubs, catalog sales, and social networking. I've seen authors addictively chase unproductive reviews when they could have used the same time to promote in other ways.

Do not judge book reviews by how well they produce sales. I have a traditionally published friend whose book was reviewed by *Newsweek* and her book still did not earn royalties over her advance.

Finding reviewers isn't easy and your publisher may not help much. No offense, publishers. I know many of you do a terrific job. Let's face it, you can use help, and you don't need to deal with disappointed (irate?) authors. And, authors! We are ultimately responsible for our own careers. Sometimes when we wait to take responsibility, it is too late.

One of my writing critique partners was published with a fine small press. When she learned her publisher had not sent advance review copies of her literary novel to the most prestigious review journals before their strict sixteen-week deadline, she was naturally upset. They explained it was a snafu. She and I used some of the alternative review-getting methods in this chapter. But mostly (because she had me to nag her), she moved on to other marketing strategies to make up for the neglect.

Most large publishers do send out advance review copies. Still, they are relying more on bloggers and other online entities for reviews. They are beginning to understand that grassroots publicity—reviews or otherwise—can produce a very green crop.

Because thousands of galleys sent to the important review publications lie fallow in slush piles, the chances of having your book reviewed by a major journal, let alone getting a glowing review, is remote.

Beware of publishers—even traditional publishers— who don't respect tradition. My first publisher supplied review copies upon written request *from individual reviewers*. They did not honor requests that were generated from their authors' initiative. This method is cumbersome, unprofessional, and discourages authors from trying to get reviews on their own. Further, publishers should *offer* review copies to a list of reviewers—even those grassroots bloggers—who have been responsive to their authors in the past.

Ask potential publishers about their marketing process before you sign with them, but—even if you feel assured after having that conversation—it's best to assume you are on your own. We'll discuss how to do that next, beginning with how to get reviews from the biggest and best.

-∞-

BIG-JOURNAL REVIEWS may still be yours. Books that have been ignored by *The New York Times* have become bestsellers; others that received rave reviews never made it to that same publication's bestseller list. It is all a game. We can choose not to play, but if we don't play, we'll never know if we could have won much less experience the thrill of winning.

To win, you need to know the rules—especially the be-on-time rule—and you need to be very, very lucky.

- When you sign your contract with a publisher, negotiate. You want advance review copies of your book sent to the major journals before their twelve-to-sixteen-week deadline. Big influencers in the publishing world pay more attention to a query or a review copy that comes directly from a publisher than one from an author or an independent publicist.
- If you are unable to get your publisher to accommodate your needs, you can:
  o Buy extra review copies from your publisher to send to the reviewers. Ask for the list of review journals they submit to and expand on it by sending copies to others you think might be interested. Find my lists at howtodoitfrugally.com/reviewers.htm.
  o If your publisher will not have your book ready for release before that sixteen-week cutoff date, self-publish your own advance review or readers' copies (also called ARCs) and distribute them yourself. You learn how to do that in the next section of this chapter. Most publishers own the rights to your book so you must ask their permission to do this.

How they supply review copies and what they charge you for them is something else you should discuss with them before signing a contract.

> **Caveat:** Distribute your own ARCs only if you are willing to risk the expense for limited results, and to take the pains to do it according to the firm and fast industry rules discussed in this chapter.

Making your own ARC or galley takes tons of planning, but you can do it.

Few use the term "galley" since print-on-demand has made publishing so quick and easy, but it is important you know this word for old-fashioned bound manuscripts because you will occasionally see it used to describe digitally printed review copies. Many use the term ARC—though no one seems to agree on whether the acronym stands for "Advanced Review Copy" or "Advanced Reader Copy." The word "ARC" seems to keep everyone in the industry using the same vocabulary to communicate.

Start the galley/ARC process by fudging with the release date of your book. Ask your publisher to list the official release date about twenty weeks to six months from the day your book is set to first roll off the press. I know you won't want to wait, but that lead time will do the same thing for indie authors and publishers it does for big publishers. It will give you time to get a professional publicity campaign going and including the intricate review process.

Delayed release dates are an industry standard. A book's delayed date *is* the release date. It is the one you and your publisher *say* it is and the one you use in your media releases and other documents. It isn't a fake date, so you needn't feel guilty.

Now you must decide if you're going to buy books from your publisher or produce your own ARCs. When making this decision, keep copyright laws in mind. If you do produce your own ARCs, you'll need to reformat your manuscript. It's obviously much easier if your publisher will provide ARCs to you at a favorable price. You will both benefit.

If you must make your own ARCs, self-publish using a printer of your choice or a subsidy press (a publisher who charges you for their services). Your cover needn't be finished; plain vanilla (generic) covers are just fine for ARCs as long as they are labeled as such.

I like Creatspace.com for ARCs. If you're careful not to get roped into the pay-for services Createspace provides, you can upload your book free and pay only for the copies you order. It costs two to five dollars per copy including shipping and you may order any quantity you need, even just one.

Many authors use Lulu and I know some who have used Fidlar-Doubleday, Inc. Find a list of printers in the writers' resource section of my Web site at howtodoitfrugally.com/digital_printers.htm.

Print your ARCs with a violation notice. It should read something like: "This is an Unedited Review Copy. Uses Other than Review Constitute a Violation of Copyright Law." If this notice can't be printed on your book, it can be labeled or stamped on the book.

Your review copies also need your book's essential information on the first page, inside the front cover, on a label, or, if the reviewer requests "no defacing of," on a sell sheet tucked inside the cover. Include:

- Official release date—the one you and your publisher have decided on.
- Title.
- Author.
- Illustrator when applicable.
- ISBN.
- Number of pages.
- Retail price (the price a customer in a bookstore pays for your book).
- Trim size (the size the finished, final copy of your book).
- Define as hardcover, mass market paperback, trade paperback, or other specification.
- Number of illustrations and/or photographs.
- Publisher's name and contact information—that could be you, the name of your own publishing company if you are self-publishing your book, or the name of the publisher you've contracted with.
- Distributor's name and contact information.
- Agent's name and contact information.
- Publicist's name and contact information.

If you're using finished books as ARCs, apply pre-printed labels on the inside of the front cover or on the first title page of the book. If you print books expressly to be used as ARCs, add a page to the front of the book with the above information on it.

> **Caveat:** Check submission guidelines for each journal you query. *Midwest Book Review* asks for books that have not been "defaced." For them, essential information on a separate sheet can be folded inside the front cover. You can also send a review copy to them when your book becomes available because they do not specify that twelve-to-sixteen week deadline.

You're now ready to send your ARCs out with your releases or media kits according to each review journal's guidelines.

The big journals that require a fourteen to sixteen week lead are:
- *Booklist, American Library Assoc.,* ala.org/booklist.
- *Entertainment Weekly Magazine,* entertainmentweekly.com.
- *Kirkus Reviews,* kirkusreviews.com.
- *Library Journal,* libraryjournal.com.
- *The New York Times Book Review,* nytimes.com/books.
- *Los Angeles Times Book Review,* latimes.com.
- *Chicago Tribune Books,* chicagotribune.com.
- *American Book Review,* americanbookreview.org/.
- *Small Press Review,* dustbooks.com. Poetry and fiction only.
- *Publishers Weekly,* publishersweekly.com.
- *Amazon.com,* Editorial, 520 Pike St., Suite 1800, Seattle, WA 98101.
- *Ruminator Review,* ruminator.com.

- *Book Page,* bookpage.com. Submissions needn't be brand new titles.
- Trade magazines associated with an industry related to the topic of your book. Use *Bacon's Directories* at the reference desk of you library to find them.
- The book or arts and entertainment section of your nearest metropolitan newspaper. Find a list of other major newspapers and some other review help at howtodoitfrugally.com/reviewers.htm#newspapers.

> **Caveat**: Many journals do not consider self- or POD-published books for review, but occasionally they do review books published independently. Those privileged authors feel it was worth sending an ARC so professionally wrought the gatekeepers couldn't ascertain that it did not come from the most respected publisher or publicist.

The following review journals are amenable to reviewing alternative forms of publishing though no reviewer, review journal, or site guarantees review for all submissions:

- *Independent Publisher*, independentpublisher.com.
- *Midwest Book Review,* midwestbookreview.com/get_rev.htm.
- *Foreword Magazine,* forewordmagazine.com.
- Book clubs for general readers and clubs for niche markets (think Writer's Digest book club and Dash Direct Club for cookbooks). Find a list at literarymarketplace.com/lmp/us/index_us.asp.

> **Caveat**: When you submit galleys or self-published ARCs, some journals ask you to send a final copy of your book when it is finished as proof that it was released.

The lists I've given you are compiled for the frugal author. They can be expanded a thousand fold if your budget allows. Work with your publisher. Do not duplicate his efforts.

Check for changes in the particulars of a journal's contact information and submission guidelines. Look for:

- The names of current reviewers. Try to address your review packet to someone specific.
- A current address. An incorrect address or name marks your material as unprofessional.
- The genres and categories they specialize in.
- Other submission requirements.

> **Hint:** Send a book or ARC with your query only when submission guidelines ask for them. For all others, wait to send your ARC until the reviewer indicates an interest in reviewing your book based on the query letter you sent to them.

-∞-

ALTERNATIVES TO MAJOR REVIEW JOURNALS are available if you miss the deadline for the biggies. We have to love them because they give authors and small publishers more control over the success of their books.

Here are the advantages of using review alternatives:

- Some review blogs, Web sites, and journals specialize in specific genres. That allows you to target your readers.
- You can often build relationships with those who run these journals—on line or in print. That

can lead to even more publicity—like an interview or publication of an excerpt—for your book. And for your next book.

- Most do not have deadlines, or limit reviews to the copyright year.
- Many accept reader reviews and many readers are elated to be asked to share their opinions with others. It may be a first for them.
- Reader reviews usually include links to your Web site, your own blog, and your online sales page. Click-and-buy is an easier sale than delayed purchases produced by print journals.
- Blog and online reviews are gaining prestige.
- Blog tour services that contact online reviewers for you have sprung up. They are often inexpensive. They get reviews for you, and their contacts become your contacts. Keep reading for a short list of some of my favorites.

> **Hint:** I set up my *New Book Review* blog to help writers get more exposure for their books and to more fully utilize the book reviews they already have. Lacking a book review, an author may submit a synopsis. Find submission guidelines in the left column of the blog at TheNewBookReview.blogspot.com.

Some of these alternative reviewers may ask for "e-books" or "e-galleys," which may confuse you, especially if you did not publish your book as an e-book. They probably want you to send them a digital file of your book rather than a paperback by post.

Use search engines to find review sites and reviewers. To get a review from online review sites, you need submit only a query. They post the request to a bulletin board asking for a volunteer to read your book. If no reviewer volunteers, you will not be reviewed. For starters try CompulsiveReader.com, BookPleasures.com, AllBooksReviewInt.com, MyShelf.com, and ReaderViews.com.

> **Hint:** Before contacting a review Web site or an individual reviewer, read posted reviews to determine if they are right for your book. Don't query—much less go to the expense of sending an ARC—to a reviewer, a site, or a blog that specializes in genres different from yours.

Sending an electronic copy of your book attached to an e-mail query seems like a time saver, but don't. Many reviewers won't open e-mail with attachments so your query may not get read. Offer to send an electronic copy in another e-mail or through your e-book publisher or a hardcopy by post. And *don't* try to convince reviewers to accept the e-copy over the paperback. It's insensitive; if they accept your book, they should be able to read it in whatever form they prefer.

-∞-

ALTERNATIVES TO THE ALTERNATIVES are useful avenues for exposure long after your book's release.

Here are some possibilities:

- Don't overlook staff members at bookstores. Many do reviews for the bookstore's newsletter. Sometimes they hang brief reviews on the shelf where the book is displayed. Bookstore book buyers and event directors may be interested in your book, especially if you live in the same town as their store.

- Ask a writer friend from your critique group to write a review. Send that review to art and entertainment and book editors with a query for a review and permission to print your friend's review if they prefer to.
- If you've had difficulty getting a Web site or newspaper to assign a reviewer to your book, try advertising. Though the editorial departments should not be influenced by the advertising departments, you may find interest in reviewing your book increases after you've signed up for an ad.
- Subscribe to online newsletters. As you read them, look for review resources. Sometimes the newsletter will print one of your existing reviews.
- Go in the back door. When a review journal doesn't accept your book for review, research their individual reviewers, and query them directly. Use search engines to find them or call the journal and ask for contact information. You may have more luck if you send a personal query directly to the reviewers who write for these sites right from the start. Find some individual reviewers at:

lorraineheath.com/review_sites.htm.

> **Hint:** I'm thinking of publishing a couple of chapters of my next novel—sort of a combination ARC and chapbook—to send to a long list of booksellers with query letters suggesting we plan well ahead for a reading or

workshop. In the query I'd make it clear that I would be pleased to send the finished book to them once it is available.

- Submit short, ready-to-go copy requesting a review to Dan Poynter. Put "Review Wanted" in the subject line of an e-mail and send it to: danpoynter@parapublishing.com. He'll put your request in his newsletter. Authors often get five to ten offers for reviews, mostly from readers who post their reviews at online bookstores or on their own or others' blogs.

-∞-

NOW YOU HAVE A REVIEW, WHAT? Depending on the reviewer, your review may get published where it will rarely be seen or where it will be seen thousands of times. You have some control over that:

- If your reviewer doesn't normally write reviews, ask her to send her review to her friends and to magazines that publish reviews that are not written by their own staff writers. If she is an author or a professional in the field your book addresses, she will benefit from the exposure.
- Ask your reviewer—even one who writes for a review journal—to post her review on Amazon.com, B&N.com, and other online booksellers that have reader-review features.
- Ask permission from the reviewer to reprint the review and then post it on your blog, on your Web site, and in your newsletter. Use quotations from the reviews to give credibility to selected media releases and queries.

- Once you have permission to use reviews, send copies of good ones to bookstore buyers. Go to midwestbookreview.com/links/bookstor.htm for a starter list of bookstores.
- Send quotations (blurbs) from the reviews you get to librarians. Include order information. For a list of libraries try Midwest Book Review, midwestbookreview.com/links/library.htm.
- Use snippets from positive reviews as blurbs in everything from your stationery to your blog. (Check "blurbs" in the Index in this book for other ideas for their use.)
- Post blurbs from reviews you get on your Amazon sales page. Read Chapter Twenty-One to learn how to use the benefits Amazon and other bookstores offer.
- Include the *crème de la crème* of your reviews on the Praise page of your media kit.

-∞-

FACING REVIEWER PREJUDICE head on is essential. Many authors have trouble finding reviewers because some judge books by their covers and even more judge books by the name of the publisher or the kind of presses they are published on. This book bigotry is changing, but very slowly. If your book is self- or subsidy-published, traditionally published but printed with a print-on-demand press, or printed by a very small, unknown press, you may learn firsthand about how debilitating it is to be judged unfairly. You can fight this kind of prejudice:

- When you subsidy-publish, use publishers that have names that are not known industry wide as subsidy publishers. Or negotiate with the publisher for your own imprint. Big publishers often publish books under several names. Doubleday, as an example, is an imprint of Random House.

- Produce a great product. That means you need to learn a lot about every aspect of publishing and, when you need help, own up. Hire it out. That includes editing, indexing, formatting, interior design, and bookcover design.

- When you feel yourself at a disadvantage, don't assume that traditionally published authors don't sometimes feel that way, too.

- Don't get discouraged. Keep at it. We live in a new world of publishing. We do have control over our own careers.

-∞-

REVIEW SCAMS abound. There are a few pay-for review services that may be worth the money—in particular those that package the review you pay for with other services. But authors who are new to the industry are easy targets for those who want to make money from them. Even respectable *Kirkus* has begun a paid-for review service. Their reviews are probably as reputable as paid-for reviews can be, but booksellers, librarians, and some readers know paid-for reviews when they see them and they generally are not influenced by them.

Think about it. It is difficult for a reviewer employed by the author or publisher of that book not to be influenced by that relationship. When readers aren't sure they are getting honest reviews, they don't consider them credible. That is why paid-for reviews fly in the face of accepted journalism ethics.

In general, I advise against paying for reviews. There are a zillion other free ways to get attention for little old author-you or your book. Why pay for something few give any credence to anyway? Besides, authors can Tweet a request for a book review and probably get one from a reader or blogger. It's that easy. I maintain a list of bloggers who tweet and review books for their own blogs on my Twitter page at twitter.com/FrugalBookPromo.

SENDING BOOKS OR ARCS is a little like sending your first child off to kindergarten. She's going to be making a first impression and you want to help her along. To extend that simile, some parents are so anxiety ridden they overdo it. Clean stockings and panties and a nourishing lunch may serve her better than fussing over buttons and bows. The ARCs you send to gatekeepers must have the essentials, not a lot of frills:

- Reread the media release and query and cover letter sections of this book so you can spruce yours up before you send your kit off.
- Use computer-generated labels instead of handwriting the envelope's address.
- Send your kit and book priority mail. It looks great, isn't much more expensive than first class, and USPS supplies the envelope at no extra cost.
- If a reviewer asks for a copy of your book, write "Requested Material" on the envelope. Please

don't pretend it's been requested if it hasn't. You won't fool anyone.

- When the envelope is opened, the reviewer should find a brief cover or query letter front and center.
- When submission guidelines don't ask for a book or don't specify that material be sent by post, use e-mail to keep your costs down.
- When you contact gatekeepers by e-mail, your subject line must be professional. Your recipients need to know exactly what they will find when they open the e-mail. If they don't, they may not open it at all. It starts with "Query," and then a headline-like "Obama Congratulates Local Author on New Novel."

Section IV
Promote Your Book
by Doing What You Love

If my doctor told me I had only six minutes to live, I wouldn't brood. I'd type a little faster. ~ Isaac Asimov

This section of *The Frugal Book Promoter* is good medicine. It's good for those who think they don't like to promote but do love writing because a good portion of book promotion *is* writing. You'll learn to love some things you didn't think you could.

This section is also a tonic for those who get a thrill from marketing. What a delight to find that you get to combine two things you love to do.

Many of the promotion ideas in this section can be used online or in more traditional venues. There are marketing remedies for those who hate anything that smacks of tech and a few ideas for those who adore what tech can do. In either case, put your lab coat on and devise a plan that fits your career goals. Mix ideas from elsewhere in this book to build a marketing campaign tailored to your personality and book's title.

Chapter Sixteen

Loving Writing and Recycling

The writing-and-recycling combination is the Prius of promotion. If marketing a book were measured in miles, you'd go farther on less fuel with your writing than about anything else. ~ CHJ

This chapter on how to use your writing skills to promote is perfect for those who love writing, but it's also great for those who are shy. Put them in your mortar and mash them with your pestle until you come up with the perfect marketing mix for your personality and your title.

-∞-

RECYCLE CREATIVE WORK. When I began to think about promoting my book, I had scraps of my writing secreted away in the nooks and crannies of my computer. They were like little emerald-cut diamonds in the dark recesses of a safe. What good were they hidden away like that? Some had been submitted and rejected and some had never been submitted at all. Some were unfinished. That made them equal because regardless of the reason they were hidden, no one had read them! There were even a few that had been printed—some on obscure Web sites that had purchased first-time rights only and these cried out to be read again.

Then I noticed new literary journals sprouting up everywhere. Many were print and Web journals edited by people who care about literature even though they did not pay their authors a cent for their creative work. They seemed likely resources because they didn't already have a battery of favored contributors. I began a rescue mission. I retrieved a few stories and poems from my files and submitted them.

Some pieces I resold. Some I gave away. (Watch for more in this chapter about bartering or giving away your writing.) You can do the same thing. Start by collecting some of your old writing. Rewrite sections of your book as excerpts or short stories. As you learn new things or do new things, write about them. Put on your big-idea sombrero and think of articles, stories, or poems that relate to your book or will appeal to your readers. Then find a publisher to showcase them. Or you can do it the other way around. Find publishers who appeal to the reader you want to reach and tailor what you write for them. Each time one appears in print, a plank is added to your platform and you expose your writing style to readers, maybe even make fans of them.

> **Caveat:** When previously published material is used, the first publisher should be credited along with the author if the publisher paid for first rights or if the name of the original publisher will burnish your piece with additional credibility.

Submitting material for no pay may be an idea that makes you cringe. However, it is a time-honored tradition among poets and literary writers. People have bartered for eons and considered it fair and just. When the article you give away appears with a tagline and a link to your Web site, it will:

- Add to your name recognition (your branding).
- Help build your platform.
- Boost your search-engine ranking.
- Increase traffic to your site or blog.

> **Hint:** Print journals often have Web sites so when they publish work that includes a link to your Web site, blog, or buypage in the tagline, you get a bigger footprint on search engines, a better trafficked blog or Web site, and exposure to your other work long after the print journal has gone to the recycling bin.

A list of print and electronic publishers that have published my work, many just thirty days or so after I began my recycling campaign is on my site. It will encourage you to try this platform-building campaign and serve as a resource for approachable presses: howtodoitfrugally.com/published_works_almanac.htm.

The list may reassure those who have not yet found a publisher that your voice is worth listening to and illustrates that even a piece once rejected by the *Atlantic Review* (that, mind you, gets something like 30,000 submissions a year!) might bring readers pleasure and serve as a promotion tool. If any of these publications suit the material you have closeted away, edit and submit! That may be all it takes to turn you from a literary couch potato into a spirited PR genius.

Many of these publishers reimbursed me with nothing more than a thank you, a lovely link, byline, tagline, and, occasionally, copies of their journal, and I felt it was worth my while. When you work with editors, you develop new relationships. We all must choose our goals. Choose to network, share, and expose your work.

-∞-

WRITE NONFICTION ARTICLES associated with your title or genre. You can place them one at a time using traditional market directories to guide your submissions or by using article banks, online sites where publishers go to find professional content. Here is a list of some of those article banks:

- o PowerHomeBiz.com.
- o Articles123.com.
- o Netterweb.com/articles.
- o Allnetarticles.com.
- o Womans-net.com.
- o Ezine-writer.com.au.
- o Clickforcontent.com.
- o Freezinesite.com.
- o IdeaMarketers.com.
- o Family-content.com.
- o Ezine-writer.com/article-lists.html.
- o Ezine-writer.com/top10.html.
- o Writers.net.
- o ThePhantomWriters.com.
- o eHow.com.

Caveat: Do not post or offer any article in trade that you may want to sell later. Many journals buy only first rights; if your piece has appeared on the Web, it will not qualify under many publishers' guidelines.

These tips will help you get more promotional mileage out of your articles regardless of how you disseminate them:

- ▪ Include information about your book in the article itself if you can figure out how to make that information pertinent to the article. Editors who use free material won't mind a little self-promotion if it is relevant and isn't blatant.

- Submit a resource box or sidebar (those helpful little informationals that are sometimes surrounded by a border) with your article. They often appear with feature articles on the Web and in print. Include your own book on the list of resources. Sidebars give editors added value and those who pay for their articles will pay more for articles that include a thoughtfully written one.

- Invite editors to visit your Web site in search of free material and to sign up for your notices about available articles. Capture their information and categorize it so you can better serve them in the future. My Web page with free articles is at howtodoitfrugally.com/free_content.htm. You are invited to borrow material in several categories for your own blog or newsletter.

- Don't date your articles with limiting content. Use "recently" instead of a specific date. Ditto for copyrights. The copyright insignia (©) and your name is enough.

- A program like SpamAssassin.com assures your editors that the content in your e-mailed article will prevent filters from bouncing their newsletters if they choose to use them. Add a note to each contribution that says, "This article was checked by (whatever program you used)."

- Keep a list of editors who used your material or might need it. (For more information on how to use these names, see the section on syndicating later in this chapter.)

- Avoid sending an article to an editor twice by tracking where you send each of them.

Submit your article with a title, a byline, and a credit line exactly as you would like to see it in print. (Look up "taglines" in the Index of this book.) Don't expect your editors to do it for you. They may not use your suggestion, but it is *your* job to make it easy for them to do *their* jobs.

-∞-

WRITE A COLUMN OR BLOG. Columns and blogs are far more productive than you may imagine. As an example, after you've written many, you can categorize them and assemble them into a book. You may start out writing columns and blogs for free, but it may turn into something that will help support your other writing.

A logical way to land a regular column of your own is to examine the articles you've written, identify a media trend, and parlay a select few with a specific theme into a proposal or query. One of my clients, Patricia Bunin, did just this with some very short anecdotes on her senior experiences. She believes that the idea sold primarily because they were short. These little essays or articles became the clippings or samples that helped convince an editor of her expertise.

To round your pitch, you come up with an appropriate column name, some facts that convince an editor you can attract readers, and enough courage to approach the right editor.

When my husband and I closed our last retail shop, I took old, yellowed clips from columns I had written before we had shops into the *Pasadena Star-News*. I was sure the features editor would politely show me the door, but I figured nothing ventured, nothing gained. The editor immediately assigned me a column called "Savvy Shopper" for that newspaper and its affiliates. Sometimes being brazen is an advantage. Sometimes we need to be in the right place at the right time. We can't be if we don't put ourselves out there.

Don't assume the samples you have aren't good enough. I thought that the way I had addressed the readers as "you" in my old columns was dated. The editor thought that was "fresh." That your samples have been published gives you credibility, but you might present something new you have written. If you have written frequent op-ed pieces or letters-to-the editor they may be an entrée to your own column, too.

Once you have experience of any kind, an editor may be willing to take a chance on something with a different slant. They need responsible writers who write well and submit on time. Find suitable periodicals in *Bacon's Directory,* either online or in your library.

Once you're accepted as a columnist, sell only the first rights so you can reprint columns elsewhere. You'll also find you can use material you've gathered in the past for your new column.

Blogs work very nearly the same way, but bloggers are at an advantage. They get to run things their own way. The disadvantages are that they don't have deadlines to motivate them and they need a little online savvy to run a blog. See Chapter Twenty-One for more on blogging.

Syndicate your articles or columns. Some columns with a specific thread like fashion or grammar lend themselves to syndication. Imagine how much better books would sell for a nationally known columnist like Liz Smith or Andy Rooney than for someone who is not known by the public. That columnist could be you.

Once you have a track record, submit a proposal to small syndication services or large ones like the Associated Press (AP). Do a search on "syndicates" for ideas. You want to know what kinds of columns they already have, where yours might fit in, and the appropriate editors' names.

Self-syndicate your column or your blog posts. You can bypass syndicates to sell your own columns to different outlets. Until you become famous, you can approach small newspapers, newsletters, etc. with suggestions for a series. You can also send out columns or post them one at a time. Or you can give your articles away, syndication style. The latter is an efficient way to recycle the essays, columns, commentaries, and rants you have written. I organized this process to meet my needs. I have no idea if anyone else does it similarly, but it disseminates writing at the grassroots level widely and quickly.

My approach is informal. I keep a separate list in my computer of all the editors I know who don't require exclusive material. I send articles I write on how authors can get free ink to one group of editors, my pieces on tolerance to another group, and so on. (See Chapter Eleven to learn how to categorize your media list.)

When you write an opinion piece, review, or rant, open your file for a particular group of editors and copy-and-paste their addresses into an e-mail address window. The next steps are:

- Use the help feature on your e-mail service to learn how to make each e-mail address blind. Your query or submission will look more personal to those who receive it.
- Think of a clear and catchy subject line.
- Include a signature line with complete contact information.
- It is unorthodox, but because eventually all the editors on my list have come to know me, I introduce my article with a short note that is generic enough to work for any editor who receives it and then paste my article beneath it. I make these points in the introduction:
  o The article is free.
  o I would like the editor to use the piece in its entirety and include the byline and tagline as submitted. Clearly delineating your expectations is not demanding; it is professional.
  o I would like notification when the article appears (along with the link that will always take readers to that specific article) so I can promote it in my newsletter and blog and on Facebook and Twitter.

> **Caveat:** This is a caveat that bears repeating. Do not attach your article. Many virus-wary editors (and others) will not open an e-mail or its attachment if one is included.

- Double check for typos (which, I'm not happy to tell you, I sometimes miss).
- Sometimes, I offer an editor an exclusive, especially if I can parlay it into extra exposure by gently asking for more than a byline and tagline. I might ask for a display or classified ad on their Web site or suggest we guest blog for one another or work in some other cross-promotional way.
- Among those who might be included on your article-placement list are Web site coordinators, bloggers, and newsletter editors—even authors with their own newsletters.

Grassroots marketing like this works. Of course, you can also target big-time editors.

-∞-

PUBLISH YOUR OWN NEWSLETTER to promote your book and keep readers involved until the next one is released. If your book hasn't yet been published, your readers will enjoy following the publishing process.

Newsletters needn't be fancy. In his column for *Time* magazine, Joe Klein told of Bryan Lentz's choice of a simple flier to promote his run for Congress. Lentz said his staff ". . . wanted something splashy." His simpler choice cost less and, he says, "They look real. People open them and read 'em like a newspaper." Klein notes,

"It was true, people [nearby] were reading the Bryan Lentz news."

That's the way it can be for your newsletter, too. I once asked my readers about my plain-text *Sharing with Writers* e-newsletters and they voted overwhelmingly for keeping them long and simple rather than short, colorful, and in HTML.

Some prefer to skip a newsletter and contribute to others' letters instead. The trouble is, there are benefits that come with having your own newsletter that you can't get by playing someone else's game. Shel Horowitz recently reinstated a newsletter (guerrillamarketinggoesgreen.com) he dropped for just that reason.

Linda Morelli, the award-winning romance and mystery writer, swears by her newsletter. She says, "I have more fun with my quarterly newsletters [than other forms of promotion]. I personalize each with news about what's happening in my world, my latest reviews and book signings, my current contest, and even my favorite recipes." Although she sends out about 100 letters by USPS to fans who don't have e-mail, she posts electronically to a much larger list.

It may be easier for romance writers like Linda to fill their letters with material that will be of interest to their readers, but it can be done for any genre. Here are some tips on how to start:

- Keep your goals in mind. Entertainment? Staying in contact with readers? Garnering support? Book sales?
- Consider the time it takes to produce a letter.
- If you plan a snail-mail edition, consider the cost *and* the increased effectiveness.
- Let your letter reflect your personality. Most letters start with a chatty piece from the author. C. Hope Clark includes a snapshot of herself doing something fun in her *Funds for Writers* newsletter (fundsforwriters.com/newsletter).
- Humor attracts and keeps readers.
- To increase readership, encourage readers to contribute articles and letters-to-the-editor.
- Include general and fun features to entertain your readers. Crossword puzzle, anyone?
- Ask your readers for suggestions on content they would like to see included.
- Post each newsletter on your Web site. Some of your regular subscribers will revisit your archived letters and the sites you link to in your newsletter, including your own.
- Use a signup window on your Web site and blog so visitors can subscribe to your letter.
- Recycle your feature articles and tips onto your blog and vice versa. Allow plenty of time between each appearance. Recycle again to others' letters and blogs.
- Include a calendar of your events.
- To encourage readers to scroll to the end of the letter, end each one with something amusing. I use pun-oriented jokes because they relate to the fun of words. Publicity Hound Joan Stewart

uses doggy jokes and solicits new ones from her readers.

-∞-

WRITE BOOK REVIEWS. Why not? You read anyway. Reading contributes to the quality of your own writing, and it doesn't take much more time to write a review for your Web site or blog or for online bookstores after you've finished reading a book. Here are other advantages:

- The bylines and taglines on your reviews expose your name to a most important audience—people who read books.
- Include your Web site link in your tagline to improve your position on search engines.
- Reviewing connects you to the editors and other reviewers at review sites, folks who can help you get your book reviewed when the time comes.
- If you write reviews regularly for a review site and your editor is willing to write you a letter of assignment, you may apply to tradeshows like Frankfurt and Book Expo America (BEA) for a press pass. Such a pass affords you many other benefits. See "tradeshows" in the Index of this book to learn more about them.

Mary Gannon, deputy editor of *Poets & Writers* magazine, says reviewers take "a lot of heat…for some free books, a few bucks, and a byline." However, it's usually only the most famous reviewers who are disparaged for their criticism and only the radical or caustic ones at that.

Hint: The how-tos for writing a review are not in the purview of this book, but Mayra Calvani and Anne Edwards' *The Slippery Art of Book Reviewing* will help you write professional reviews whether you are using them to promote your book or hope for something more from reviewing. To buy the book, go to budurl.com/Reviewing.

Whether you are compensated with cash or with exposure for your book, your reviews will be good writing samples and publishing credentials as your career moves forward. Here are a few sites to try:

- Rebeccasreads.com gives very specific guidelines for reviews.
- Myshelf.com looks for reviewers who offer them exclusives.
- Simegen.com runs a reviews section.
- Compulsivereader.com.
- MidwestBookReview.com.
- Bookpleasures.com.
- Don't forget to pop your reviews up on online review sites like B&N.com.
- And don't neglect readers' social networks like Bookholics.com, Shelfari.com, and Goodreads.com. Choose the one that appears to attract the most readers in your genre. Find more information on using them in the Chapter Twenty-Two on social networking.

> **Hint:** I developed a type of review that I consider to be original, if such a thing as original exists. In Reviews for Riters, I assess a famous writer's work as if it had been submitted to critique group. I look for writing techniques she uses superbly or not so well,

ones that emerging authors can emulate—or not. It's a cross between a how-to article and a review. I found editors of sites that cater to the needs of writers enthusiastic about them. You might build such a niche with your own idea. Find mine at howtoditfrugally.com/free_content.htm.

-∞-

WRITE FOR ANTHOLOGIES. Anthologies are collections of similar articles, poetry or stories assembled by an editor or group of editors. It is a wonderful way for new writers to get recognized.

It's easy. Watch for calls for submissions in newsletters and magazines like the ones listed in the Index of this book, then send something you've written that matches the publication's needs. Sometimes they pay you for it, sometimes not. No matter. Your name and your book will receive exposure with an added measure of credibility because you are published within its covers. Often you receive much more than you gave.

Some authors complain that they don't get paid, don't get paid enough, or that they are expected to buy the anthology and to promote it. These grievances seem shortsighted to me. You would probably *want* to buy a couple of books your work appears in to give to special people in your life and to editors who may then give you (and the anthology) some publicity. Inclusion in an anthology is, after all, part of your platform, a kind of clip that points to your experience and success.

Further, if you're contributing to an anthology as part of your marketing campaign, it's to your advantage to promote. If all the contributors do so . . . well think of the promotion power behind that!

These doubting Thomases also overlook that many of the finest review journals and anthologies do not pay their authors, and that these publications are accepted entrées into the upper echelons of the literary world.

Work published in anthologies is recyclable, too, providing you did not sign over all your rights to the publisher. A writer who recycles her work may feel less resentful about not being paid or by other demands.

My first anthology was a cross-promotional effort. We all knew our collaborative e-book would only be as successful as the sum of the participants' promotional efforts. We were to give our e-book away rather than sell it. We shared our promotional coups using an e-group on Yahoogroups.com, became friends, joined one another in other projects, supported one another. Where is the exploitation in that? The process worked so well, I began to consider using anthologies published by traditional publishers, university presses, and others.

Anthologies sometimes pay their authors and almost always credit them with a tagline or other acknowledgement. Here are other advantages:

- Anthologies may offer awards. One of my stories appeared in an unpaid anthology but it also carried with it the "Red Sky Press Award." Awards, especially those chosen by prestigious judges like Rose A. O. Kleidon, Professor Emeritus in English at the University of Akron, can be used to promote in dozens of different ways. See the Index of this book for more on "contests" and "awards."

- Anthology editors may plan group book signings to promote the collection. A bookstore signing planned by *A Cup of Comfort* editors helped prepare contributor JayCe Crawford for the release of her book. Anthology editors should not object to your passing out your business cards or bookmarks at their events. In addition, after you've participated, you have an entree to the bookstore's events coordinator.
- The release of an anthology, book signings for anthologies, or any other related events or awards are opportunities for an author to send out her own media releases; this is not just exposure, it's credible exposure.
- Some anthologies give a portion or all of their net profit to a charity.
- When you participate in an anthology, you may meet someone in the publishing world from whom you can learn new things or meet people who will introduce you to others with similar interests. Hooray for networking!

Authors should be cautious. But they shouldn't reject an opportunity of being read and maybe even discovered based on someone else's bad experience or paranoia.

-∞-

WRITE FOREWORDS AND INTRODUCTIONS for other authors. When I was asked to write my first foreword for a book, I had no idea of the benefits of doing so, but it sounded fun. Eric Dinyer is an artist who had a concept for a gift book called *Effort and Surrender: The Art and Wisdom of Yoga.* I was surprised when Andrews McMeel Publishing used my name on the cover—nearly as prominently as the author's. The book was sold in Walmarts across the nation. That's not shabby exposure! The gift book is gorgeous with a little window in the cover that showcases Eric's artwork. It was a perfect addition to my branding campaign. Since then I have been asked to write other introductions and forewords. I never find it necessary to refuse. Authors don't usually ask unless you are a match for them.

An author might pursue these kinds of assignments by letting it be known they are available when they network with other writers and artists or on their Web sites.

-∞-

WRITE TIP SHEETS. A tip sheet is the way to editors' hearts. It is a list of quick, readable entries that relate to a specific subject. Editors use all the tips in an article like "Ten Great Tips for Writing Scintillating Headlines" at once or just one of the individual tips to fill nooks and crannies in their layouts. They know their readers love them. The subject line "Tip Sheet" is a most welcome message in an editor's e-mail box.

It is true that fiction writers must tweeze their material to make a PR technique like this work, but the results are worth the effort. Nonfiction writers will likely find tip sheets come popping off the pages of their books. Here are some ideas:

- List events in a timeline. This is ideal for the writers of history, regency, and other period romances or historical novels.
- *Time* magazine itemizes individual statistics to suggest conclusions. Your list of stats would deal with an aspect of your book, say the rebuilding of urban areas if it is about revitalizing inner cities.
- The publicity firm I once worked for instituted The Ten Best Dressed List. This was a publicity coup that built more than one career. Do a "best" or "worst" list that relates to something in your book.
- Editors like "Top Seven" or "Top Ten" lists. These lists adapt themselves to how-to books.
- Lists of the unusual little tidbits are good. I used one about Utah's idiosyncrasies to intrigue radio show hosts when *This Is the Place* was released. I put my list in a "Did you know" format. "Did you know that residents of Utah consume more catsup per capita than any other state in the union?"
- Because quotes have mass appeal, *Time* magazine uses them in a column called "Verbatim" each week. Recycle short quotations from your book. Tweeters love quotations and often extend their life by retweeting them.
- With a few adjustments, I could submit the list on writing tip sheets that you are reading right now to sites where authors congregate. I would need to add a title, byline, and a credit line complete with a buy link that would help market this book.

> **Hint:** For tip sheet ideas go to Top7business.com. It features a new list of seven ways to solve a problem each day. Submit a tip list suitable for their online publication.

-∞-

WRITE OP-ED ESSAYS. You are probably familiar with the op-ed sections of the newspapers you read, but you may not know they are called that. Not all papers identify these sections the same way. They are usually found near the letters-to-the editors section or on the page opposite their daily political cartoon. Though they are opinion pieces, they tend to be longer than letters-to-the-editor and usually carry a tagline identifying the author as an expert. (Check "taglines" in the Index to learn more about how to use them.) The authors of letters-to-the-editor are not compensated, but the authors of op-ed pieces often are.

Once you are a published author, it will be easier for your work to be accepted for op-ed sections. Send a convincing query letter to the editor in charge of the paper's editorial page. Sometimes newspapers print an additional roster of editorial staff and writers on the editorial page or on their Web sites.

> **Hint:** Pitch your op-ed ideas to newspapers that covered current events related the topic of your book. Do it immediately. To newspapers, the word "current" is crucial.

-∞-

WRITE PROMOTIONAL E-BOOKS. There may be as many different kinds of electronic books as you're likely to find in any bookstore. On their shelves, you see hardcover books, trade paperbacks, mass market paperbacks, books bound with twirly wires, pop-up books, large-print books, tactile books, and more.

E-books are all electronic but they, too, come in all sizes from whitepapers (short how-tos or informationals) that should, by all rights, be called e-papers to full-blown books. Some are given away. Some are sold. They are offered as .pdf files, ready for readers to read on their screens or to be printed out. E-books can also be downloaded to multimedia readers. Surely one of these iterations can be used to your advantage.

And just how do you use them to your advantage? Lots of ways. When your book is published as an e-book, in addition to a traditional have-and-hold book, you let your readers (who, after all, are your customers) get your book in whatever form *they* want and lets them get it fast. Some books—books on tech, as an example—require frequent updates. E-books allow you to do that. You can reach niche markets without much upfront expense, too. But mostly—tada!—e-books are great tools for promotion. Here are some ways to do that:

- Write a whitepaper or e-book to give away. Don't think that because it's free it can be slapdash. The idea is to let the e-book you're giving away attract readers to your other books—the ones they must buy. Having said that, you are giving it away so it could contain advertising in the back of the book that leads the reader to your other work and that of others.

213

- To get wider exposure than you could on your own, coauthor an e-book. Share your contacts, your publishing expenses, your promotion ideas, your time, and your different skills.
- Write an e-book to entice others to do something you'd like them to do, like sign up for your newsletter. Like buy another of your books. Like subscribe to your blog. Okay, let's admit it. They're little bribes. You can use others' e-books as bribes, too. It's a great way to help one another in a way that benefits you both. As an example, Shelley Hitz offers this e-book on social media tips free to my readers: self-publishing-coach.com/support-files/social-media-tips-from-the-experts.pdf. It's a round robin kind of promotion; I contributed to this e-book at no charge.
- Write a sequel to your book and publish it as an e-book to spur sales that have become stale. Or the other way around. James Patterson gave away an early novel to create a flurry of media attention and attract readers to his new one.
- An e-book format can breathe oxygen into a book that is about to expire. If your book isn't already available as an e-book, publish it that way and promote its new availability in a travel-easy and frugal format. To do that you must own the rights. Otherwise, encourage your publisher to do it or allow you to do it.

> **Hint:** Copy for some e-book devices must be specially formatted. Making a .pdf file of your Word file won't cut it. Smashwords.com publishes for an assortment of devices and they have a tutorial that helps you with this task. Or download that tutorial from Gene

Cartwright's iFOGO Village at ifogovillage.ning.com/group/smashwords. IFOGO also offers formatting service to those who don't want to tackle the job on their own.

My students often complain that authors make less money on e-books than paperbacks. Yes . . . and no. Think of this as Economics 101. There you learn about the importance of volume. Think of it as Marketing 101. In that course you learn about word-of-mouth and exposure. The more people who read your book in any format (and love it), the more you'll sell. But here are the reasons I make all my how-to books like this one and *The Frugal Editor* available as e-books:

- They can be offered inexpensively to starving or budget-conscious readers.
- They can be published fast. Once written, I was able to have the first edition of *The Frugal Book Promoter* ready to use as a syllabus of sorts for my UCLA Extension Writers' Program class in less than thirty days.
- It is easy to update them.
- The number of pages is not an issue; you can include whatever you think best fills the reader's (or your story's) needs.
- People who live in other parts of the world can access your book quickly and inexpensively.
- An author can publish an e-book absolutely free.

I'm sold on e-books. I even make the poetry chapbooks I publish myself available as e-books. People who love poetry take their Kindles when they travel to Paris as readily as people who read nonfiction business books.

The anatomy of a free e-book might be just what you need to make one work for you. The free e-book I published as a cross promotion with other authors was one of best, most long-lasting promotions I've done. Let's call it the new math for free publicity where E-book + E-gift = Promotion. Oops. Error. Make the answer FREE promotion.

I met Kathleen Walls in an online group. She asked more than two dozen authors from several countries to contribute to an e-book that would be given away. *Cooking by the Book* could be used as a gift of appreciation to the support teams it takes to edit and market a book and to the legions of readers who cook but had never read any of our other books.

Authors who had at least one kitchen scene in their books were invited to contribute to *Cooking*. Each author's segment begins with an excerpt from that scene. The recipe comes next, and then a short blurb about the author with links so the reader can learn more about the authors and their books.

This e-tool was a cross-pollinator. Contributing authors publicized it any way they chose as long as they gave it away. Here are some of the ways we used to distribute *Cooking by the Book*:

- Some offered a free e-book as part of a promotion and let people e-mail them for a copy. This was the least techy approach and it allowed personal contact with readers. It also allowed us to collect and categorize our readers' e-mails to use in later promotions.

- Some set up an autoresponder that sent our e-book directly to our readers' e-mail boxes when they sent requests to an address we provided. This automated approach requires little but promotion from you after you've once set up the responder. I sent the first chapter of my novel using Send Free (carolynhowardjohnson@sendfree.com), but it could as easily been a full e-book.

- Some sent readers to our Web sites where they found a link to download a .pdf file of our free e-book. E-books distributed like this are more effective if they include an offer or call-to-action—perhaps a discount on a series of your books—within its pages.

- Some let others distribute our e-book as a gift to their clients, subscribers, or Web site visitors—either with a purchase or as an outright gift. When you use this method, you get to set the guidelines for its distribution because you provide the free e-book.

- If we were doing this promotion today, we could offer our free e-book through Smashwords.com. To make free e-book editions work for you, your book must include ads, links in the text, or both to entice readers to your Web site or to buy your other books. You're publishing it to *market* your other work.

- You may find other ways to distribute your e-book or alter these processes to meet your needs.

Contributors to our *Cooking by the Book* benefited from their efforts and from contacts with other authors. We even had some superior promoters among us:

- Most of us set up a promotional page for the cookbook on our Web sites.
- One promoted it in her newsletter.
- Mary Emma Allen writes novels, but she also featured the cookbook in the columns she writes for New Hampshire dailies *The Citizen* and *The Union Leader*.
- David Leonhardt incorporated the cookbook into a Happiness Game Show speech he delivered over a dozen times.
- We all gave away coupons offering this gift at book signings. Because e-books cost nothing to produce, they can be given to everyone, not just those who purchase a book. Some made bookmarks featuring this offer.
- I put an "e-gift" offer for *Cookbook* on the back of my business cards.
- If we were doing this promotion today, we'd all blog about it and use Twitter, Facebook, YouTube, and other social networks.
- We treated the promotional book like a real book. We got blurbs and reviews. Reviewer JayCe Crawford said, "For a foodie-*cum*-fiction-freak like me, this cookbook is a dream come true." That review popped up in places we didn't know existed.
- We used them as e-gifts to thank editors, producers, or others online.

Our most startling successes came from sources we had no connection to at all. The idea for using a promotional e-book like this was featured in Joan Stewart's The *Publicity Hound*, in *Writer's Weekly*, in the iUniverse newsletter and more. They probably found it especially newsworthy because it worked so well for writers of fiction.

When I queried radio stations for interviews with angles related to this cookbook, I had the highest rate of response I'd ever had, and that was in competition with a pitch for *This Is the Place* just before the Salt Lake City 2002 games and an intolerance angle on the same novel right after 9/11.

Each year Mother's Day beckons us to repeat our publicity blitzes, because, if you haven't noticed, mothers tend to do *lots* of cooking.

> **Hint:** I love Createspace.com for publishing both e-books and paperbacks, whether or not they are to be used as promotions. You can probably do everything yourself and absolutely free except for the copies you buy and the low-cost premium membership, if you choose to go that route. There are even templates for covers there. If not, I can coach you through the first one and you'll be set forever more. Contact me through my Web site, howtodoitfrugally.com.

> **Special E-Book Offer:** I offer a free e-book for subscribing to my Sharing with Writers newsletter. Find the offer on most pages of my Web site, upper right corner: howtodoitfrugally.com.

–∞–

TRANSLATE WORKS YOU LOVE. You could translate poems, plays or about anything else. You might choose something famous or something obscure. If someone else has translated the same work, that's okay. You will bring your unique sensibility to the project. Edna Mine Karinski is a children's author at heart, but she is translating Mitsue Katsue Karinski's *Harvest Moon* from the Japanese as a personal tribute to her mother.

Chapter Seventeen

Learning to Love What You Thought You Couldn't

I like to take Wooden's advice a little further. You *can* do what you think you can't do—and learn to like doing it. I hope more authors accept this challenge because some scary aspects of marketing could keep our books from reaching their potential—and even keep us from publishing.

For some, speaking evokes as much fear as spiders or snakes. And we think contests only set us up for rejection. If you think you could never learn to love public speaking and literary contests, try. They are the brightest stars in the panoply of book promotion.

-∞-

SPEAKING IS THE STAR OF PR AND LIFE. The ability to speak in public will bring credibility to your résumé, and publicists dream about working with a client who can speak or is at least willing to learn.

If you are frightened, let the birth of your book nudge you toward learning this skill. If after giving speech-making an honest effort, you decide not to give formal speeches, all your other appearances—from book signings to recording videos to leading critique groups—will benefit from your new speaking skills.

If you think of speaking as sharing, you may find it fits your personality as well as a pair of comfy slippers. There are techniques that make being in front of a crowd less stressful. As an example, at your book launch you can take your microphone to the edge of the stage, sit down, and talk as if you were speaking one-on-one with those who have come to wish you well. At a seminar you can use a mike with a long cord so you can go into the audience to answer questions—a casual and effective way to touch those who have come to hear you. Beginning actors minimize their fear of performing before others by focusing their attention on a lucky-penny talisman they keep in their hand instead of on the crowd. If you've ever taught or conducted meetings successfully, think of speaking on topics related to your book as an extension of those skills.

Here are ways to make your speaking appearances more effective and comfortable for you:

- Give handouts crammed with valuable information to the audience, preferably something they'll keep. Print your pitch, the image of your bookcover, and your contact information on each sheet.
- Use an old-fashioned flipchart—a giant notebook that fits on an easel. Write as you talk as if you were taking notes in your senior English class. You can use this technique as a

cheat sheet by outlining your presentation before you start speaking and filling in the secondary categories as you speak.

- Breathe deeply before you start speaking. Have a glass of water on hand. If you've also provided munchies for the audience, the entire situation will feel more relaxed.
- It might motivate you if you think about this: Authors sometimes make more money speaking than they do from their books.
- Learn to use PowerPoint. Although I'm not fond of PP presentations because they tend to reduce eye contact with a speaker's audience, this little miracle from Word's Seattle campus can work a little like having a cheat sheet at the ready.

So, you're ready to give speaking the good old college try, right? Here are some possibilities:

- Go to Toastmasters' meetings. Find them online.
- Take a speech class at your local community college.
- Read Pam Kelly's book. She teaches master classes in speaking to UCLA's instructors and I learned everything I know from her. Find her book at budurl.com/PamKelly.
- Subscribe to Tom Antion's newsletter. He's the online speaking guru. Subscribe by sending him an e-mail at orders@antion.com.

Now you're ready to unearth potential speaking engagements. You watch the calendar sections in weekly and daily newspapers for coming events and locate entertainment agencies and organizations related to the topics you speak on in your yellow pages. You write a query letter to each lead, only this time you're asking for speaking engagements. You wait a couple of weeks, call to ask if they received your letter, and follow up with a verbal pitch. Pitching on the phone is easier than in person. And it's very good practice for speaking in general. Here are some other sources for finding places to speak:

- Fraternities and sororities.
- Night clubs and coffee houses.
- Corporations.
- Professional organizations.
- Charitable organizations.
- Political groups.
- Reading clubs.
- Libraries.
- Schools, especially college classes that are associated with some aspect of your book.

You can also propel one speech into others. In your handouts, include a form that asks the audience to recommend another organization that might benefit from your presentation. It will be more effective if you:

- Request that they turn the form back to you at the end of the meeting.
- Design your form as a self-mailer with pre-paid postage so they can send it later.
- Ask for specific information like the name of the organization, kinds of programs preferred, officer in charge of programs, phone number, and e-mail address.

- Offer a discount or other perk (like your free e-book!) for the referral.
- Offer your service at a reduced rate or at no charge to charity events.

You may choose to charge for speaking. Occasionally an organization offers only an honorarium. In either case, they should let you display and sell your book. And you should not be shy about listing your book as a resource in your handouts.

I always ask those in charge of programming to mention my presentation in their newsletter and media releases and include a picture of my bookcover and my Web site address.

Handling hecklers in public is one reason some authors don't care for speaking, but think of it this way. It's better for authors to learn to handle iffy situations at a small public venue than on national TV.

Here are two secret words. Determine. Defensive. You *determine* you will not be *defensive* in advance. We are now public persons and must resist the urge to react. Take a deep breath and decide that these folks are not hecklers. They are probably tactless or ignorant and neither are reasons to be offended.

A fellow author who is subsidy-published once e-mailed me this question for my Q&A *a la* Ann Landers column in my newsletter:

> **Author:** During my question and answer period at a book signing, a man asked me rather rudely why

someone with my credentials should choose to subsidy publish and mentioned that he had found typos in my book. In an interview earlier I was questioned about Jack Kelley's fabricated stories in *USA Today*, as if I had something to do with them.

My Answer: Try to give people like this a break; assume they just want information and turn the question away from you and to the publishing industry in general. What's considered good about each form of publishing and what isn't. How the publishing industry, just like others, is not perfect. You might be armed with an anecdote of your own so the heckler (if that is, indeed, what he is) is disarmed by your candor. Humor is helpful. On a similar occasion I told my questioner how *The New York Times* reported that major publishers were inflating their first-run figures for books in order to create buzz in the media and that compared to this kind of an…er…indiscretion, a typo or two hardly seems like a sin of great proportions. You might then turn the occasion into something positive by mentioning how your book or another published by your subsidy publisher was recently optioned for a movie or received an award.

After an upsetting moment we might examine our reaction to see what we can learn about ourselves. Did we feel insulted because we lack confidence in our choices? Do we feel our skills are inadequate to address criticism? Is there something deeper at work here we might tackle in the interest of self-improvement?

During a book tour (yep, a real *tour*—meaning several stops in a short period of time to promote one specific book) in Georgia, I was confronted by a woman who asked if I knew the Mormon religion was a cult. In Utah where I was raised, I frequently encountered intolerance because I was *not* a Mormon. I handled the situation well enough (but not perfectly!), returning her question with a question about how she would define "cult." Nevertheless, the experience helped me see how deeply rooted the hurts I experienced as a child and teenager were, that I hadn't, in fact, "gotten over" them as I thought I had, and that I am offended as much by bigotry aimed at others as at myself. Self-examination helps authors handle encounters of the hard-to-take kind more effectively.

-∞-

AWARDS SET YOUR BOOK APART. I pity the poor reader these days. Reviews can't be relied on for unbiased opinions, so a reader may have trouble telling which book is most likely to set her heart a'beating. As she shops, she often turns to the blurbs or endorsements on the back of the book. She may read a few of a book's first pages. But a book that has won an award from an organization like Jeff Keen's USA Book News award (usabooknews.com) or the New Millennium award (indiebookawards.com.com) or, yes, from universities like Columbia's Pulitzer (pulitzer.org), will probably clinch a sale faster than many other sales techniques.

Authors who have won literary contests (contests run for poetry, short stories, novellas, novels and other literary entities, usually sponsored by journals, publishers, and the like) also get bragging rights they can put into their media kits, query letters, and Web sites. That makes it easier to sell a promotion idea (or a next book!) than it would be for someone who is new to writing. Gatekeepers—anyone from acquisition editors to feature editors at newspapers—can be influenced by a contest. Make that a contest win, place, or show. It may be what's needed to set you apart from the many authors clamoring for attention. In fact on a slow news day, just about any award looks like a nugget of gold to a busy editor.

So why are authors so ready to hate contests? Fear of rejection is an easy answer. An article in the revered *Poetry & Writers* magazine mentions that writers often consider contests rigged and resent the fees (usually from free to $25 for literary contests and from free to $125 for book awards). The magazine article pointed out that publishers and organizations become dependent on the fees they charge for contests and note that rarely does an unknown author win. I'm not sure the last part isn't sour grapes; the point of many contests is to find delicious new voices that will keep the not-so-voracious appetite of publishers for new material well fed. If it is the truth, perhaps we should do something to hone our own skills to approximate those of more established authors.

There are other benefits to contests. Some offer critiques of entries—a value that cannot be overestimated in terms of learning more about the contest-winning process and one's craft. Some publishers sponsor contests to attract submissions of great new manuscripts.

> **Hint:** Some of the most prestigious contests only accept nominations that come directly from publishers.

You may need to gently prod your publisher if you know of a contest you think your book is right for.

When it comes to marketing, a contest win is a contest win is a contest win—whether you win, place, or show.

Here are some guidelines for using contests to gain exposure and expand your credentials:

- Choose contests that fit the size of your pocketbook. No-fee contests work well until you refine your contest IQ. Those include following submission guidelines to the nth degree and selecting contests that suit your material and your voice. Pick contests that impose fees at least as carefully as you might select a tomato from the produce department at your market. Journals that award prizes to the best work submitted for their pages in a given year are a good, frugal way to start.
- Choose contests based on the kind of writing you do. Read up on past winners. Examine past winners for genre, voice, length.
- Find contests from a source that lists less popular contests as well as those that have names attached to them like Hemingway, Faulkner, and Pulitzer. Keep reading this chapters for a short list of contest resources. Go to howtodoitfrugally.com/contests.htm for a list even beginners have a chance of winning.
- Pay attention to the contest's guidelines, *except* for the one that calls for no simultaneous submissions. This rule is patently unfair to the author. You know it and they know it. It's a rule, not a law. It is a courtesy, however, to

notify those contests or journals you have submitted to if your entry wins elsewhere.
- To increase your chances and to keep you from worrying about each entry, submit work to several contests at a time.
- Keep track of entries so you don't submit the same material to the same contest twice.

> **Hint:** Some journals still don't accept online entries. Don't recycle paper copies that have been returned to you. Editors complain about entries that look as if they have spent a night in the rain.

Find suitable contests on the Web, in books, and through organizations. Here are a few leads:
- Use the Deadlines section of *Poetry & Writers* magazine to find reputable contests. Most are very competitive and charge fees. Find them at pw.org.
- CRWROPPS is an announcement list for contests and calls for submissions. To subscribe go to groups.yahoo.com/group/CRWROPPS-B/.
- A fat volume called *Writer's Markets* (budurl.com/WritersMarkets) publishes an updated edition each year. It lists contests, publishers, agents, and tons more. Buy the book and get online access to updates.
- Check professional organizations like your local Press Women, the National Federation of Press Women, and the Wisconsin Regional Writers' Association (WRWA), which accepts writers from anywhere.
- Do a Google search on "writing contests" plus your genre.

- Subscribe to *Winning Writers* newsletter at winningwriters.com. I love this one for finding free contests.

Once you've won a contest—finalist or first place—you are newsworthy:

- Add this honor to the Awards page of your media kit. If it's your first award, center it on a page of its own. Oh! And celebrate!
- Write your media release announcing this coup. (See Chapter Eleven to learn to build a targeted media list and Chapter Twelve to learn to write a professional media release.)
- Post your news on media release distribution sites. Find a list of these sites at howtodoitfrugally.com/media_release_disseminators1.h
- Notify your professional organizations.
- Notify bookstores where you hope to have a signing and those where you have had a signing.
- Notify your college and high school. Some have press offices. Most publish magazines for alumni and their current students.
- Add this information to the signature feature (see Chapter Twenty) of your e-mail program.
- Add this honor to the biography template you use in future media releases—the part that gives an editor background information on you.
- Use this information when you pitch TV or radio producers. It sets you apart from others and defines you as an expert.
- If your book wins an award, order embossed gold labels from a company like labels-usa.com/embossed-labels.htm. You or your distributor can apply them to your books' covers. If you

win an important award, ask your publisher to redesign your bookcover or dustcover to feature it *a la* the Caldecott medal given for beautifully illustrated children's books. If you don't know this medal, visit your local bookstore and ask to see books given this award. It's one of the most famous and most beautifully designed.

- Be sure your award is front and center on your blog, your Web site, your Twitter wallpaper, and your social network pages. Don't forget your e-mail signature.
- Your award should be evident on everything from your business card to your checks and invoices. I use the footer of my stationery to tout my major awards.
- If your book is published as an e-book only, ask for the contest's official badge or banner to use for promotion. If they don't have one, make one of your own using bannerfans.com/banner_maker.php.
- Frame your award certificate and hang it in your office to impress visitors and to inspire yourself to soar even higher!

Robert W. Schaefer, one of the readers of the first edition of *The Frugal Book Promoter,* wrote to tell me that he would appreciate a plan of attack for getting an award for his book. Here's what I told him.

- First and foremost, write a great book. One with great content. One that is organized well. A reminder here. It's almost impossible to do this without some personal guidance, which is why I recommend writers' conferences (see the next section of this chapter), and well-vetted writing classes in your genre.

Caveat: When you change genres, take another class. Do it even if you have been successful at writing in another genre. Authors who have achieved stature should be especially cautious about embarrassing themselves by launching into another arena without knowing all the new stuff they need to know. Poetry is not fiction. Writing a romance requires some skills science fiction does not, and vice versa. Journalists have a great start, but they'll find that knowing more about some elements of fiction like dialogue may enhance their news stories as well as help them write a better novel.

- Get your book edited by a professional editor. You'll have an easier time of selling it if you do this *before* you begin the submission process. Because many publishers have cut their editing budgets, you'll be more assured that the job is done well enough to have it qualify for an award. Read my *The Frugal Editor* (budurl.com/TheFrugalEditor) to know more about editing and how to choose a qualified one.
- If you are self-publishing, hire an excellent book cover artist. Mind you, I didn't say a graphic designer or fine artist. People like Chaz DeSimone (charlesdesimone.com) know things about book cover design and marketing pitches that others don't know.
- If you are self-publishing, hire a good formatter or interior book designer, one who knows the intricacies of frontmatter, backmatter, headers, footers, and page numbering.

- If you write nonfiction, learn the art of indexing. It isn't as easy as the word processing programs seem to make it, but I think it's one uphill battle that's worth fighting on your own because no one will know your book—know what you feel is important for your reader to know—like you do. There are, of course, professional indexers who will work closely with you. If your publisher provides an index for you, check it to see if important categories or details have been overlooked.
- Follow the guidelines in this chapter for finding the perfect contest, one that is a match for your book.
- Attack this process with confidence and be willing to make an investment of time and some money.

As you can see, the more you know about publishing, the better equipped you will be to produce a product you can be proud of (and, hey! Your book *is* a product!). You may even produce a prize-winning book. You wouldn't expect to become a computer programmer without knowing how the hardware worked, now would you?

-∞-

WRITERS' CONFERENCES WORK if you work them right. I hear grumblings about writers' conferences all the time, but when I ask, I usually find that authors went to conferences with unreasonable expectations or they selected conferences knowing little about them. Trust me on this, a series of respected writers' conferences may be the near-equivalent of an MFA for a time-starved writer juggling creative aspirations and the requirements of a day job.

Writers' conferences are valuable because they immerse you—albeit for a few short days—into your art. They expose you to a broad array of what you need for success. They tend to make us all aware of how much we don't know and how much we need to know to publish and promote.

Authors often go to writers' conferences hoping they will snag an agent or publisher. The trouble is, they do this before they've been to enough conferences or taken enough classes to polish their craft. After experiences like these, they throw up their hands in horror and decide to self- or subsidy-publish, but if they haven't honed their skills enough to attract an agent or publisher at a conference, it's possible their book is not ready for publishing on their own either. Many times they are frustrated because:

- They attend the wrong conference at the wrong time in their sojourn from first draft to publishing. They may be looking for an agent before their novels are complete or their sample chapters and proposals for their nonfiction book are written.
- They set unrealistic goals for the conference.
- Their expectations for what a conference should provide are too narrow and or too broad.

When seasoned authors express surprise at how involved they must be in the promotion of their own books, I am convinced anew of the need for conferences. It's difficult to come away from most conferences without getting a handle on what a book requires to make it visible.

Conferences staged by large universities, writing schools, or well-known magazines may give more up-to-date, accurate advice because they vet their presenters and can attract the most experienced writing instructors. That makes them invaluable. Authors should look at the credentials of a conference and its presenters before they register. Even a great conference may not be a match for their genre or their level of expertise.

Aside from the credibility a reputable conference will give to your platform, here is what you'll miss if you never go to one:

- You'll miss a chance to learn about traditional and alternative publishing. If you aren't well-advised, you will doubt your own choices when things go awry (and a few things *always* go awry—it's the way of the world).
- You'll miss all those writing secrets that seminars offer. You can't hear a secret if you aren't in the room.
- You'll miss out on contacts with more publishers, agents, and marketers than you're likely to meet elsewhere in a decade.
- You'll miss the greatest possible critique partners. Conference-goers tend to be excellent critiquers because they cared enough to learn about their craft. If you don't already have

skilled critique partners, forming a new group should be one of your goals for a conference.

- You'll miss a chance to corral one of the reputable agents in attendance.
- You'll miss the chance to practice your pitch and may never learn how a good one works.
- If you don't attend a well-known conference, you can't add it to your list of achievements in the query letter you send to agents and publishers. Having attended a respected conference is an indication of the investment you have in your career.
- If you don't attend a conference, you'll never know what you missed—both the good and the bad.

Choosing a conference can be tricky. Many conferences are expensive. Even free online conferences can take a lot of time. This is one of those occasions when it pays to be picky.

Determine your goals and choose a conference accordingly. Some focus almost exclusively on craft and often call themselves retreats. Some make an effort to offer seminars in book marketing. Others tend to be entrées to agents and publishers, and some offer information on publishing like the legalities of copyright law. Some do a little of everything.

Study up on conferences. The library has back issues of *Poets & Writers* that include reviews of conferences. Use your networks or Google to get opinions and suggestions from writers who have attended.

Here are a few more conference-perfecting ideas:

- Do not choose a conference based on its exotic location unless your first interest is a vacation.
- If you choose a conference that offers critiques of your work by publishers or agents for an additional fee, spend the extra money to participate. And if you wait until later, you may have to kick in another full conference fee for the privilege.
- If signing with an agent is what you are really after, wait until your book or proposal is fine-tuned to go to a conference.

> **Hint:** If pitching an agent is your primary goal, be sure agents who specialize in your genre will be there by reviewing the conference Web site. Register for the conference early enough to be assured of an audience with your choice.

- Determine the thrust of the conference you will be attending. Because of proximity and prestige, UCLA (uclaextension.edu/writers) has access to Hollywood as a resource. This makes their conference one of the best for screenwriters. Other conferences have their own specialties.
- If you want to find time to concentrate on your writing, you may prefer a writers' retreat rather than a conference.
- Examine the credentials of the conference presenters. If you write persona poems, you may want to study with a teacher who has had success writing that specific kind of poetry like UCLA's Suzanne Lummis. A person who is interested in writing courtroom dramas will

benefit from an instructor who has published in that genre.

- Other bona fide educational institutions that offer onsite and Web classes are Gotham Writers' Workshop in New York (writingclasses.com) and The Image Warehouse, Athens, TX, which also publishes a journal (imagewarehouse.org).

- Until you're sure you can utilize an expensive conference to its fullest, select seminars offered by some online conferences like the Catholic Writers' Conference (catholicwritersconference.com), the Muse Online Writers' Conference that I cosponsor with Lea Schizas (themuseonlinewritersconference.com), and Promo Day (jolinsdell.tripod.com/promoday) founded by Jo Linsdell. They are all free, though you are encouraged to make small donations to defray costs. It's also a good idea to take the same precautions selecting a free online conference you would take choosing an expensive on-site conference. Time is money.

> **Hint:** Bring a small pouch of tools with you to conferences. I use a bag I received with an Estée Lauder gift-with-purchase. Toss into it color-coded pens, snub-nosed scissors (sharp ones may not get you through airport security), a small roll of cellophane tape, your index labels, paperclips, strong see-through packing tape (in case you must ship materials books and other materials back home), ChapStick, hole puncher, breath mints, a tin of aspirin, elastic bands, Band-Aids, and your personal medication. If you

are presenting throw in a hammer, tacks, razor, a small pair of pliers and a mini measuring tape, Mine even has a spool of very fine wire for hanging large posters. Don't unpack this kit when you get home. You'll need it in the future for other conferences, book signings, book fairs, and other promotional events.

You can use a conference to promote, too.

- Some conferences offer tables where participants can leave promotional handouts for their books or services. Before you leave home, ask your conference coordinator how you might utilize this opportunity.
- Ask the conference coordinator if they publish a newsletter or journal. If so, send the editor media releases as your career moves along.
- Take your business cards to the conference.
- If you have a published book, take your bookmarks to give to others.
- If you have an area of expertise that would interest a conference director, introduce yourself. She may be busy, so keep your pitch very short and follow up later.
- Record the names of fellow conference attendees and presenters who might give you endorsements for your book in the future.

Chapter Eighteen

Publishing Dreams vs. Marketing Needs

The one thing that never disappoints an author is holding a new book in hand. The one thing that pleases us unexpectedly is how much writing a book forces us to grow. ~ CHJ

Other than watching our books hit *The New York Times* bestseller list, what most authors dream about is signing books. You see yourself in bookstores and at book fairs and tradeshows like Book America Expo (BEA). You're at a table signing books with a Franklin Christoph fountain pen and a long line of admiring fans waiting to breathe your essence, touch your ink.

That's a lovely dream and dreams do come true, but making venues like these work well takes a lot of work. After their first big book tour, some authors decide there are other ways to promote that give them more bang for their buck, more marketing power for the time they take and the stress they create.

I want you to realize your dreams but I also don't want you to make all the mistakes I made when I started marketing my books. If these kinds of appearances are your dream, go for it. But know that if for any reason you can't do a tour, all is not lost. There *are* other ways to promote—many more effective. And there are other dreams to catch.

-∞-

TRADESHOWS ARE NOT WHAT YOU THINK. Authors don't sell books at tradeshows like Book Expo America. We give them away. We're selling only in the sense that we're promoting them to the people who come to tradeshows, people who will help us sell them, people like publishers, editors, librarians, and bookstore buyers.

Many tradeshows will not let booth participants sell merchandise directly from the tradeshow show. Tradeshows are about marketing, though customers may place orders with vendors for future delivery. It's safe to say that tradeshows exist for every industry. In general, they are huge, very busy, creative places. They're also confusing and can be very expensive to participate in.

It confuses many writers that these shows often call themselves book fairs. To keep our terms straight, we'll speak of book fairs as those where readers (and yes, others!) come for a fun day of book-browsing and maybe some buying.

Probably the most famous tradeshows in the world of publishing are Book Expo America, London, and Frankfurt. Library organizations hold regional tradeshows for easy access by librarians. To help you see the difference between tradeshows and book fairs, two of the most famous book *fairs* in the U. S. are the one founded by Laura Bush in Washington DC and the one sponsored by the *LA Times* in Los Angeles.

Authors dream of being part of tradeshows but often don't get to participate because booths are expensive, travel is expensive and access is closed to individual authors and they don't know how to get around those restrictions.

Services have sprung up to fill the void. Some organizations offer to put your book on display in their booths at these publishing-industry shows for a more reasonable cost than renting a booth on your own. Booths can easily run over $1500 and these services usually cost $200 to $500. But your book will get lost among dozens, if not hundreds that they "feature."

The sponsors of these booths often claim to have great success selling the foreign rights to books or pitching self-published books to large publishers. If authors can't be on the premises to show, talk about, and sign their own books, the money spent for these services will almost certainly be wasted. The fee is paid up front, so the caretakers of the booth will not be invested in the success of the books on display. The sales person in the booth will never have read the book or met the author. There is usually no way to hold the organization accountable for lack of a success they didn't really promise to begin with.

If you are considering a service like this, ask if they are willing to provide their service and get paid only if they produce results. When I say "results" I don't mean a list of publishers who have "shown an interest." The lists I was given were either not detailed enough for me to reach the "interested party" or were generic lists given to all their clients. Many of these services do their best,

243

I'm sure. I just think that you can probably spend your money more effectively.

If you can afford to be in these booths *in person*, here are the advantages:

- Bookstore buyers, acquisition librarians, and the media do attend tradeshows and you might generate interest for your book with some of them.
- Tradeshows can be great learning and networking experiences. Publishers, distributors, warehousers, book-oriented media, foreign rights agents, and publicists will be there. And they expect to be pitched! Most tradeshows even include great education programs taught by the best in the industry.
- If you're there on a press pass (and you may be able to get one if you are a bona fide reviewer or writer on matters of publishing for any branch of the media), you will have access to the press room where you can stock their shelves with your media kits and pick up others kits, too.
- You may someday be a presenter or panelist at one of these shows. If you are an expert on some aspect of publishing and have some speaking credentials, put your expert query letter skills to good use and see what happens.

Finding tradeshows is easy if you connect with a great list-serve group or forum like the ones sponsored by Small Publishers Association of North America (spannet.org) or find my list of publishing-oriented tradeshows on the Writers' Resources pages of my Web site at budurl.com/BookFairsTradeSws. Google this list of library councils for more information:

- American Association of School Libraries.
- California Library Association.
- Illinois Library Association.
- New England Library Association.
- New York Library Association.
- New York State Reading Association.
- Ohio Library Council.
- Pennsylvania Library Association.

You may need to show publishing credentials to get into a tradeshow, and, even then, access can be expensive. Those with press badges and those who have rented booths need not pay an entrance fee.

Tradeshow signing opportunities are more plentiful than you might think. Here are some backdoor suggestions short of renting an expensive booth of your own:

- If you have won an award from an organization like USA Book News (usabooknews.com), they may invite you to spend some time in their booth to sign your books. In fact, before you enter a contest, ask the administrator if they offer this benefit. There may be a small charge for this time to help defray costs and you will be expected to give away the books you sign rather than sell them.
- If you have a distributor or wholesaler, they may extend opportunities (usually for a fee) to sign your book in their booth.
- If your book was published by a large publisher, they may provide you with free booth time.

- Some publishing-oriented organizations like Book Publicists of Southern California (bookpublicists.org) or Independent Book Publishers Association or IBPA (ibpa-online.org) may have a cost-sharing booth. As with a display at any tradeshow, to do well you must be *in* the booth, *talking* to people who drop by.

Sometimes those who have booths are allowed to apply for one or two signing spots at the back of the hall on the tradeshow floor. These are coveted signing positions, even more prestigious than signing positions in individual booths. Attendees line up to get free books, talk to the authors, have pictures taken with them, and have their books (sometimes ARCs) signed. I got one of these treasured spots for *This Is the Place* through the Small Publishers Association of North America (SPAN) booth. It was a dream come true, even though I had to buy and then give away 300 books. A promotion like that is worth the expense and time. For the dream. For the outside chance that some amazing opportunity will come from it. And because it will give your book sales a boost. It was a much more successful marketing venture than the signing I did a few years later out of my distributor's booth or the one I did out of an award booth.

As with any promotion, an author doesn't just sign up for a signing, pay the rent for her booth, and hope. The event must be promoted and that's where those contact lists we talked about in Chapter Eleven come in handy. Of course, you put all of the applicable skills in this book to work for your appearance—media kits, media releases, and query letters. I have even included an sample invitation to one of my BEA booth appearances in the Appendix of this book for you to use as a template for your first tradeshow appearance.

-∞-

BOOK FAIRS ARE FOR THE PUBLIC. They attract lots of people in the publishing industry, but they also are for readers who might *buy* your book on the spot! Still, you want to prepare for encounters with the media—producers, directors, bloggers, and others interested in new content. The promotion you do for your book fair appearance isn't only about encouraging people to come buy your book! That promotion builds your credentials among general readers and influential people in the entire publishing world.

Like tradeshows, you can do book fairs the expensive way by renting your own booth or the frugal way by sharing with others. The benefits of doing it with others are the same as with any cross promotion. That is, you and your partners or other participants gain exposure from each other's contacts and you share the costs and booth responsibilities.

But like tradeshows and about any other promotion you do, book fairs aren't magic. When authors assume book fairs are about sales rather than exposure and credibility they set themselves up for disappointment. In fact, if you don't use a book fair booth as an opportunity to network, to promote, and to gain credibility for being there, don't do it. Book fairs are like marriage. We love them only when we work hard at them.

Hint: One of the best things you can do is send invitations to every library event planner and acquisition librarian in the vicinity of the book fair venue.

I used to sponsor book fair booths at the *LA Times* Festival of Books. Slowly and at considerable cost—one year at a time—I learned what works and what doesn't. My booth partners and I used tons of value-added promotions including:

- Catalogs we produced ourselves that featured booth participants' books. We used the fair logo to give the catalog credibility. We sent it to book buyers, local media, and influentials like movie directors and producers (because that fair is in the middle of Hollywood land). We all shared the costs of printing and postage.
- Videos and/or trailers using a similar plan. Each year's video was used in our booth and each participant had access to it for their blogs, Web sites, and other promotion.
- Much of the work we did for videos and trailers was recycled onto CDs to be given away. CDs can be reproduced in large quantities very inexpensively. One of our participating authors offered our freebies to visitors saying, "A CD for your PC?" Fairgoers loved them.
- We offered free books donated by other generous authors with the purchase of any book from our booth.
- A drawing for a gift basket was successful because it garnered the contact information of many readers. We shared that information with one another, too.

- We produced totes and bags featuring our bookcover images and our booth number. We gave them to folks to carry the books they had purchased from us. These bags then became advertisements for our booth as our customers carried them around the grounds.
- Some of our booth participants wore T-shirts emblazoned with images of their bookcovers, their Web site addresses, and our booth number.
- Each participant produced posters that we used to decorate the booth.
- Volunteers passed out freebies (like the catalogs we produced, goodie bags, and CDs) to the fairgoers as they entered the campus.
- We also had mini training sessions for our booth participants in which we urged them to talk up one another's books, guided them through promotion possibilities and display techniques, and gave them resources for promotion materials.

Book fairs are not all equal. Some are right for one title but not another. Some charge $35 and some $1300 for a booth. Book fairs are more valuable tools if you have a connection to the region, if you tie your booth to a local charity, or if the genre of your book fits the theme of the fair or at least the section of the fair your booth is located in.

One way to ensure success at any fair is to be a featured guest or presenter at a fair where the book fair administration promotes you in their advertising campaign. And then you double down with your own promotion and end up with a royal flush.

Another is to choose a fair that benefits an organization. Lori Hein, author of *Ribbons of Highway: A Mother-Child Journey Across America* did well at a book fair that benefited her daughter's elementary school. Her signs informed book fair revelers that three dollars would be donated from every book sale and she sold twenty-five books. She says, "Two weeks later I'm still riding the coattails of that one book fair." She did a lot of things right:

- She chose a fair where she had personal ties.
- She chose a fair that was aligned to the title of her book; a school fair and a book about a parent-child relationship were a great team.
- She used good signs.
- She was specific about the amount she intended to donate.
- She passed out fliers and cards complete with a good pitch and contact information to encourage after-fair sales.

Here are other things you can do to increase the effectiveness of your booth and make the experience more enjoyable:

- The *LA Times* offers listings in an advertising section that goes out to their subscribers and other readers before the fair. It seemed expensive but people who contacted me six months after the fair mentioned they had found my title and Web site address in that section.
- Fair administrators also offer booth extras like electrical hookups and lighting. Lighting is an

important part of great retailing and you *are* retailing when you sell books from a book fair booth.

- Be kind to your back. Take a roller board or a hand cart.
- Send media releases to local press, TV, libraries, bookstore event coordinators and buyers, and book discussion group leaders.
- Take pictures to use in future promotions like your Web site, your blog, and your Facebook pages.
- Offer a special "fair-only discount" to interested readers.
- Wear a nametag that says "AUTHOR" in large letters the entire day, even when you go to lunch. Use indelible ink on broad satin ribbon, clip it into a swallowtail shape, and hang it from your nametag. Readers are impressed with authors; let them know you are one.
- If you are a fair speaker or panelist, use that designation to find an entrée for your book in the booths of participating bookstores before the fair. They may stock your book after the fair.
- Keep a guestbook; building a contact list should be one of your primary goals at any event you do. Remind those who sign in to *print*.
- Give souvenir buttons to anyone who walks up to your booth. Don't just hand them out. Ask if you may pin them to your customers' shirts; they become your walking billboards and you make a friend. Used like this, buttons are one souvenir that works.

- Use specially-designed car magnets and decals and even (less effectively) bumper stickers. The car or truck you bring your books in will be parked at the fair all day.
- If someone from the press visits your booth, don't just smile. *Ask* them for coverage. *Pitch* them ideas. *Help* them get the story they want. Better still, the story they didn't know they were after.
- Be hospitable. Set out a bowl of treats.
- If you'll be standing on the grass wear warm, comfy shoes and socks and bring a mat.
- Bring along a helper, preferably a chatty one.
- Dress the part. Literary authors could consider a scholarly look—perhaps a turtle neck and Harry Potter-style spectacles. As a conversation starter, Kathleen Walls, author of *Ghostly Getaways*, wears a bride dress like the one on the cover of her book.
- Take a kit of essentials including tape, a hammer, pliers, and tacks. Re-supply anything you run out of when you get back to home base. Re-use your kit at the next fair.
- Pack a lunch. Even if you have a friend who can relieve you, you are the star attraction. You're there to meet your public, not disappear into the food zone.
- Take sunscreen and a hat in case your awning doesn't arrive or in case the fair doesn't provide them as part of your rental.
- Consider buying mugs or T-shirts imprinted with your bookcover. You probably won't have much luck selling them, but they make nice gifts

if an editor, producer, or director should stop by and show an interest. Of course, if the weather turns foul, you might sell a lot of imprinted umbrellas or rain bonnets.

- Make notes in the moment on each business card you collect and follow up on leads as quickly as possible.
- Don't forget your thank-you notes. Send them to those who bought your book and to the fair coordinators. Maybe you couldn't be a presenter this time, but if you keep in touch, next time you might be the celebrity *du jour*.
- Did I mention great signs? Use a banner and collapsible stand like the one I bought from my friend George at GSsigns.com. They are not inexpensive but I found my banner proclaiming "Award-Winning Author Now Signing" complete with a photo made a big difference for attracting readers to my table when I was signing.

By now you know you don't need to *sell* your book. It will sell itself if you're marketing it well. Still, at a fair you benefit from tried-and-true sales practices. Stand, don't sit. Practice your pitch and adapt your pitch to your audience. I might say, "*This Is the Place* is a coming-of-age story about a young woman about your age" to a young adult. I tell older readers how many awards it has won, including the Reviewer's Choice Award. You can also practice some responses to sales resistance:

- If a browser says, "I already have too many books on my nightstand," the author doesn't try to sell something they've just told you they don't want. Instead you say, "I know what you mean. However, if you are a member of an organization that could use a presenter, I do those, too," as you hand them a card or flier or even a free book.

- If a browser says, "I'm writing my own book," the author says, "That's wonderful. I edit books," or "I have a signup sheet for my newsletter. In it are tips and tons of resources for authors!"

Evaluate your fair experience (or any other marketing event) right afterward. I do this so I can refine the procedure the next time 'round, or avoid it altogether. Fairs are a bit like having babies. You are determined to never do it again immediately afterward, but you tend to forget about the pain and are ready to start again in about six months.

> **Hint:** I often use one idea I found in an old evaluation: Keep your nametag—the one you used at a fair or presentation—in your glove box or in the box of books you carry in your trunk for sales on the road. If you come across a fair in your travels and decide to stop by, wear the tag as you walk the fair. You'll be surprised at how many attendees will want to talk to you about your book.

-∞-

BOOK SIGNINGS AND BOOKSTORE TOURS are a little like bathing suits. They look better in our dreams than they do in the dressing room. Like itsy bitsy bikinis or strongmen's tiny suits, cold book signings can be chilly and, until we have an adoring fan base, they are seldom hot, hot, hot!

I witnessed a book signing for Anne Rice at Vroman's Bookstore in Pasadena, CA. People were lined up around the block—and doubled back. Rice's fans had been there for hours with her big, fat books in hand— newly purchased—waiting for her to arrive. I was on the way to a movie next door. When I came out, the line was just as long, but the faces were all new. Heaven (and Vroman's accountants) might be the only entities with a firm take on how many books she signed in two hours or how many more she would sign before her writing hand became too sore to function.

I mention this because signings have their place. That place is just about anywhere if the author is famous. Or if she is a master promoter. If she is not, that place is in the middle of her own little pond.

An emerging author may have more than one pond—a small lake where she works, a puddle of a community where she sleeps, a pool where she was raised—but, unless the author, a publicist, or a publisher has stirred up huge waves in that larger national-book-buying ocean, she may find it discouraging to sign outside an area where she is known.

Someday, after decades of growth, you may have a book signing like Rice's. Until then, my own book signing story may be closer to what you might expect. My launch and the signings I did in locales where I had contacts were successful (by much more humble standards than Rice's!) but still tons of work and not much fun.

Before my first book was published, I spent three decades as a founder and owner of gift stores and worked for a short time as a publicist and journalist. After that many years in the business of selling and PR, I knew before I ever had a book published how to plan and work an event and what to expect. Or so I thought. Some authors have experience in these related fields, some don't. Some are good at them, some not. Some like promotion and sales, others don't. Even with a strong background in these fields, the major successes I gleaned from book signings was learning what to tell future readers of my how-to books what works well and what doesn't. My greatest pleasure was meeting those who knew my work and came to wish me well.

I've had signings that surprised bookstore event directors. "Wow! Fifty books! And this is your first book. I'm going to call our Van Nuys store and suggest they set something up for you, too!"

And I've had signings where I just wanted to go home, take a hot bath, and bury myself in blankets.

That does not mean I have discarded book signings from my repertoire of promotions. I have, instead, set up rules that fit both my emotional needs and my goals for promotion. Aside from keeping signings within familiar territory, here are some of the guidelines I use:

- I sign only at events where I am a speaker, reader, workshop leader, or panelist. To walk into a bookstore without what is known in the entertainment trade as a warmup, does not work well.

- I do not think of book sales as the prime purpose for doing book signings—they are occasions for exposure in person and in the press, for branding and for fun.
- I want to sign where I have contacts that allow me to get broadcast air and ink space from the event. I want to sign where I can send out invitations to people I know or to people a friend of mine in that area knows. Then I know the marketing value of the event will be worth my time—even if the turnout was not.
- I only sign for stores that will do their full share of advance publicity. This includes:
  - Exposure in their newsletter, in the local media, and on the Web.
  - Posting signs or distributing fliers or bookmarks in the store before the book signing.
  - Utilizing local press and online event calendars. Trumba.com has a good online calendar, but Google's is free.

You may choose a full-blown book tour of several bookstores across the nation or keep your appearances near home. You do it because a tour fulfills a life's dream or because you believe your particular book and skill set are suited for tours. If so, take a card from the deck of T.C. Boyle, literary author cum promoter extraordinaire. In *Poets & Writers*, Joanna Smith Rakoff says T.C. is "not content with nice reviews and decent book sales...he wants to be a phenomenon." That's how you approach book signings if you choose to take on that assignment. You take the responsibility for making each appearance the very best it can be.

Make your book signing sizzle. Here are some ideas you can use:

- Coordinate your plans with whoever is in charge of your bookstore's events. Event planners need to know what you need—for both the setup and the promotion.
- Ask the store manager to occasionally use the store's PA system to introduce you to customers, especially if you are not reading.
- Arrive an hour early to set up. Many stores will not have prepared for your visit, even when you previously discussed your needs with them.
- Ask the sales associate at the cash register if you can display a stack of your books on the counter. This area is called "point-of-purchase" by the retail trade—for obvious reasons.
- Although some bookstores stock their own "autographed copy" stickers, have some made just in case. Apply them to the covers of the signed copies you leave for the bookstore to sell after the event. Don't worry. You will use all your stickers at your launch and other places you appear. I had my labels printed on gold foil by an address label service I found in my Sunday newspaper throwaway.
- Offer to send autographed bookplates or labels to the bookstore manager when she reorders so she can put them into your books. Many bookstores have special areas with autographed books from past signings on display. Bookplates were originally a way to personalize books in one's library with contact information so that loaned books could be returned easily. They can

be purchased at bookstores in the new-fangled sticker variety. You can also use mailing labels printed on your computer with your logo or bookcover image. Authors can continue to send signed ones to bookstores. It's a great way to stay in touch with buyers and event managers.

- Design knock 'em dead signs to bring with you. Verbiage should have the same level of pizzazz as loglines used for screenplays. Color and images are important. So is quality.
- Put your signs everywhere, including your car parked in front of the bookstore. Perch a 5 x 7 tent card or sign with an easel on the top of that stack of your books at the point-of-purchase. Use a small business-card size tent card or Post-it on the shelf where your books are normally displayed. Put signs on your signing table, one in the window, maybe even the bathroom near a vase of flowers. Send a large poster to the store to use at least one week before the event. Design these signs so they can be recycled for other events.
- Display your books face out using plastic or wire display stands. They're like plate stands or small easels. Find them at craft and art stores or at footprintpress.com/stand.htm where you can get a discount if you use the code FRUGAL.
- Ask the bookstore manager and sales associates to mention you to customers who go through checkout. They could say something like, "By the way, have you stopped to say hello to our award-winning author who's signing books

today?" as she points to the pile of books on the counter or to where you are set up.

- Talk to the sales associates. They are the ones who spread the word about books. Give a signed book to a salesperson who is especially interested and ask her if she would recommend it to customers after she reads it.
- Bring something to give to those who buy your book, certainly, but also to those who pause to talk. Everything you hand out should include information for ordering your book on them. Possibilities are:
  o A bookmark.
  o Your promotion/business card.
  o A token souvenir (see "Other Souvenir Items" in Chapter Thirteen).
  o A recipe. Even if your book isn't a cookbook, a recipe from a kitchen or cooking scene will be well received; it might include an excerpt or quote from that foody chapter.
  o Give away a list. An example is, "The Year's 10 Best Reads." Include your book and contact information.
  o A flier offering a free e-book. (See Chapter Sixteen's "Write Promotional E-Books.")
  o Snack foods. I love the M&Ms that can be custom printed with your title or name. I had "Frugal Editor" printed on lime green ones and "Frugal Promoter" on yellow ones.
  o Find them at mymms.com.
- Use a guestbook. Encourage people to *print* their e-mail addresses for future promotional

purposes. A contest or drawing may persuade them to sign.

- Bring a friend to help. Her duties are to ask people to sign your guestbook, serve as your unofficial photographer, and chat with you when it is slow.
- Take pictures.
  - o Slip a snapshot into the thank-you notes you send to bookstore personnel after the signing. I've seen bookstores use images offered by an author in their newsletters.
  - o Use some of the photos on your Web site, for signs you make for your next signing, and in your scrapbook.
  - o Tuck some into your query letter to other event directors to show how special you make your signings.
- Review your elevator pitch (see "Pitching Your Readers" in Chapter Ten) until it sounds natural when you use it on people who walk by.
- Bring your own fine-tipped markers for signing. Know what message you'll write before your signature, but personalize it when you can. When you dedicate a book, check the spelling of the recipient's name before you start writing.

> **Hint:** I bought a lightweight canvas bag with rollers to use as permanent event storage. It includes all my promotion items and a pouch of small tools I need to set up so I don't have to borrow from busy store personnel.

Book signing myths abound. Be especially cautious about information you find on the Web. Listen, learn, but consider the source. Many authors and PR "experts" repeat gossip rather than what they know from a reliable source or from professional experience or first-hand practical experience. Here are some fallacies that run rampant among authors:

Fallacy #1: *You can't have an effective promotional campaign without a book tour.* Most authors today choose to do scattered signings—not complete tours—because most pay travel expenses themselves. It is less costly to sign in cities you plan to visit anyway. Besides, the Web is a viable alternative because it has made it so-o-o easy to reach so-o-o many people.

Fallacy #2: *If you sign books before you leave the bookstore, management can't return them.* I have a big box full of books—some signed, some not—that were returned to my publicist (eventually) after a whirlwind of book-signing gigs. They are proof that bookstores can and do return signed books. And, yes, my publicist did have an agreement with the stores that signed books could *not* be returned. If you are unlucky enough (or unprepared enough) to have a dismal signing, be aware that the store manager will not be thrilled about keeping a half dozen books—signed or unsigned—in her inventory. Even if your book sales went well, follow-up sales may not match that success. A bookstore is in the business of selling books, not stocking them.

Fallacy #3: *If you take extra books along with you and need to use them, the bookstore will pay you upon delivery or within thirty days.* I still have unpaid invoices from the signings I did in 2001 for *This Is the Place*. Rarely do bookstores pay in less than sixty or ninety days. Rarely will they pay without reminders. Never will they pay unless you provide an invoice. I always ask if a bookstore can pay before I leave the premises and only one, R&K Bookstore in St. George, UT, did so. And they offered before I asked.

> **Hint:** Even with this dismal prospect, it is better to provide a few books you never get paid for rather than inconvenience a reader.

Fallacy #4: *You can ensure success of a signing by running an ad in a local paper or by buying a list of names in that locale.* Lists are important. *Targeted* lists are a whole lot better. Lists you've assembled from your own contacts are pure magic. And one-time ads are rarely effective unless your name is John Grisham.

Fallacy #5: *Bookstores are the only venues for book signings.* There are all kinds of places for you to sign books, places that you have personally supported in the past and that will, now, return the favor. Some nontraditional venues make signing an adventure and possibly more profitable. You will think of your own, but here are some suggestions:

- One critique group of romance and mystery writers sponsors signings at supermarkets that carry mass market books.
- Align yourselves with a charity. Everyone recognizes the extra value. A signing sponsored by Romance Writers of America (rwanational.org) benefited the Laubach Literacy Programs. Writers can join similar efforts of writing-oriented organizations.
- Museums are possible venues. My first launch benefited the Autry Museum of Western

Heritage. They donated a well-equipped theater, promoted the event, and allowed me to serve a buffet. The Museum kept forty percent of the book sales. Commercial bookstores' pricing policies are about the same. The difference is that booksellers are a profitable venture rather than nonprofit.

- Match nontraditional venues to the genre of your book. Mysteries at a police department as an example. Coffee houses and universities work well for a variety of books.
- My grandson's private school offered to sponsor a signing, as least in part because *This Is the Place* is a coming-of-age story, but also because of our past support, I'm sure.

The untour book tour is a little like the Mad Hatter's unbirthday party. It isn't quite the real thing because it's not a non-stop tour of multiple venues. Untours can be lots less expensive and a lot of fun.

You can plan two kinds of untours. One is the tour of bookstores you do piecemeal—a bookstore in one town today, another fifty miles away next month. A more popular model is an online tour, also known as a blog tour or virtual tour.

You plan an untour of bookstores when:
- You will regret it if you don't do a tour of real stores rather than blogs and Web sites.
- You have determined that there is no way your publisher is going to foot the bill for one like he does for the Stephen Kings in his catalog.

- Your budget is not large enough to duplicate an extensive tour but you still want a taste of a real tour.
- You're willing to spend a lot of time organizing the tour and promoting the tour.
- You don't mind doing your tour in segments, which means, of course, dragging it out over several weeks and months and—possibly— traveling in bits and pieces during that time.

The secret of an untour of bookstores is to piggyback your bookstore appearances onto your other travel needs like trips for pleasure or business. That doesn't necessarily mean only one bookstore appearance a trip, but it might if you can only give one additional day or evening to your book. Here is your plan of attack:

- Each time you leave your home base, the trip becomes an occasion to promote. Juggle your other plans to accommodate your tour. Plan every aspect of it before you go.
- Try to get events at several noncompeting bookstores in the same city or region. Choose widely separated venues only if your other plans take you to each location.
- Choose independent bookstores when possible. Indies are more likely to be interested in your book and will probably expend greater effort to promote your event. After you send your query, follow up with telephone calls to the event directors. A friendly nudge never hurts, especially if you're armed with another reason they would benefit from having you.
- If you meet resistance, guarantee sales of books the bookstore purchases for the event. That

means that if the store doesn't sell them within a given time, you or your publisher will buy them back. Negotiate. Ask if they will keep a certain number (usually six) signed copies for thirty to ninety days. If they hesitate, offer to pay the return postage on them. Having said that, know that getting paid for your books may require a lot of additional work on your part.

- Show bookstore owners how you can increase their profits with a signing by outlining the support you can give them with contact lists and the publicity you will get for them.
- Plan events that fit the title of your book and your energy level.
- Promote *each* signing and the tour as a whole. Use every trick in this book. Feature editors, the weekend calendar sections of the local newspaper, radio stations. Leave no pebble in place.
- Plan tours in areas where you have a base of support, where there is special interest in your topic.
- Bookstores aren't the only place to do a signing. If you can't get a bookstore in a specific area to host you, ask a friend to open their home to their reading friends. Ask an organization—perhaps a sister group to one you belong to in your hometown—to let you speak and sign.
- Go on a tour well equipped. That's hard when you fly, but it can be done.
- Expect the unexpected, even an unplanned radio interview or an opportunity to add another reading to your agenda might pop up.

- Let friends or relatives help. In fact, choose locations where someone will use their influence, invite their friends, or lend you a car or a bed.
- Keep essential information on your iPhone, in your travel journal, or on a calendar you keep at your side. "Essentials" even include directions from your Motel 6 to the bookstore.
- At each stop, make time to drop off promotion packets at libraries and other bookstores and introduce yourself to their staffs. These packets might include an adaptation of your media kit, fliers, small posters to post on bulletin boards, and a copy of your book.
- It might be less expensive to spend your vacation money and expand an untour into a do-it-on-your-own full tour. Because *This Is the Place* is set in the 50s and features a rusty old Buick convertible, I thought touring Route 66 in a classic car might be a good idea. It didn't pan out, but local TV stations would have loved such a picture-perfect tour.

> **Hint:** If a publisher sponsors your tour, take what you know about promotion from this untour chapter to supplement your publisher's efforts so you'll love doing it and your book can soar!

I met a self-published author who decided he didn't care if his budget balanced. His book was his hobby and he was darn well going to enjoy it. He parked a monster vehicle near the Rose Bowl during a University of Southern California vs. UCLA game. It was professionally painted with the image of his nonfiction bookcover, endorsements, his photo, and Web site address. He had dispensers for fliers specially made to fit on both sides and the back of his venue-on-wheels so people could help themselves to trifold brochures with buy information in them when he wasn't around. This huge vehicle was home, office, and mini museum for artifacts that illustrated the theme of his book. After I talked to him for fifteen minutes, I was exhausted. I walked away shaking my head, pitying the poor publishers who had been short-sighted enough to reject the book of this powerhouse marketer. And, by the way, this might be classified as an untour with this difference: Between separate travel segments, this author's big, bad bus was always on duty.

Your stay-at-home tour are usually called blog tours or virtual tours. They merely substitute reviews and interviews and donated articles on blogs and Web sites and sometimes online radio interviews using your telephone for real bookstore signings. That means you can handle everything with your bottom planted firmly in a chair in front of your computer.

These virtual, blog, or stay-at-home tours can be substituted for your untour of bookstores or your real do-it-yourself book tour. They will save you tons of money and effort. You can do blog tours yourself or hire them done.

There are advantages and disadvantages to doing it either way. If you do it yourself, you save money. If you hire it done, you save time and increase your relationships with bloggers and radio hosts—people you might not otherwise find—to use in future promotions. So, if your budget can take the hit, this is one time that spending a little is worthwhile.

Here are three such virtual tour services, each a little different from the other. Explore them, compare prices, and decide which best fits your goals and title. You may find you can use more than one effectively:

- Aggie Villaneuva for an online blitz of interviews and reviews at PromotionAlaCarte.com/shop/interviewsandreviews.
- Denise Cassino helps you achieve bestseller status on Amazon with a tour and viral blast at Mybestsellerlaunch.com.
- Nikki Leigh for virtual tours at BookPromotionServices.com.

When you are touring virtually, don't forget to:

- Use your social networks and newsletter to drive traffic to the blogs and sites that feature your work.
- Put the contact information of those who joined your effort on your media list.
- Send thank yous.
- Get permission to re-use the reviews and interviews. Once granted, install the best ones on your Web site and in your media kit and, after a time, rerun them on your own blog. You can even link to podcasts and videos you used during your launch.

–∞–

LAUNCHES ARE THE BEST of book signing-related events. If I had my druthers, I'd focus on one large launch per book, perhaps for charity, invite tons of people, and have a *party.*

Launches are nothing more than glorified book signings. Well, okay. They can be as difficult, expensive, fantastic, and rewarding as a wedding. But you use all the skills in this chapter you'd use for signings and tours—every single one—stir in whatever pizzazz will make your heart zing and go for it. They are almost always held where the author knows the most people and they almost always are the one thing authors do to promote their books that do not disappoint.

Section V
You and the Media:
What's New, Old, and In Between?

To me anything with a chip is high tech; to my grandson, my limited edition, '85 Apple signed by the Woz himself is an antique in spite of its chip. ~ CHJ

What we we've talked about so far is mostly basic—techniques that have been around forever, like using query letters to get exposure. They are principles that underlie marketing success, old or new. Sometimes they're basics with a new twist. The thing is, media can't be neatly divided between old and new and shouldn't be. Not only do the same principles work everywhere, but most new media is firmly rooted in old media soil. Whether toddlers or seniors, they're all media. They can work together or apart. Together is better.

If we learn one thing from marketing, it may be that discriminating—on the basis of age or anything else—is destructive to our success. Some mediums are better for your title, your talents, and your pocket book than others, but those are the determiners, not how long they've been around.

So, let's learn how to make the most of every possibility open to you—online or off. Local, national, or international. Old or new. No holds barred.

Chapter Nineteen

Radio and TV: The Ageless Pair

Is radio old or new? I think of it as old, but Internet "radio" hosts are out there disagreeing with me thousands of times every day. ~ CHJ

Some authors are frightened by promoting on media like radio and TV, and others petrified of anything associated with a computer. But lots of what is accessed through a computer—streaming radio, videos, trailers—grew out of what came before it. When we think about it, the similarities are astounding. Authors can easily avoid whatever media frightens them and concentrate on the media in their comfort zone. I urge them to do just that, especially when it comes to radio and visual media like TV. Once they've had some success with one, it's easy to apply those skills and confidence to others.

-∞-

GETTING MEDIA INTERVIEWS is about the same no matter what kind of media host you are pitching. A TV host. A feature writer at *Parade*. Bloggers. Radio hosts of any ilk—"real" air radio or Internet streaming radio like BlogTalkRadio. You've already learned how to do that in this book. Apply these time-tested techniques to anything your heart desires.

Use your search engine to find radio, Internet radio, bloggers, and TV hosts who are looking for guests. To find new resources, use Twitter lists compiled by book marketers who tweet. Compile your list and the next time a big news story related to your book hits the news, send out your query for a guest spot. Check the Index of this book to quickly review your query-letter skills and get busy. Fran Silverman's *Talk Radio Wants You* (budurl.com/Silverman) lists all kinds of radio resources including Internet radio programs.

> **Hint:** If you have been writing and recycling articles (see Chapter Sixteen), you have an entrée with those editors and bloggers who may refer you to people looking for guests in other media.

-∞-

BEING INTERVIEWED by radio hosts or bloggers with small audiences is a good place to start because you gain experience and expertise with each appearance. Besides, grassroots exposure feels more personal to its audience and often commands more loyalty.

British author Samuel Butler once said, "The advantage of doing one's praising for oneself is that one can lay it on so thick and exactly in the right places." However, for radio and TV, you need to "lay it on" tactfully enough so that you are invited back, invited on other shows, and don't make yourself laughable before your audience. Here's how you do that:

- Make a list of the points you want to make about your book. The conversation can often be tactfully directed to include them.

- Before the interview, ask your host if she would like you to submit questions or talking points. If she is open to that courtesy, design the content to meet her needs and yours. The sample interview in your media kit will help you with this project.
- Listen or watch archived shows or arrive early to get a handle on how the host works and what will be expected of you.
- Show you understand the broadcast business by offering soundbites (clever, memorable ways of saying things) during the interview. Anticipate what an interviewer might ask and come up with some of these golden coins of wisdom; that's easy for you because you're a writer, right?
- Your broadcast may appear on the radio or TV station's Web site, on iTunes, or YouTube. Ask for a permalink (a link that takes you to the exact page your podcast or video appears on) or HTML code for it. The latter will make your interview appear like magic on your blog or Web site. Self-Publishing Coach Shelley Hitz shows you how to do this with her YouTube video at youtube.com/watch?v=rpLsdNFz51c.
- If possible, linger a while or contact your interviewer by e-mail or phone immediately afterward. It's thank-you time. One way to thank your host is to link to the interview from your Web site and tweet and blog about it like crazy. Tell your host you are doing it; she needs to see what a valuable guest you are.

- Give signed copies of your book to anyone who was of special service to you during your interview.
- Follow up about four weeks later with a proposal for another interview, one with a different slant than the one you just did. Remind the producer that you would be pleased to serve as an expert should they need one. Talk a bit about your next book, too.
- Don't forget to put the host and producer on your list of media contacts.

Your radio interview will be a success if you have been working on your speaking as suggested in Chapter Seventeen where we talked about skills that are useful over and over again in marketing our books—and in life.

If you are still nervous about speaking, radio is a good place to start. It's so much easier to be a proficient guest on radio than on TV. You already know how to talk on the phone. Most of us are pretty good at that.

After you've prepared talking points with your host, get a glass of water, take a deep breath, and sit back and have a normal conversation. Or better, stand and pace—it helps your voice maintain its energy. If the host forgets to mention your Web site, blog, or newsletter, do that on your own at the close of the program or when that information feels integral to what you are saying.

Tie something you say to the needs of your host's specific audience. This isn't all about you. It's about the radio audience. The easiest way is to mention the show's broadcast area or other demographic when you thank your interviewer.

TV is easy, once you've perfected radio presentations. You need only add a couple more skills to what you learned with your radio appearances to look professional on TV. Skype has begun to change the time and travel expense drawbacks to appearing on TV so it's often as convenient (and comfortable!) as radio.

Minimize the scare factor by pitching for local TV appearances first, preferably something sponsored by an organization you are associated with or hosted by someone you know.

I was dumfounded when I was accepted for my first TV interview. I walked into Glendale Community College's public information office, told them I had come back to campus to upgrade my computer skills to help with my writing and that my first book had just been published—all in one big, gulpy breath. I hadn't yet asked for an interview when I heard, "We'd love to interview you." This interview aired on local cable TV. It was taped by students who were learning skills needed for the television industry using the school's state-of-the-art studio on campus. I learned a lot about interviews from this experience, but the most important lesson I learned was to muster the courage to ask.

Everyone knows the upside of pictures. It's that "pictures are worth a million words" thing. The downsides of TV are:

- You often must travel to be in the studio and that expense is rarely covered by either the TV producer or your publisher.
- Unless you are a celebrity, have written a controversial book, or have a spitfire TV publicist, it is hard to land a national TV spot.
- TV is especially harsh on those who have not learned its secrets. (Those secrets are coming. Keep reading!) It's a good idea to review some of them in this chapter before each appearance.

Learning new TV skills takes a little courage. Actor Daniel Day Lewis said, "The thing about performance is that it is a celebration of the fact that we do contain within ourselves infinite possibilities." Here's how you prepare for your own TV celebration:

- Breathe deeply before the action countdown. Breathing lowers your voice and relaxes you.
- Beginners should keep their eyes on the interviewer. You don't want the camera to catch a distracted glance.
- As you develop skill, occasionally look into the camera as if it were the person you are talking to. That's your audience. There! In the camera's eye. Watch how TV anchors do it.
- Advanced TV performers learn to watch the camera lights on sets where more than one camera is used. Don't try this without training and practice.
- If you tend to blush when you're excited as I do, tell the makeup artist. He can tone down the amount of rouge he would normally use.

- Bring a copy of your book and keep it in your lap. When you make a point about it, show the cover to the camera with confidence.
- When a woman sits, she crosses her legs at the ankles. Men keep both feet together on the floor.
- Choose clothing in medium or light hues. Avoid white, black, and patterns. Select a fabric that breathes under hot lights.
- Don't wear epaulets or other designs on your shoulders. If they don't stay in place, you'll look as if you're hunching.
- Avoid jewelry that jiggles, clanks, or glares.
- Women should choose neutral-colored fingernail polish. The camera person may take a close up of your hands holding your book. Very long and brightly-colored nails draw attention from your cover.
- Linda Morelli, romance and mystery author, suggests controlling exaggerated facial gestures. She says she once "rolled my eyes heavenward. I've regretted doing that ever since."
- Be on guard before, during, and after the interview. Don't say anything—on or off the record—that you wouldn't say on the air. Even seasoned politicians have found that a live microphone clipped to their lapels can be a lethal weapon.
- The audience and interviewer are friends. Relax.

Those are the TV secrets you can't do without. But there are two more. Tada! One is the use of written word superimposed on TV screens and the other is the mysterious voiceover. Here is how to handle them:

- Watch for stage dressings. At one interview, the producers had blown up my bookcover and used it as part of the backdrop. If I hadn't noticed, I might have used the book I brought as a prop. Instead, I placed my book on the coffee table that was between my interviewer and me. It looked natural there, but I didn't need to hold it up when I referred to it.
- Messages called chyrons sometimes appear on the screen during your interview. They may include toll-free numbers, Web site addresses, and your book's title. Ask the producer if they plan to use them and what they will say so you can avoid duplicating those messages and use your on-air time more effectively.
- Similarly, there may be an introduction you don't hear. If there is, it helps to know beforehand what they will say.

Getting a CD of your performance can be useful. Bring a blank and a pre-addressed envelope so it will be little trouble for the producer to send you a copy. Your copy can be edited—even made into a montage of interviews—to get future appearances. You may hear these referred to as "reels."

Send a media release about your appearance to the local press—but not to competing TV stations. If you can get a photograph of you with the host and a prestigious backdrop (one that says CBS TV, as an example) you could send copies to the press with your release.

-∞-

TELEVISION IS A MANY-SPLENDORED THING. Network TV. Local TV. Affiliates. Cable TV. Public-access TV. And, though we don't think of them as TV, videos *a la* YouTube and other online entities. Each provides an author with its own set of opportunities and disadvantages.

Many authors arrange TV interviews in cities where they'll be vacationing. Others try for TV bookings in their home town and then fill in with national radio.

> **Hint:** When pitching TV, be sure the producer "sees" your idea—the possibilities for action, for color, for an interesting setting. Your idea should also be well conceived to fit with current news and the station's audience.

Local TV needs you. You may have a small station in your home town; it may be hiding in a strip mall, at your local community or private college, or in an office building with hardly a sign to identify it. It may be in a dark room with equipment that doesn't look much more sophisticated than the video camera your eight-year-old asked Santa to put under the tree. But it's there, waiting for you and your marketing ideas.

These stations look for hometown personalities and people who can speak to local issues—whether they are local or not. There may even be a local program that features authors and books.

> **Hint**: If you are going to appear on TV, contact the most suitable bookstore in that station's broadcast area. Tell the events coordinator or book buyer that when you are on air you'd like to refer listeners to her

store if she has sufficient stock. Do this in plenty of time for her to order books. Offer to do a workshop or a reading at her store after the broadcast.

Network TV is one area where a great publicist with a sizzling Rolodex can help you. When she lands you an appearance, you or your publisher must be prepared to pay your travel expenses. Some stations occasionally use Skype, but usually only for extremely accomplished experts on topics like politics and nuclear physics.

I once was interviewed by Peter Kulevich on CBS TV in Palm Springs. I live within two hours of that resort town, and my author friends and I had a good ol' time sitting on bar stools at The Chart House watching Peter and me on the evening news. I got the gig because I was participating in an event to promote National Literacy Day. I had bombarded the TV studios with my releases and Peter had taken the trouble to check out my credentials on my Web site. This is an example of getting media attention by doing something community or charity related.

To find locally produced programs (network or otherwise), use your yellow pages or *Bacon's Directory for TV*. It lists shows, their producers, their direct phone lines, and addresses. You can pay *Bacon's* (or someone else) for lists, but why do that when this resource is available at libraries?

> **Hint:** An exception to my "Find-Other-Ways-to-Promote-Yourself-Than-Paid-Advertising" rule is using the *Radio-TV Interview Report* (rtir.com) to let more than 4,000 producers know about your book

and your expertise. It works better for nonfiction authors, but fiction writers can often find angles in their work that makes them experts in an area that will interest producers.

Public-access TV is an opportunity for you to get what you want by doing it yourself. In some markets you can lease a half hour on public-access TV for under the price of lunch for two. A year's programming may cost $1500, cheaper than a single small ad in a metropolitan newspaper. The TV station provides the camera, studio, editing facilities and—if yours is a forward-looking cable provider—may even offer free how-to classes in tackling the project.

Federal law requires these stations to offer air time— sometimes for free (if a charity is involved). Some don't like that rule much, so if you are interested in this kind of publicity for your book, you may have to dig— even prod—to get them to admit you as a bona fide show host. This kind of TV is also called lease access.

Many who love books have managed to put together public-access programs that showcase publishers, other authors, and themselves. Others start a series that showcases their own expertise. If an author's book tells how to achieve financial security, their TV show carries the same message. An author could also make it a one-time special, promote it like crazy, and use clips from it for online video sites.

Connie Martinson loves books and libraries. She started her book show using pure seat-of-the-pants motivation. Her story is an inspiration to those who want to try this method of promotion, and if you should live in or visit the Los Angeles area, she is open for queries. Find her at www.conniemartinson.com.

> **Hint:** Instead of developing your own show, piggyback on programming provided by others by querying them to be a guest, a fellow commentator, or co-anchor.

The public broadcasting systems include both radio and TV. National Public Radio (NPR) was defined by Morley Safer of CBS News as the "never-never land of broadcasting, a safe haven from commercial considerations, a honeypot for every scholar and every harebrained nut to stick a finger into."

The Public Broadcasting System (PBS) and British Broadcasting System (BBS) are NPR's close relatives. Safer obviously understands a public figure's need for "a safe haven from commercial considerations." Maybe he knows a few of us authors, too. These entities are just what we need to give us a foot up.

> **Hint:** Once you've landed an appearance, that experience will help you get other bookings. It's about showcasing your credibility.

Get an NPR gig by pitching to the host or producer of a specific show like "Fresh Air." Listen to an assortment of each show's programs so the idea you present to them fits.

Pitch the NPR shows that have the highest ratings first because they may not accept a guest who has appeared on a competitor's show. If one of the biggies features you, however, some lower-rated shows will be pleased to hang onto their coattails.

> **Hint:** Find a sample query letter by Christine Louise Hohlbaum in the Appendix of this book. It got the author an interview on NPR, and it's annotated so you can see why it was effective.

Videos of all kinds including interviews are really nothing more than TV online, right? And they are the hardiest little marketers ever. I have a few video interviews and they were making the rounds on Web sites about the time I was signing at a book fair. It was about three in the afternoon, hot, and I was getting tired. Suddenly an author walking the fair with her publicist stopped dead in her tracks. "There she is," she squealed. She ran over, told me she had seen my video while she was surfing her iPhone. She decided right then that *The Frugal Book Promoter* was the how-to book she wanted and she determined she would order it even if she found something else at the fair. She was so excited about this serendipity, she bought all my books including my novel and chapbooks of poetry. And so did her publicist. Moral: Videos work, even the ones on iPhones and Facebook.

There are all kinds of ways to tackle videos. You can go all out for something that has a chance of going viral, or you can produce simple ones to spruce up your Web site or blog. You can use humor or an educational format. You can do an interview. You can do one video and reuse it everywhere or do new ones for different events. You can do a series of tutorials or mini how-tos. You can make them yourself or hire them done. They can look like little movies or more like slideshows. Call them what you will, but do them.

If you want to hire someone to help you with visuals, here are some suggestions:

- For trailer-type videos that really market your book, try Reno Lovison at authorsbroadcast.com.
- For slideshows like the ones we used on TV screens in our booths at book fairs, try Joyce Faulkner at katieseyes@aol.com.
- For a professional product from interviewer Rey Ybarra and the lens of his magic cameraman, Randy De Troit, go to budurl.com/ReysVids.

Chapter Twenty

The Old Internet

Pretending the Internet is new, new, new and better, better, better is convoluted thinking. Wikipedia is just an old-style encyclopedia delivered faster using less reliable experts who don't get paid to write it. ~ CHJ

With new Internet developments come new ways to market. Okay. Nearly new. The principles of marketing and basic marketing skills travel easily from pre-Web days to the present. And much of the old Net (if we can call anything on the Net old!) is as useful for marketing books as when they were first introduced. Maybe more so.

We often rush to predict the demise of the tried and true, and authors—who are often not the most Web-savvy of individuals—rush to drop Web tools that have served them well. Web tools they are familiar with. Web tools that fit the publishing world even when they may feel outdated to those who are in the know about the latest Internet links and kinks.

–∞–

YOUR WEB SITE might feel old in the newbie world of the Internet. New twists and turns keep coming up and some—like the idea that you can use your blog as a

Web site—work well for some authors. But not all authors are created equal. Authors, genres, and even titles within genres may call for different approaches. Commercially successful authors like Scott Turow have their own Web sites. Some, like Nora Roberts, personalize their sites by writing the copy in first person. Publishers, big and small, are coaxing and commanding their authors to build Web sites.

One thing is certain, though. This is not an aspect of your promotion campaign that you can dismiss without risk. No matter where you are in the publishing process, now is a good time to set up a Web site. Doing it early on will give you a handle on your needs. It will give you a chance to explore your branding. To see if you only need something very simple. To understand how your site may grow in order to serve your readers.

Some sites like Authors Den provide beginning authors with a free start, a way to grow by graduating to paid levels and a taste for what is ahead. Fiction writers may find a site like this continues to fill their needs. Nonfiction writers may see they need to grow their sites. I continue to use Authors Den (authorsden.com/carolynhowardjohnson) as a backup for when my own site crashes and to do other things with it like distribute my newsletter. It is also an excellent way to network with thousands of other authors.

It is impossible to know what you will need in the way of a Web site, but it is certain you need one. Here are a few of the most elementary features you will need, features often overlooked by beginners:

- A contact link. You'd be surprised at how many authors forget this or think their need for privacy precludes using one. Ask your Web designer. There are ways to maintain privacy and still honor your readers' need to get in touch with you.
- A media room where gatekeepers can download your media kit and high resolution photos of you and your book's cover. Include a place where media folks can sign up to get your new releases sent directly to their e-mail boxes and a place where you can showcase future plans.
- Your recent media releases. Because you will add a new release to your site frequently, this page will help your site place higher on search engines, too.
- A special giveaway that lets visitors see what your book is about, or encourages them to subscribe to your newsletter, to visit your blog, or to buy your book.

  > **Hint:** Free is and always will be a magic word. Offer something free. See the section in this book on free e-books and white papers in Chapter Sixteen.

- Mentions of your awards or even a special page to tout your awards and honors. (Learn more about using awards in the Index of this book.)
- Endorsements galore. I try to use a blurb on every page of my site. See more on blurbs in Chapter Ten.
- Nonfiction writers should include the Contents page from their book.

- At least one favorable review of your book, with permission from the reviewer to reprint it.
- Eventually a page where your readers can buy signed books directly from you.
- Look at your media kit folders. Things in it like your First Person Essay, your Ten Tips sheet, your Sample Interview can be recycled onto your Web site, even though they will also be available to those who download your kit.
- Link liberally from one page of your site to another.
- Get a book on Web *basic* web design. Web design, like so much else surrounding publishing, isn't something you need to know everything about, but the more you know, the more easily you can work with a webmaster to make decisions or to feel equipped to go it on your own.

> **Important:** Regardless of your plans for your Web site, get your domain name now. I use GoDaddy.com. Scott Turow and Nora Roberts use their own names. If you lag, you could lose yours to folks who scoop up authors' names and then try to sell them back to them at a huge profit.

As you can see, this is a basic list. I don't want to scare beginners off. Sites vary depending on the kind of books an author writes. It is okay to begin piecemeal and add features as you go. I do encourage you to learn enough about building Web sites to feel confident about adding new content. I found waiting for a Webmaster to make every change I needed frustrating and expensive.

I also like the idea of letting an expert—again, someone familiar with the needs of authors—help you build your site. MaAnna Stephenson (blogaid.com) is my blankie. She teaches her authors as she builds their sites. When your site is ready for public scrutiny, it will look good, do what you need it to do at the stage of publishing you find yourself in, have the potential to grow in any direction your career takes you, and you'll feel able to handle the day-to-day needs of Web site marketing.

Here are some extras to add as your site grows. They are strongly recommended by most experts:

- How-to author Peter Bowerman notes that most authors' Web sites don't have a frequently asked questions section (FAQ). I don't, but I intend to work on it. If you don't know what those FAQ questions are now, it won't be long before you will.
- A site map will help your visitors navigate your site easily. They will love you for it.
- Credits and links to the sites of your Web site designer and photographers.

NEWSLETTERS are one of those old promotion tools that still work in spite of rumblings that blogs have supplanted them. If I were ranking ways to promote on the Web, producing a newsletter would easily be in the top five. Newsletters are discussed in Chapter Sixteen that covers what you can do to promote by doing what you love most, which is write. That love of writing is more than enough reason for most of us to go the newsletter route to promote our books.

Hint: Most authors of nonfiction understand how a newsletter can benefit them, but newsletters work for fiction writers, too. One of my favorites is from mystery writer Billie A. Williams. Subscribe to see how she does it at http://tinyurl.com/4s4f47u.

-∞-

E-MAIL is another promotion tool that—to hear some tell it—is tottering on one leg. But it is the way you communicate with most everyone on the Net. There are advantages to reaching people with e-mail:

- Your message goes right to people's e-mail boxes. Direct e-mails avoid the extra clicks that communicating through social networks often requires.
- Your e-mail signature passively promotes for you every time you send an electronic message.

     Hint: If the e-mails you send out require an extra click (and that includes the e-mail distribution you use to distribute your newsletter), reexamine your process. We Internet users are getting lazy. That extra click may be a deterrent. Further, it increases the chance of a broken link or other things that can discourage the recipient from reading what you send.

- The subject line of e-mails is a sales message even for folks who don't open your e-mail.

Your e-mail signature needs to be more than just your name now that you are—or soon will be—contacting editors, producers, fellow writers, and readers. They want to know more about you, and some *need* to know more about you. Use the automatic signature that most e-mail services provide to give them that information. Once you have your signature set up, it promotes for you—no cost or time required.

To create an autosignature, use the Help menu in your e-mail program. Do a search for "signature" or "signature file." Some e-mail services allow you to include a thumbnail picture of your bookcover or a banner. A banner is really just a long logo and shouldn't be confused with popup banners on hard-sell Web sites. See my signature in Appendix Six. Try these ideas, too:

- Change your signature often or at least every time a new promotional idea comes to you.
- Provide a link to articles about you or by you with a line that says something like, "See what the *Chicago Tribune* said about (your title here)" with a link to your buypage.

  Caveat: If you use links other than those to pages on your own site, check them frequently to be sure they are still live.

- Offer something free in your e-mail autosignature to encourage people to click on the link to your Web site or blog or to subscribe to your newsletter.
- Are you an expert? Let 'em know! "Expert on publicity, media relations . . . ."
- Use a brief invitation to upcoming public appearances such as "Visit my booth at the Virginia Book Fair," with a link for more information.

- Design your signature so it blends with your brand. To quote my mother, "You wouldn't wear a polka dot blouse with a plaid skirt, now would you?"

Caveat: When you send out media releases, queries, or submissions to unknown editors, remove art or photos from your signature. They may render the message unreadable for certain Internet servers and editors may not want to risk a virus by opening your mail.

Your other online signatures are important, too. It's only common courtesy to use a signature when you communicate in those little comment windows on blogs or social Web sites. I know they provide an avatar (logo) and a link to your Web site automatically, but an e-mail address or link is *not* a signature. You wouldn't send a thank-you note by mail without a signature—even if the stationery was imprinted with you name. Your signature is an opportunity to promote your book *and* to serve others by making it easy for them to contact you.

–∞–

DIRECT E-MAIL MARKETING is not spam. The people on rented lists have given permission in one way or another to distribute certain kinds of information to their e-mail boxes.

People you have personally communicated with can also be contacted. Do, however, use an unsubscribe message to allow uninterested folks to remove themselves from your list. There is no point in sending something to someone who truly does not want to receive it.

Direct e-mail is not something that works for every book. It is not an easy method of marketing to master, so you either need to be prepared for the grade-fifteen learning curve or hire it done. And that is not cheap.

Some authors who use direct-market e-mail—generally writers with how-to books—use it to great advantage. To learn more, start with Chris Baggott's *Email Marketing by the Numbers: How to Use the World's Greatest Marketing Tool to Take Any Organization to the Next Level* (budurl.com/EmailDirectMarketing). Google "direct e-mail services" to get an idea of cost for a *series* of blasts—a *series* because a single e-mail will not work any better than a single ad in a newspaper. It's a whole campaign or nothing.

I like a not-very-commercial, front door approach to e-mail marketing. You send releases, announcements, or personal notes about your new book to your own targeted lists of folks (see Chapter Eleven to learn more about assembling your own lists). Tailor each message to the group you are sending it to so it feels as one-on-one as possible. A businesslike approach is perfect for some groups. For others, a chattier note may work better.

-∞-

AN AUTORESPONDER can make many promotions more effective including anything you do with e-mail. An autoresponder is a techy gadget or Web site that gets a sample of your writing out to those who request it—all automatically. You are used to getting them yourself. It's an autoresponder that sends you a welcome letter when you subscribe to a newsletter.

You can use autoresponders many ways, but few use them to build interest in their writing. That's a missed opportunity!

These programs also help you collect e-mails of those interested enough in your title to request information be sent to them. Explore an autoresponder service like sendfree.com to see how they work. After you've posted a provocative excerpt on an autoresponder, you'll be assigned an address that you must promote. I know! Promote it? But it's usually like that: We must promote the promotion to make it effective. Here's how you do that:

- Add your responder address to your e-mail signature.
- Post it on suitable pages on your Web site. You may eventually need more than one auto-responder address.
- Follow up with a personal note to those who requested information on your autoresponder.
- Add their address to your list of readers.
- Put a little pitch for readers to get your first chapter by autoresponder in your letterhead and other stationery and promotion material.

For those who want to see how an autoresponder works—even for fiction—send an e-mail to carolynhowardjohnson@sendfree.com, and watch for the quick response in your e-mail box.

-∞-

LIST-SERVES, YAHOO GROUPS, Google groups. It matters not what you call them. They are groups of like-minded folks run by moderators. They are useful tools that aren't being used as much as they once were. There *are* some where members get off topic, but with a little effort you can find a few helpful ones that are moderated well. They work well for you because:

- They are targeted. You can find groups interested in the subjects you write about. Groups interested in writing. Groups focused on book promotion. Groups that simply allow you to promote at will. Groups that broadcast opportunities.
- You can choose to receive daily digests or individual posts delivered to your e-mail box so you can work these groups the way it is most convenient for you.
- You build long lasting relationships.
- You can find people interested in cross promotion—often more quickly than on some of the social networks.

These groups are eager to have you jump into the fray. Ask questions and share your knowledge with fellow members. Notice how others are succeeding. Look for people to review your book, interview you, publish your articles, and publish your next book. Include full contact information in your signature each time you post. Keep your new friends' e-mail addresses.

Hint: As you read posts on your e-groups, pay attention to other members' signatures. They may include resources you can use such as the names and links of publishers, agents, contests, and blogs.

Chapter Twenty-One

New Net Game Changers

As surely as the greatest artists of history changed the way the world sees artistic pursuits, the Net has shaped a new landscape for readers and writers. ~ CHJ

"Game changer" is a label that's being over applied to just about every innovation on the Web, but it is doubtful many would argue with the idea that blogging and online bookstores have shaken the publishing industry like a nine-point earthquake. Social networks are not far behind.

-∞-

BLOGS are often classified as social networks because people can interact with a blogger by leaving comments and because they do interact well with other online networks. Still, most of us think of them as quite different from MySpace, Squidoo, Twitter, and others. We see them as more connected to old media or rooted more in print media like periodicals. Not the Pleistocene, but older than some.

Your blogging worries are probably overblown because you've heard the diary myths. That you must post something on your blog every day. That you have to expose all your darkest secrets. That blogging doesn't work. That blogging takes too much time. Don't believe the rumors. Blogging is far more connected (read that interactive) with a broader audience than anything we've ever experienced with old media. Blogs are amazing tools that can be shaped to your needs, so put aside preconceived notions.

The advantages of blogging are many. Here are the reasons you should blog instead of working at some other promotions that may not be as effective:

- Blogging is creative and that's right up your alley. I talk a bit about blogging in Chapter Sixteen. It covers ways to promote doing what you love most, writing. And blogging *is* writing.
- Blogging is a good way to introduce readers to your voice, promote loyalty, and, in the long run, sell books.
- Blogging helps build name recognition and builds a huge footprint on search engines which makes it easier for readers to find you on the Web.

> **Hint:** Blogger/Blogspot is an entity of Google and that is a big reason that material on that blog content service appears so quickly in the Google search engine. It is also why the Google Alerts, a neat research tool that allows authors and others to know what's being said about them on the Web, arrives in the e-mail boxes of people using that service so quickly.

- Blogging helps you network with others in the publishing world, including publishers, agents, other authors, publicists, and other bloggers. Keep reading for ways to connect with others and promote your blog.

Building a blog is easy because some whiz kids designed something called content management service (CMS) for you to use and they often offer it to you free.

If you don't already have a Web site, don't have anyone to help you add a blog to your Web site, or just want to blog the easy way, start blogging right now using the steps listed below. Guys and gals at Google have made blogging especially easy with blogspot.com (also called blogger.com). With it you can start a blog with five (only five!) essential steps.

Start with the free Google account you may already have. If you do, the words "My Account" will appear as a link on Google's homepage. It's in blue in the top right corner of the homepage. If not, use a link on that page to set up your account.

1. Once you have an account, you'll find a whole bunch of services that Google offers—also free. Many of them are miracles disguised as links, but right now we're only interested in the little orange icon (or logo) with the "Blogger" link next to it. Click on that link.

2. Find the link that says "Create a blog." Click.

3. The first prompt will ask you to name your blog. Choose wisely. Go to the Index

in this book and look up "branding" before you choose a name for your blog. The name you choose shouldn't limit your focus too severely nor should it be so broad it won't appeal to the audience you seek for your book.

> **Hint:** For now, ignore the "advanced option" section. If you start with these five steps, and forget the rest for a while, you'll feel more comfortable and it will probably take less than five minutes.

4. Next choose a template. Choose something simple. Play with colors that fit your branding campaign and the looks of your book or Web site. Avoid dark backgrounds. They are hard to read.
5. Your next window says "Start Blogging." That may be oversimplified, but it's close. Take your time to browse the "Settings" and "Design" tabs.

See how easy that was! Now explore new "Segments" or "Gadgets" a few at a time. They are on your layout or design page. Tweak or start over until you have your blog the way you want it. Nothing is written in stone. It costs you nothing to enjoy the process but the time you might otherwise spend playing online solitaire.

If you are not a freshman computer user and have a Web site of your own, consider incorporating your blog into your existing site's format. The frequent fresh content of a blog makes the search engines happy. It will make you happy, too, when you see your site move up in the online search-engine ratings. Having your blog or Web site listed on the first page of often-searched-for keywords is a good thing for your book.

Other places you might choose to house your blog are typepad.com and wordpress.com. You choose where your blog will live the way you would choose a new home—based on the features you like best. Or you choose Blogspot.com because I told you it is easy, sufficient for most authors' needs, and did I mention free?

> **Hint:** Blog beginners who want to go all out with WordPress, a blog service with lots of bells and whistles, can get help from Miller Mosaic Social Media Marketing at millermosaicllc.com/services, or get one-on-one training or up-to-date how-to books on WordPress at blogaid.net/wordpress-training.

Your blog is pivotal to promotion. We use our blogs to promote, obviously. What isn't so obvious is that the blog itself must be promoted. One of the most important ways to do both things is to integrate it with all the other entities you use for networking on the Web. You link to your blog on every suitable promotion you do. Here are a few ways to do that:

- When you post an article on your blog, invite contacts on your other social networks like LinkedIn and Twitter to drop by and comment. Make your invitation into a teaser and include the permalink to your blog. A permalink is the very long address you find in your browser window when you click on the blog's title. It takes visitors to a specific blog post rather than to your most recent post.

- Install an invitation to subscribe to your blog on your Web site and on your social network profile pages. Tell visitors how they will benefit from doing so.
- Link to your blog from your autosignature.
- Include content that keeps people coming back, like freebies, contests, games, breaking news. What you use depends on your target audience.
- Add your links to your blog for Digg, del.icio.us, Technorati, and others. These services let folks research topics that interest them. They may add your blog to their reader lists, and Digg (vote) on the posts that you write. These sites are sort of research-oriented social networks in and of themselves.
- Add widgets to your blog. They are images—often logos—with links. They do things like let readers easily spread the word about your posts on their social networks and lead visitors to your book's buypage on your favorite online bookstore.
- Partner with other bloggers to help spread the word about your blog by trading articles, interviews, and reviews and to come by your blog to comment. These partners also tweet about your blog. You do the same for them.
- Put your blog on Kindle where readers subscribe to blogs targeted to their interests.

Usually for about $1. It's a promotion, not a get-rich-quick thing. Tony Eldridge shows you how with this video: marketingtipsforauthors.com/1115/tipsPublishBlogKindle.html.

- Stephanie Meyer, author of the famous *Twilight* series, catapulted her book to bestseller lists by visiting blogs targeted to her young adult audience and commenting on the posts. She added something of value to these blog posts, mentioned her own books, and included links to her sales page and to her blog.
- Trade links with other bloggers. These links go on your blog rolls, the portion of your blogs where you link to related blogs as a service to your readers. You'll find a gadget on Blogger that lets you do this easily.
- Ask people with similar interests to be guests on your blog. You contribute to their blogs, too. Then promote each other's blogs using the social networks that you built.

Keeping your blogging time corralled is easier than you think. There is a rule-of-thumb that you post often because search engines like activity, but there are no blog-frequency cops. Here are six time-saving ways for you to keep an active blog and keep your time expenditure within reason.

1. *Using guest bloggers* is like spreading love. Others write one or several guest posts—even a series—on a subject that fits your blog's focus. It's a good way to save time and a good way to network. Your guests may then promote your blog and, by extension, your book.

305

Guest-bloggers can submit directly to you and you do the posting, but in the "settings" feature of your blog is a feature called "permissions" that allows the guest to do their own posting. I like the former method because you can better control your blog and the editing process.

> **Hint:** You may also guest blog for other bloggers. This will get you (and your blog, Web site, and book) in front of other audiences. If you include links in your guest-blogger credits (sometimes called taglines), some people will click on them and be carried back to your other online entities. Some call these active links "incoming links" or "backlinks." Search engines love links that lead to your blog! Google spiders search for these links. They think they are so important they raise your blog in the search-engine rankings when your blog has lots of them.

2. *Get partners for your blog*. Find compatible fellow authors, readers, agents, publishers, or bloggers who agree to write one or two posts a week. It's like dividing the blogging pie. You write an equivalent number of posts. When you combine your talent and time, the power of the project increases incrementally both in terms of promoting the blog and in the sheer posting power. Search engines love blogs with lots of new content. The drawback to this method is that the spotlight will not shine solely on your book and your promotions.

> **Hint:** You may still wonder why you'd want to share your blog with a fellow author. Sure, you need to be selective, but maybe you need to review the advantages of "cross promotion" by looking up that

entry in the Index of this book. There are certainly advantages to both sharing and doing it yourself.

3. *Recycle articles, tips, bargains,* and anything else you can think of from the other writing and promoting you do. Everything on your blog doesn't have to be new or exclusive, and everything you write for your blog may be cycled back to those other promotions. Check Chapter Sixteen on recycling articles.

4. *Use the carnival concept.* A carnival is a blog or blog post that lists the best articles or helpful sites related to your blog's focus in the wonderful Web world. Put all these links in a single post and include a little synopsis or pitch for each.

Some blogs post nothing but carnivals. Tony Eldridge, a former marketing professional, blogs on book marketing (blog.marketingtipsforauthors.com). He finds great posts by subscribing to related blogs and listing his favorites every Friday. Carnivals save writing time, but you might spend more time reading other people's blogs to find good content.

5. *Outsource your blogging* to a writer who is familiar with blogs. He or she might charge per blog or per month for a given number of blog posts.

Obviously your blog won't be free if you choose to do this, but you'll balance that expense against what blogging space would cost if you were paying for display advertising. Factor in the value of the time you will save, too.

You will need to supply the information for each blog until your new freelance helper becomes familiar with the many facets of your books. At that point, he may come up with ideas for you and thus expand what you could do for yourself. Two such writers are Mindy Lawrence (mplcreative1@aol.com) and Terese Morrow (keybusinesspartners@yahoo.com).

6. *Use videos* to tell your stories if you're a faster talker than writer. Learn five ways to use videos from marketing expert Tony Eldridge at

> http://blog.marketingtipsforauthors.com/2009/08/5-ways-to-use-video-on-your-site-and.html.

Bloggers' block is a myth. Writers worry about writers' block but they needn't extend that disability to their blog posts. Reassuringly, there are only a few guidelines and tons of material to blog about.

To attract and keep readers, a blog must include practical or entertaining information. It is not that hard and the process of doing it helps a writer focus on the strengths of his or her book to find yet undiscovered aspects of it that help promote it.

Authors often ascribe to the notion that getting ideas for posts is easier for some genres than others, but it's possible for all of them because they all share some qualities by virtue of their being books.

Here are things that most authors have in common that are supremely bloggable:

- Yourself. Specifically the "you" who writes. Your readers may well remember you long after they've forgotten the title of your first book.
- Anything in the news that relates to your book. Nothing is off limits. For a horror writer the news may be the latest mass murder (isn't there one of those every year?) For a children's story about bunnies, Easter is a blogging opportunity.
- Talk about writing and publishing in general. You think people aren't interested? How many people have said, "Oh, I'd love to write a book!" to you in the last year?
- Every writer knows other writers or soon will. Link to the articles on their blogs and Web sites. When they're doing something that will interest your audience, blog about it.
- Talk about your promotions, like your latest two-for-one book offer or your Kindle special that gives readers a taste of your writing style.
- Talk about your coming events. Book signings, your launch, your seminars, your speaking gigs.
- How about your opinions. I loved a recent blog that ranted about the confidence-corroding nature of the term "self-promote."

  Hint: Phyllis Zimbler Miller and I wrote an article that shows fiction writers how to use blogs effectively, including blog ideas for different genres of creative writing. Go to fictionmarketing.com.

On their blogs writers may also:
- Review others' books, especially ones that relate to yours in some way.

- Create contests. Let readers submit material for blogs. Make a contest of that, too.
- Interview other authors or experts in fields related to your book. Some bloggers use the same questions for all their guests, but in the interest of more entertaining blog posts, tailor your questions to the interests and accomplishments of the interviewee.
- Quote from blogs and Web sites with a focus related to yours. Some blogs are nothing more than one inspirational quotation a day. Some blog posts are nothing more than a list of great quotations.

> **Hint:** Copyright law has a free-use clause. You may quote short excerpts for reviews, essays, and articles and some others at no charge and, yes, without permission. Some online bookstores use quotes of up to twenty-five words in their blurbs.

Getting unique ideas for your blog is easy. Glean ideas for your blog or any of your other marketing entities as you go about your day—everything from shopping to watching TV. Authors are notorious for taking busman's holidays. We get ideas for our poems, our characters, and our narratives when we travel. We even dream them. Blog ideas come to you the same way.

> **Hint:** Carry a notebook and pencil with you everywhere. When I don't have writing equipment, I tear pages and ragged little clippings out of magazines, newspapers, and even junk mail.

Examine your own book for a handle on subjects to blog about, for ideas for future media releases, and for feature ideas you could pitch to editors. There is no point in doing this exercise twice or three times. Let's get organized and make a thorough examination once a month that will work for more than just our blogs.

-∞-

ONLINE BOOKSTORES are rooted in tradition however recent they may seem to us. One of the major differences, of course, is that Internet thing—connectivity. Brick and mortar bookstores encourage browsing. So do online bookstores. You can connect with authors at bookstore readings and seminars. You can connect with authors online, too. But at online bookstores that association is less sporadic and readers (and authors!) can review and recommend books almost as if they were bookstore sales associates.

There is some overlap between the old and new. Brick-and-mortar bookstores have an online presence, and the big ones have online stores. Many stores offer e-book access. Some have their own e-book readers like B&N's Nook.

But as game changers, online bookstores have been instrumental in the blossoming of e-books and e-readers. They may also become the instrument that contributes to the demise of the chains of traditional bookstores, though—just as radio survived TV and TV seems to be surviving the Net—the old fashioned printed word on paper and assembled into a book will never disappear. Nor will the indie bookstores that cater to the specific interests of its customers.

I'm going to be daring here because authors—especially new authors who dream of seeing their books in bookstores—won't like hearing this: You can do without having your book in brick-and-mortar bookstores and sell lots of books, but these days a book cannot reach star status without online stores.

This section on using online bookstores to their fullest potential is the most essential advice in this book beyond the need to market in general. Really. Don't let anyone fool you into thinking you can relegate book sales to your own Web site sales page and succeed. Or only to bookstore distribution. Not if your goal is to sell books to those outside your mother's sewing circle.

-∞-

AHHH, AMAZON. Theodore Roosevelt said, "The mightiest river in the world is the Amazon. It runs from west to east, from the sunset to the sunrise, from the Andes to the Atlantic." The Amazons of mythology were warrior women. All the Amazons, including Amazon.com, perform amazing feats. When it comes to book *sales*, Amazon.com strides on the sturdiest of legs. She sells your books here and overseas, as e-books, hard covers. or paperbacks. Talk about great branding!

Because books from small and large publishers, subsidy- and self-published authors, and other content are found on Amazon's pages, she is a unique buying and selling tool. She also exposes your book to a very important demographic, *readers.* Still, promoting your book on Amazon is like climbing a trellis where thorns grow among the roses; you must read and adhere to the strict guidelines of any Amazon feature you use.

Because Amazon is fickle (it's always adding a feature or taking something away, always changing page designs, always changing the names of their features), I can only give you general guidelines for the benefits they offer. Here are a few of my favorites you can access once you have opened an Amazon account:

- Authors get a Profile page, much like the ones on any social network. Amazon has called it Author Central and Author Connect. Who knows what it calls it this week. It lists your book, an author biography, and coordinates other Amazon features you participate in. Use the magic of Real Simple Syndication (RSS) to install your blog on this page.

  > **Hint:** RSS is a way that anyone (yes, *you!*) can distribute what you do once—say, on your Web site—to make it appear magically on your blog, too. Or on your social networks. You simply copy and paste either computer code or Web site addresses. It is a time-saver and effort-expander like none other I can think of.

- A "So You'd Like To . . . Guide" is a feature that lets you post articles, essays, rills, or rants on any subject you wish. At the bottom of the article you type in the ISBNs (but Amazon calls them ASINs) of books or other products related to the subject of your piece. The guide you produce may appear on the pages of those books or products you listed. I once used guides for lists of recommended books and texts for the classes I teach. They made it easy for my students to simply click-and-buy when they felt a resource was one they needed in their own library.

- "Listmania" lets you list products or books you feel are exemplary or useful. Listmanias are built much like the So You'd Like To…guides, but require less work. Each individual Listmania does not, however, attract the readership of So You'd Like To . . . guides. Amazon tracks readership (and ratings) for you so it's easy to see exactly how many hits each of your lists attracts.

- Sales figures on some online bookstores help visitors know how well a book is selling but they're confusing. I wouldn't be surprised if Jeff Bezos, founder and CEO of Amazon, can't explain the method they use to calculate their ratings. In fact the book categories a publisher or author chooses for a specific book can influence its rating. The only practical use for ratings is that authors can tell when their book's sales have slowed down. Don't you believe it when you hear that readers pay attention to the ratings. The only time most readers notice is when sales of your book propel you to one of Amazon's bestseller lists.

> **Caveat:** Don't try to beat any of the booksellers' ratings games or make too much of a bestseller status. Author David Vise received some bad publicity for allegedly trying to rig *The New York Times'* bestseller

list by buying huge numbers of his own books. It doesn't hurt to Tweet about bestseller successes, but those in the industry are distrustful and rarely fooled or impressed by most of the other shenanigans some authors think up.

Don't spend too much of your valuable writing and promotion time tracking your ratings, either. If you fear you're addicted, subscribe to a time-saving service that watches ratings for you at: booksandwriters.com. They have a free trial period.

- Most online bookstores have a search engine that allows researchers and readers to find your book by keying in title, author, or keywords. You want to be sure the keywords that best describe your book lead readers *to* your book!
- Most online bookstores offer a "Look Inside" feature that lets readers read a few sample pages from your book. You will hear some authors disparage this feature, but trust me. It helps sell books, especially well-written books.
- Amazon lists both its top reviewers and those it designates as Vine reviewers. The former are reviewers who have reviewed the most books on Amazon. The latter are readers Amazon selects and sends books and other products to in exchange for the promise of a review. These features are wonderful tools for finding individual reviewers. Many reviewers in both categories also review for other blogs, journals, and Web sites. Match the interests of a specific

reviewer to your book before you send a query letter asking for a review.

> **Caveat:** Occasionally an author will try to become a top reviewer. Reaching for this hallowed ground may be an impossible goal because several reviewers may spend every waking hour reading and writing about books. Harriet Klausner has reviewed over 7,000 books. You, I'm sure, would rather write another novel or have a root canal than try to beat that record.

- The reviews offered by Amazon and other online review sites take on a new importance for authors. Those who post reviews there find they can be networking goldmines and can give their names a new literary luster. Authors must necessarily be avid readers; it only takes a few moments to add a thoughtful review on sites that allow these voluntary posts. Choose a great title. Edit well. Read the submission guidelines. Add a brief tagline (see more on Taglines in Chapter Ten) that abides by the bookstore's rules. (See more on writing reviews in Chapter Sixteen.) You may also post your reviews as videos on some bookstore sites.

> **Hint:** If you cannot recommend a book, don't post a review. That doesn't mean that noting a book's weaknesses isn't valid. It's just that there is no point in slashing and burning a book an author has invested himself in. Besides, that kind of review isn't likely to help your branding unless the

image you are trying to create is that of a curmudgeon.

- Amazon's "Advantage" feature lets any independent publisher or author post a book to Amazon. There may be a fee for this although there is no fee to publish books on Kindle. Most subsidy publishers and traditional publishers list their books on Amazon, but if yours doesn't, get permission from your publisher to do it yourself.

  Caveat: Check your contract and proceed accordingly. Insist your publisher get with it. If they resist and your contract doesn't limit you, you can do it on your own.

- Customer Discussions are featured on every book's sales page. Authors can begin discussions on aspects of their books and see what ensues. They can go to the sales pages of other authors and enter existing discussions. Avoid blatantly promoting. Make your contributions helpful and thoughtful.

Manage your book's sales page on Amazon. This duty should be handled by your publisher, but sometimes publishers don't do it. Or they don't do it in a way that presents your book in its best light. You're tired of hearing this I know, but no one knows your book like you do. No one cares as much about your book as you do. Some of the things you can or are expected to manage yourself are:
- The blurbs from reviews. You may want to add an excerpt from a reviewer to the ones your publisher provided. Carefully follow fair-use

guidelines. "Fair use" is a legal term and worthy of an entire book. To learn more about it, search "copyright," "quotes," and "blurbs" in the Index of this book or search for more information on the Web.

- Images other than your bookcover. Readers can use this feature, but so can you. I've used them to include the logos for awards my books have won, for cover images of other books in the same series, for snapshots that illustrate the spirit of a book, and for the headshots of collaborators.
- You may post videos on your Amazon page.
- Amazon's New and Used feature lets you sell slightly damaged books and excess stock. Find the "Sell Yours Here" tab on your book's sales page. Click and it will guide you through the process. When quality isn't important, I occasionally order a used copy of my own traditionally-published books from this feature because I can get one cheaper there and more quickly than from my publisher.
- There are windows for readers to add tags on each book's sales page. Your book's rating on Amazon and the impression your page makes on readers are affected positively when lots of readers add tags to this feature.
- There are buttons for readers to vote as "helpful" (or not) near the reviews on each book's sales page. Voting for reviews encourages readers to peruse the reviews, which is good for the reviewers and good for your book. It is okay to encourage readers to add

tags, post reviews, and vote for content as long as you don't try to influence their choices.

Amazon myths abound. If you haven't already heard, the gossip mills churned out by authors who naturally love to talk will soon notify you that the writing (like reviews and So You'd Like Tos..." you post to Amazon becomes Amazon's property and cannot be published elsewhere.

I asked Amazon's customer service about their claim to own material posted there. They made it clear that they own only the right to "reuse" what you post, but that you may continue to use the material as you see fit.

This explanation comes from Amazon's customer service department and applies to any of their disclaimers/guidelines that use the term "non-exclusive":

"When a customer posts a 'So You'd Like to . . . Guide' to our site, the customer is granting us the nonexclusive right to use the guide. This means that once a guide is submitted to our site, the guide is ours to use as we see fit for as long as we wish. As this license is non-exclusive, the customer who has written the guide can also use the guide as he or she sees fit. The guide can be included in a book or posted on another site."
Nicole L., Amazon.com Customer Service

You will also hear that efforts on Amazon like those I've described do not result in sales. Sales are, indeed, hard to track, but if marketing works, targeted marketing like this works better.

Here's the thing. No marketing campaign works in a vacuum. You make online bookstores part of a many-speared campaign and cross promote them, your campaign will work. They'll work less well without a smart presence on online bookstores.

> **Hint:** Online bookstores are prime targets for unethical promotion practices. Please review Chapter Four on the importance of ethics in all you do for your book—online or off.

-∞-

OTHER ONLINE BOOKSTORES work similarly to Amazon. It seems once your book is doing well on Amazon, lots of others pick it up, even Harvard's online bookstore. It's nice to have a presence on some of these others, but you can't be personally involved with them all. Furthermore, loyalty counts. So direct your online book sales to one of them. The more sales you make on a single bookstore, the higher your ratings go. The higher your ratings, the more you get to be seen on that bookstore's bestseller lists (if they have bestseller lists). Here are my favorites, in order of preference:

- Amazon—the ones in the US, UK, and Canada but also the one in Germany where books in English are also widely read. I like them because they are so highly trafficked and do so much for authors.
- BN.com. But don't believe it when you hear that when you direct sales to their online store and your book does well, it will be more likely to be stocked by the Barnes & Noble brick-and-mortar stores. This company makes it very clear

it operates as two separate entities.

- Powell's Bookstore (powells.com), known for their used books, their voice, and their assortment of targeted newsletters. They have a brick-and-mortar store in Portland, but they are strong online and encourage online reviews.
- Harvard Bookstore, just because it's fun to have one's book there.

There are, of course, many others that encourage reader reviews.

As you explore these online bookstores, you may notice that many have so many interactive features they have begun to function like social networks. It so happens that using social networks is the next topic on our agenda. When you can, use the power of online bookstore's features and apply the social networking skills you'll soon learn (or already know) to these bookstores sites.

Chapter Twenty-Two

Using Social Networks

Social networks are rooted in the human psyche. We have belonged to them and they to us since homo sapiens first took to caves. ~ CHJ

"Social network" is a term that has recently taken on a whole new meaning. Social networks once included groups like book clubs, service organizations, groups loyal to schools and teams, and our writers' critique groups. Today we think of super-powered social networks on the Web first!

Because Web social networks are new (and so large!), they can be difficult for authors to manage. They can be fun, be useless, or be amazingly effective networking tools. They can also soak up your time. Much depends on how you use them. This chapter explains a simple system I use to manage them as tools for promotion, one that flexes as the sites and my needs change. Whatever system you use, you can adapt it to your needs and to the networks' frequent innovations.

-∞-

SIMPLE SOCIAL NETWORKING is essential for busy authors. An author needn't be conversant with every feature of any given social network to use it effectively. Knowing the basics suffices.

I install a profile page on the networks I am invited to join—when time allows. It doesn't hurt to have that presence. I respond to invitations I get and leave it at that. Except for three. They are Facebook, Twitter, and LinkedIn, but many authors put lots of effort into at least one of the bookish networks, Goodreads, Bookaholics, or Shelfari.

Choose networks that suit your title and personality. As an example, eCademy is good for those who write textbooks or write about world affairs. I also like many of the small networking groups at ning.com because they tend to focus on specific categories of interest. John Kremer has one at bookmarketing.ning.com and Gene Cartright has one at iFOGOvillage.ning.com that has expanded to include things like free Web site services for its premium members and a separate site to showcase novels for producers and directors looking for new material.

Here is a simple method for making online social networks work for you and your book:

- Sign up. Build a profile. Invite folks you identify as avid readers or with whom you want to build better marketing relationships.
- Accept anyone who wants to connect with you on a network unless they offend your sensibilities. This is business, not social (regardless of the name "social network"). You can't tell who might be interested in reading your book. Even people who are selling something may also read.
- Use an avatar (that's the little identifying logo

that most social networks offer their participants). Select one that will help sell your book at a glance. Your bookcover may be a much better avatar choice than your headshot.

- Integrate the networks you use. That is, hook one to the other using Real Simple Syndication (RSS). Some are already integrated in the network's structure for you. As an example, your LinkedIn posts will go directly to Twitter if you opt in to that feed when you are updating your status. Integration is the power of the Web in action. One post can be seen by several of your networks.

- Post often. Try for at least once a day on each with the exception of Twitter. You can do ten a day—easily—on Twitter.

- Let your voice shine through. What you write in your posts should be tailored to your audience and reflect your personality or the book you are promoting.

- Too many social networkers collect names and then rarely use them. The idea is to make friends and call on one another to cross promote or develop projects.

> **Hint:** You may want to use some advanced features like Facebook's amazingly targeted (but certainly not very frugal!) advertising opportunities. (See my warning against paid advertising in Chapter Nine.) Or use their "like" pages (once known as "fan" pages). Definitely use their "share photos" feature. Mark Zuckerberg, Facebook founder, says that feature appeals to folks' most basic inclinations. And their events feature can be

used effectively once you have many friends—especially if you promote your events using the full power of the interactive Web.

Entire books are dedicated to social networks. If you are determined to delve more deeply into the secrets of each, read Dana Lynn Smith's e-book *Successful Social Marketing* at bookmarketingmaven.typepad.com/savvy_book_marketer/successful-social-marketing.html.

If you want to see how great Squidoo lenses (another social network with a different twist) works, visit Jennifer Akers at squidoo.com/JenniferAkers.

Note: Many networks have an invitation feature you can use to invite friends to promotional events online or off. They are easy to use when you have only a few friends on these sites, but it can become unmanageable once you have hundreds or thousands because the sites require you to invite them one at a time, or one category at a time. I'm sure the powers-that-be have their reasons, but I find this limitation annoying and downright anti-marketing bigotry.

About those reader networks for readers? The ones like Goodreads, Shelfari, Bookaholics, and associated sites like LibraryThing? Let's not give them short shrift. In fact, if they interest you as a way to promote (and they should, especially if you write fiction or poetry), follow the simple participation guidelines I've recommended in this chapter for general social networks. But then go a step or two farther.

- Yep. Add reviews of the books you read to these sites. Any old book will do but it will work better if you focus on the books that are related to yours by genre or topic. Include a reference to your book (subtly) in the review, and a credit line—all in accordance with these sites' guidelines. If you decide to do this, go back to Chapter Sixteen and brush up on how to use reviews effectively.

- You will find lots of groups—including reading groups—on these sites. Actively participate in a couple associated with your target audience. These groups may provide some Real Simple Syndication features to connect them to other promotions you are doing. We've talked about RSS feeds elsewhere so you know what time-savers they can be. The Index in this book will help you find them. Connect these reader-group sites to your other social network profiles, your blog, and your Web site.

> **Hint:** At one time I listed only my own books and books related to them on LibraryThing and then fed that information using their RSS Feed feature to my Sharing with Writers blog. My LibraryThing selections then showed up on my blogs and even rotated automatically which helped keep content on the blog fresh.

Chapter Twenty-Three
The Dangers of Online Promotion

As a child I gathered eggs for my grandmother—too many to hold safely in the basket she gave me—and learned firsthand what the metaphor "egg on your face" and the aphorism "Never put all your eggs in one basket" mean. ~ CHJ

When we think of online danger we usually think of security risks. That topic is for another book. Sure we should take precautions, but I think our culture manipulates us with fear. Read up on security, by all means, but don't let it keep you from marketing your book.

I worry more about how—after a huge investment in time and talent—a social network can close down your account. Here are my stories. Call them the school of hard knocks.

Here I am, flipping through the pages of *Time* magazine and there *it* is. A chance to be listed in an encyclopedia called Wikipedia—right up there with Proust and Chekhov. And an author could actually see themselves there before they die!

This article wasn't directed at authors and it didn't suggest anyone who longs for fame get it instantly by adding her biography on what this news magazine's editors call The People's Encyclopedia. But what a fun opportunity for writers! So, I tried it. It took quite a bit of my time.

Naturally, I used the link to my Wiki page a lot. No point of having one if you don't promote it! Then one of my techy newsletter subscribers tells me my page is no longer there. She gives me a link to a very secret, hidden page that discusses *why* I am no longer there.

Wiki operates with free labor, people who consider themselves experts. Many are. But among them are those who relish their power. Or those who are so successful they think they are always right. It seems that two of the awards on my page could not be verified online or the award-issuing entity didn't (in their opinion) measure up. Keep in mind, I have a couple hunks of engraved crystal to prove the authenticity of my awards, and the one that apparently didn't measure up was a local newspaper of a fairly large Southern California city. They also didn't like that I am self-published, but hadn't bothered to notice the traditional publishing I've done. I decided not to buck this kind of prejudice. It's not worth it to me.

Another time I was booted from Facebook. They didn't like that I accepted too many invitations to be friends at one time—or wasn't doing it in a way their programs recognized as legitimate. My daughter's Facebook friends thought the whole thing was a hoot. I was not so amused. It only took one letter to get that fixed, but if it had taken me more, I would have happily (well, okay, maybe a little ticked off!) dropped that networking effort, too. The world is full of marketing possibilities. There is no point in making oneself miserable with one, whatever their strengths . . . or flaws.

Then there are self-appointed watchdogs who despise the abuse of author-friendly Web sites enough to spend their promotion and writing time to police and report violators, which sometimes causes problems even for the innocent. Isn't that what vigilantes did in the Old West?

Others prefer to take the promotion low road by dissing their competitors' work, including writing unfavorable online reviews. If that happens, you can appeal to the powers-that-be on the Web site in question and they sometimes will remove the offending comments or reviews. Sometimes not. (Please see Chapter Four on ethics.)

Occasionally something goes wrong with a site. It goes out of business or has technical problems, and you lose your great list of loyal readers. Yeah, we should back everything up, but, hey. We're just human!

How does all this affect you? Let's learn from them how *not* to treat your fellow authors. We should support one another, partner, cross promote. The universe is big enough—generous enough—for us all to succeed.

I want you to put your marketing efforts into work that builds on itself. You do that by focusing on the marketing that works for you, but not to the extent that you could lose all your promotion power to the whims of another. Protect yourself. Back up your networks. Spread your efforts around, and integrate them.

And don't let the nitpickers get to you.

Section VI
Well Traveled, Oft Forgotten

The noise of the Web can be so deafening we don't hear the muted call of marketing methods that have worked just fine for decades. ~ CHJ

Most online promotions in this book are extensions of marketing methods that have worked well for a very long time. This section, however, is about offline promotion tools that might be more effective than ever before.

You might ask how anything can be more effective than an online promotion that can reach so many, so fast. Because many authors have deserted traditional book promotions for the ease and allure of the Net, authors who return to the tried-and-true offline techniques face less competition and their efforts feel more creative and more personal to the recipients.

Though this section is about those old-fashioned methods, isn't it nice we have the Internet to give any offline promotions a marketing boost! You've seen tags like "As advertised on TV" and "Watch for our brochure in your mailbox." We can add tags like that to our online efforts to draw attention to the marketing we do *offline*. We can even suggest that online readers sign up to receive our offline promotions.

333

Chapter Twenty-Four

Reading Groups

Writers could once find folks who love the smell
of ink and the feel of paper in reading groups.
Now authors who want to share their writing just
want to find groups who love to read anywhere—
online or off. ~ CHJ

Authors can enlarge their circle of fans by reaching out
to readers' groups. You may belong to one. Members
read an assigned book then come together to discuss it.
Such groups exist everywhere, even in cyberspace.
Often the author of a chosen book will visit with such a
group, read for them, and sign their books.

This is where your marketing campaign comes in. If
you can locate a group that reads the kind of literature
you write, convincing them to choose your book is
usually not difficult. They tend to be starved for contact
with real live authors like you. The trick is to offer them
more personal service than other writers. Arrange to
sign hard or paperback copies for those who belong to
online groups. To do that, you collect addresses from
the virtual attendees and send the members well-
designed, hand-signed, and dedicated bookplates. These
could be sticky labels—either the fancy kind you can
buy at bookstores that were traditionally used to specify
book ownership or the generic (and frugal!) Avery label

variety. They then affix these labels, signed and dedicated by you, to the inside covers of the books they bought to read. Authors of either fiction or nonfiction may also gift their readers with free e-books that relate to their topic of their books in some way.

Real live, in-person reading groups still work best. Faces and handshakes forge relationships. Find reading groups at:

- Your work place. Check the bulletin board and company newsletter. Offer to read excerpts to your fellow workers even if you find no reading groups there.
- Synagogues, mosques, and church groups.
- Service and social groups and organizations.
- Bookstores.
- Libraries and museums, both public and private.
- School and parent groups.
- Lists in newspaper and magazine calendar sections.
- Use search engines. My search on "reading groups" reaped resources in the millions including organizations that sponsor reading groups in specific genres like mysteryreaders.org/groups.html.

Once connected, make the event a unique experience. Have a contest. Give away a memento. Serve goodies. Stay in touch with members. When you make book club members feel special, word gets around about you and your book.

Chapter Twenty-Five

Catalog Sales

Catalogs are show business. They spotlight a product for the purpose of selling merchandise, but they also create a buzz, project an image, tell a story, leave an impression. They create celebrity for their sponsor and for each of the products within their pages. ~ CHJ

The primary reason for your book to appear on the pages of a retail catalog is sales, but that exposure is also extraordinarily good publicity.

Your book's appearance in catalogs issued by mail-order-only catalogs or retailers (like Geary's of Beverly Hills) qualifies as publicity because you don't pay to appear in them and they increase interest in any book they feature through exposure to targeted audiences. The secret is in finding catalogs that match the subject of your book so you can pitch their producers.

You can also use cross-promotional catalogs published by a group of authors or other organizations. They usually rely on each participating author to distribute the catalog—online or by mail—to achieve mass readership. There is usually a fee for these catalogs to cover the time and expense of putting them together. You could sponsor one yourself and charge others for the time it takes to set it up and coordinate the dissemination.

-∞-

BONA FIDE RETAIL STORE CATALOGS include everything from catalogs for department stores to boutique clothing stores to gift stores to gadget stores. When you find a fit for your book (such as your nonfiction book on the life of Picasso for a catalog produced by a chain of art galleries) the advantages are:

- The retailer or catalog producer buys your book and features it in their pages. This is not an ad that that you pay for.
- The catalog company probably pays the freight for their book shipments from you or your distributor, unlike most bookstores.
- Unlike most bookstores, catalog producers do not return what they cannot sell. They probably won't even ask for returns unless you suggest it. And why would you? This is their usual way of doing business. When in Rome, do as the Romans do.

> **Hint:** These no-return sale terms should be included on both order forms and the sales contract you present to them.

- They reorder when their stock is depleted.
- They want a title that fits their product mix and sells, though the cover art must appeal to them, too. They don't much care if your book is current.
- Most don't require exclusivity.

- They must be sure they have stock to cover their sales, so their orders will be substantial enough to make both you and your publisher smile. Many small-to-medium size publishers have no experience with catalogs and you may need to show yours *why* they should smile, how to handle billing, and other matters.

Disadvantages are:
- Learning curve ahead! You'll need to expertly pitch your book and negotiate sales to catalog buyers who have different needs and policies from bookstore buyers.
- Because catalogs buy in quantity they demand a hefty discount. If you or your publisher cannot give fifty percent or more, there is no point in pursuing them. However, if you only break even on catalog sales, it may be worth the trouble for the publicity benefits.
- Some authors and publishers fail to print enough books to supply a catalog's immediate needs. Authors who use print-on-demand technology must have access to fast turnaround time.
- Nonfiction books are generally—but not always—more suitable for catalogs.

Here's how to find catalogs that might be interested in your book:
- Do an engine search on "retail catalogs." About 600,000 lists and individual catalogs will appear. Narrow the search to include only catalogs for which your book is a fit.

- Go to a bookstore or library and ask to see their *Catalog of Catalogs*. Find one or more categories that fit your book and tada! You've found another way to see your bookcover in print and realize sales at the same time.
- The fast but more expensive way to find leads is to purchase John Kremer's specialty retailer and catalog databases from bookmarket.com/orderform.html. Scroll down a bit for his list of catalogs.
- Become familiar with the catalogs that come to your home. Ask your friends to share their catalogs with you. When you find an appropriate one for your book, go for it!

> **Hint:** If your publisher isn't interested in partnering with you on this project, ask them for a large-quantity price break, stock your own books, and handle the details yourself.

-∞-

COOPERATIVE CATALOGS are cross-promotional efforts that work well for groups of promotion-minded authors. When they are distributed online, people who receive the cooperative catalog and are interested in your book click on a link in the catalog that takes them to the buypage on your own Web site. Sometimes they are distributed by mail, as handouts, or as newspaper inserts.

Some of the authors who participated in the book fair booths I sponsored partnered on a catalog with some Military Writers Society of America authors. Rather than distributing our catalog online exclusively (the inexpensive way to do it), we printed them and sent them third class to lists of media folks, librarians, and bookstore buyers provided by the participants.

By using the participants' own contact lists, these catalogs were received by people who might have a special interest because of locale, subject matter, or other connection to a featured author. Participants were asked to drop a postcard to those same people before the catalog was issued asking them to watch for it in their mailboxes. We thought this personal approach would attract more interest than either an online catalog or a catalog received with no pre-promotion fanfare.

We used the catalog overrun as handouts to fair visitors—all of whom were readers by definition.

In addition to a small charge for the time it takes someone to design a catalog and administer it, you will probably be expected to promote and distribute any cooperative catalog you participate in—online or off— using your contact list, blogs, and other promotion entities. You handle your own sales and shipping. Denise Cassino's collective catalog called Spirit of the Season (spiritoftheseasoncatalog.com) is one such catalog open to authors.

Chapter Twenty-Six

Corporate Sales

Many companies give presents to clients . . . such gifts should be kept inexpensive so they are not seen as bribes. ~ Amy Vanderbilt

Vanderbilt gave this advice on the niceties of corporate marketing long ago and though the giving of corporate gifts may not be as prevalent today as it was when she wrote her famous books, the practice is still widespread. Often businesses look for gifts that sing less of extravagance and more of long-term benefits. Books are often the answer. Maybe *your* book.

In addition to gifts for social occasions and holidays, large and small companies (including nonprofits) give gifts to their employees as awards or incentives. Sometimes they have training programs (yes, think books!) that help teach their employees and clients subjects they deem vital to their success. Generally they buy in quantity and expect substantial discounts from retail prices. If your book fits the needs of a particular industry, here are ways sell your books to them:

- To sell to corporations, you need to put your marketing bonnet on. How does the subject of your book align with a specific business or industry? How might you convince a corporation that it would benefit from utilizing your book? You must know the answers to these questions to write an effective pitch.

- If you know someone in a corporation that is a match for you book, ask for their recommendation. Send a thank you even if your collaboration doesn't work out.
- Set up a special page on your own Web site, and use sites like findgift.com to make it easy for business administrators to find you.
- Self-published authors can personalize books to meet the needs of large corporations. As an example, a special edition of *The Frugal Book Promoter* might be titled *John Wiley & Sons' Primer: How our authors might contribute to the success of their own books.* I could print a separate run that includes an introduction from their marketing department and a dedication page to personalize the book for them. I would set a minimum order requirement to make the process profitable, and I'd need to edit parts so they'd reflect Wiley's policies. You can see the process isn't easy, but there is a big profit potential and publicity value with this kind of sale.
- Contact Jerry Jenkins at specialmarketbooksales.com for ideas and services for special market book sales.

> **Caveat:** Corporate sales usually work well for gift books, cookbooks, and books with a business or health theme. However, novelists can sometimes come up with ideas beneficial to a business. As an example, I can see a romance set in the office of *Vogue* magazine

being purchased by a clothing manufacturer to be packaged as part of a swag bag like the ones the Academy Awards committee gives to stars. The book would be fun holiday reading and add a new dimension to bags of jewelry, cosmetics, and pink iPhone covers.

Once you have landed a corporate client, ask for their endorsement to help you get similar sales. LinkedIn has a feature that makes recommendations easy to get.

Traditionally-published authors should check their contracts or negotiate with their publishers before pursuing catalog sales. A book's price structure, speed of production, and reprint and copyright issues may be stumbling blocks. It's worth a try. For the profit. And for the buzz it might create for both you and your book.

Chapter Twenty-Seven

Retail Is More than Bookstores

Books aren't the sole purview of bookstores anymore. Your book is suitable for the merchandise mix of some retailer—from a tire store to a fast food chain. ~ CHJ

A category called "gift books" is a hot commodity in retail circles. Most every store you see in a mall or on the street is ripe for a title that is closely aligned with its image and its customer's needs.

Selling to specialty retailers is a useful way to market books long after the shelf life on a new release has supposedly expired and bookstores have lost interest. As an added benefit, exposure in nontraditional venues creates demand at libraries and bookstores at any stage in the market life of a book.

Unless your publisher specializes in gift books, they probably won't approach retailers other than booksellers, but you can make traditional sales calls to local retailers on your own. And you can sell to national and even international retailers using a combination book and business proposal. My booklet *The Great First Impression Book Proposal* (budurl.com/BookProposals) will get you started. You need only adapt the ideas in it and the format it suggests to do this kind of selling.

If you are convinced a particular store could sell a ton of your books, use what is called a "forced sale" technique. Offer the buyer six books in a point-of-purchase display complete with signs (header cards) you have professionally made. The store pays you only if they sell their stock and they don't have to return them if they don't sell; they may use them any way they choose. They agree to place them at their point-of-purchase (near the cash register) in that nifty display you provided for thirty days. They get to try a new product at no risk. They do not have to go to the expense of returning or paying for what doesn't sell. You present the invoice with the conditions on it when you make your sales call.

This sales tool will be ineffective only if you choose a retailer that is unsuited to your book. Even if some books end up not being paid for, they may be read or otherwise make their way into the community. You may have to give away fewer books this way than by sending sample copies to retail outlets one at time, and your sales results might be much better.

Let retail sales representatives sell books for you, too. Once you have a track record selling books as gifts, write up a marketing plan and present it to sales representative groups. You find them in "to-the-trade" buildings like The LA Mart in Los Angeles (www.lamart.com/) or the 225 Building, New York (225-fifth.com). Other population centers have them, too. Contact the buildings' offices, ask for a list of their showrooms, select ones that represent lines that fit with your book's subject matter, and set up an appointment.

When you approach these representatives, sell yourself as well as your book. Offer to do a signing at their next tradeshow, even to give sample books away to the store buyers who frequent their booth or showroom. Suggest they offer one of your workshops as a perk when their accounts buy a minimum number of books. That gives the store owners and buyers (the representatives' customers) a built-in event at no additional cost for the star attraction (yes, that would be *you*!).

Did I mention that when retailers buy from sales reps, the sales are not returnable? Ahem! That's a huge advantage to both publisher and author.

Attend gift tradeshows and track down a like-minded representative there or advertise for a representative in a for-the-trade magazine like *Gift Shop* (giftshopmag.com).

> **Caveat:** Expect to pay a percentage of sales to representatives, usually ten to fifteen percent of the wholesale price. Also expect to offer retailers a discount of forty to fifty percent from the price printed on your book. To accommodate such a discount, traditionally-published authors may need to cut a deal with their publishers. At the outset, self-published authors must set their price structure to accommodate retail sales (something they need to do anyway if they want to sell books to bookstores—online or off).

Chapter Twenty-Eight
Library Sales

The serious writer would a million times rather see a book sold to a library than to a reader, for it is his wish to have his book read not once by one, but over and over again by many. ~ CHJ

Some authors disparage sales of books to libraries. They believe that if libraries don't have their title in their stacks, a reader will find it necessary to buy a copy. And that would lead to lots more sales, right?

Wrong. The objection voiced against selling to libraries is based on one or more specious arguments. Generally, people with library cards purchase few books, and those who buy lots of books frequent libraries for research rather than borrowing. A book sold to an individual may get passed around from friend to friend, given to Goodwill or sold secondhand. An author does himself a favor if he forgets about how his book might travel once it is purchased. There is nothing he can do about it anyway.

For the purpose of marketing, getting your book into libraries helps generate buzz. Ask what your publisher does to alert acquisition librarians so you can supplement those efforts. You can do a better job than your publisher at promoting your book at libraries near your home, but if your book has a regional slant or is of national interest, search for necessary contact information to help your publisher reach them no matter where they are. Or pitch these librarians yourself.

> **Hint:** If your book is of national interest, notify libraries state by state, starting with library systems that would be most interested in the subject matter of your book. Work one state at a time and rewrite your query letter to include benefits for each.

Libraries are workhorses for readers. They also labor mightily for authors, especially when we work at growing relationships with them. Search for city, college, neighborhood, and university libraries.

- Many—not all—have a policy to buy books written by local authors.
- Contact them to see if you might be scheduled as a featured speaker.
- Get involved by offering to lead a workshop on the subject of your book or by founding a critique group for writers or a book club for readers.
- They may disseminate or post your fliers or bookmarks.
- They may allow you to do a display in their window or on a bulletin board.

> **Hint:** Research the Index of this book for "tradeshows." Note how you can use regional conferences and tradeshows sponsored by library associations.

Chapter Twenty-Nine

Postcards

Because the Web is frugal, fast, and interconnected, it has supplanted many stellar methods of promotion that worked. Perhaps they shouldn't have been discarded. ~ CHJ

Before the Web, postcards were the darlings of marketers. We now know the Web is faster, more frugal, and more connected, but postcards still make great invitations or announcements for in-person events like launches, signings, and seminars. Here's why:

- They're appealing and quick—no stuffing or folding.
- By using the sort function on your computer, you can send only to those within a reasonable traveling distance to your event.
- They are less expensive to mail than other direct mail means.
- If you send your cards post card rate, USPS returns invalid addresses back to you at no additional charge. That helps you keep your mailing list current. This service can result in huge savings in the future.
- Colorful postcards can mimic your bookcover so your book will be immediately recognizable when your prospective customer shops online or in bookstores.

- They're fast to read.
- They get noticed.
- Postcards have more staying power than many other forms of communication. People may even post them on their refrigerators.
- Postcards feel more personal because they are used less and arrive in folks' mailboxes where they now probably get less junk than they do in their e-mail boxes.
- Mailing services can handle postcard mailing relatively inexpensively using an author's own contact list, a purchased list from businesses that sell lists like American Express, or they can integrate a combination of the two.
- The response rate to postcards has always been high, perhaps because the perceived value of postcards is higher than that of so much other slush we are inundated with in this information age.

> **Hint:** Cross promotion works here, too. Four authors could share a card. Printing huge quantities of cards lowers costs per card; sharing one another's mailing lists exposes books to more readers.

Here's how to design postcards so they work for you—frugally and effectively:

- On the front (the picture side), leave a space around the image of your bookcover where you can insert your best sales tool—an endorsement or blurb.

- On the back (the address side), leave a little less than ½ the width of the card in white space at the right for an address label.
- Use the left hand of the backside for promotional information.
- Print your return address or PO box number on the back so USPS can send undeliverable postcards back to you. The return address goes to the left of the printed bulk mail insignia the post office uses instead of a stamp. Use a very small font size. You're saving the far left half of the card for details about your book. Leave ¼ inch space along the bottom for codes the post office imprints there.

> **Hint:** Leave some space in the block of print on the left to handwrite a message or to apply what I call a target label. This space is for time-limited information like the date, time, and place of your launch. It keeps you from having to print a different card for each different mailing and thus lowers the per-card cost.

Postage becomes an issue when your list gets bigger and bigger, so choose a card size that meets the USPS bulk mail specifications. The larger cards are more dramatic but your budget will suffer if you're sending out lots of cards. Guidelines are at USPS.com.

Like advertising in general, postcards work well as a sales tool when they are part of a regular and frequent campaign. The more you print, the less they cost per card. That's why I love, love, love the target label idea in the hint above.

Here are three sources for printing your cards:

- Henry Ayala at Tu-Vets.com works with authors regularly.
- Another is ModernPostCard.com.
- Vistaprint.com is popular among authors but you can do better on the price from other suppliers if you are printing large quantities of cards, say more than 1,000. Watch for fluctuating and inflated shipping costs when they offer specials or "free" offers.

Chapter Thirty
Get Quoted

In the Academy Award-winning film *The King's Speech*, Colin Firth says, "I've got a voice." After a meaningful pause, his speech instructor says, "Yes, you do." Our voices are often most heard when what we say is quotable. ~ CHJ

Quotes are pure gold publicity nuggets and they work for everyone including mothers. My mother used homilies to teach us kids—she called them "tried-and-true sayings." They work for everyone, even sports figures. John Wooden, the UCLA basketball coach and author, was as famous as his star players. His quote, "It's what you learn after you know it all that counts" will go down in sports history because it was emblazoned across the cover of one of UCLA Extension's catalogs.

Being quoted is good branding. A few of my own and those of others are in this book. When you're editing your own work, notice the little nuggets floating around in your copy that are every bit as good as those quoted in *Bartlett's Familiar Quotations*.

When you position yourself as an expert, you become a candidate to be quoted. Authors of the so-called hard-to-promote genres can be experts, too. A poet can be expert on poetry or, if she writes about ecology, an expert on that. And, as a poet, she may be more quotable than many who write nonfiction.

Position yourself to be quoted. Try starting each of your media releases with a quote. Install a "Quotable Quotes" page on your Web site and invite people to use your quotes—credited, of course. Include a line about your availability for quotes as part of the last line in your release, something like:

> "A media kit, images, and quotations promoting tolerance are available electronically or by post on request or in the media room at
> www.howtodoitfrugally.com."

A quotation even helped my husband get an endorsement from a famous Asian political figure by beginning his query asking for a blurb with "Behind an able man there are always other able men." ~ Ancient Chinese Proverb

> **Hint:** If you need quotations on marketing or writing, you'll find an assortment of mine and lots of other reprintable articles at howtodoitfrugally.com/free_content.htm.

Several quote sites allow you to post your own zingers. John Kremer advises tweeters that quotes are supremely retweetable. Some sites and organizations send a quote-of-the-day to e-mail boxes of those who opt in. Submit some of your own brilliant sayings to the editors of online quote services and publishers of calendars that feature quotes.

SECTION VII
Onward and Upward

The habit of celebrating helps me acknowledge and enjoy the distance that I have already come along the writing path. By celebrating early and often, I appreciate more of the here and now.
~ Bruce Holland Rogers

Many years ago, I happened across advice for my zodiac sign from Joyce Jillson. It doesn't matter what that sign is because it is good for all writers any day of the year:

"There are plenty of reasons to be proud. Write them down. If you don't celebrate the small wins, you don't have much to build on. It's all about momentum."

Chapter Thirty-One

Success as a Motivator

Not recognizing our own success is a destructive cycle as old as Greek tragedy because it is part of our psychological makeup. ~ CHJ

Our achievements are never enough because success demands more success. Because we are success-myopic, we don't see it when it is sitting on the bridges of our noses. It's so easy to be infected by negativity— the news about everything from war to the state of publishing is just so dreadful.

If you disparage your own achievements, you are not alone. People who do that have trouble building confidence to try for more or better. Promotion successes kick start a cycle of success only if we put them to use for us psychologically. It's dangerous for your promotion efforts (and your writing) not to nod at your victories—large and small—in the mirror.

An online coaching company for business people who need help with their presentations tells their visitors to "Visualize yourself succeeding." Short, sweet, and fine advice. Rhonda Byrne has become one of the most successful writers around advising people to use techniques that have been known for centuries, things like the law of attraction and manifestation. It's all about attitude. Her attitude certainly helped her book, *The Secret,* succeed.

Sometimes we don't celebrate or visualize success because we don't recognize when we have achieved it. Was "success" that first royalty check? Will "success" only come when our book's name appears on *The Times'* bestseller list? Was it the day we started commanding $2 a word as a freelancer? Or are these all mirages that are expunged by insecurity once we have achieved them?

The easiest way to recognize success is to write down goals. Once they're in black and white, more recent expectations can't muss up our perspective. We'll know when we deserve to celebrate. Remember when you thought you'd never get a book written? That day is here. That *is* success.

What if the goal you jot down is "to be just like Danielle Steele?" Study her technique. Take classes. Then tap into your own originality. You may not want to *be* the great D.S., but many of us want to have their voices recognized as hers is. When I feel less than successful, I reread *Word Works* by Bruce Holland Rogers. It's perceptive, witty, perfectly written. Have you heard of him? He won several awards including the Nebula (sfwa.org). He is an example that even if you are big in all the ways that count, your name may not be a household word. So if our names aren't famous, will we still not feel valued? Probably. Unless we've made a list of those goals and celebrate each time we get to cross one off our list.

Chapter Thirty-Two

Book Sales Getting Musty?

About Publishers: I conducted a study (employing my usual controls) that showed the average shelf life of a trade book to be somewhere between milk and yoghurt. ~ Calvin Trillin, humorist

There is no way to keep a book at the top of the charts forever, but if you keep reviving it, you might hold a classic in your hands. Or your marketing efforts for one book may propel your next one to greater heights.

-∞-

FIGHT THE IT'S-TOO-LATE URGE. So your book has been out a year. You're ready to write another book. You don't think your promotion is working. You think you've missed your chance.

Publicity is like the little waves you make when you toss pebbles into a lake. The waves travel, travel, travel and eventually come back to you. If you stop lobbing little stones, you lose momentum. I can't tell you how many authors I've seen give up on flinging those promotion stones into a pond about the time they would have started to see results if they had stuck with it.

It's never too late and it's never too early to promote. Rearrange your thinking. Marketing isn't about a single book. It's about building a career. And new books can build on the momentum created by an earlier book, if you keep the faith. Review the marketing ideas in this book, rearrange your schedule and priorities a bit, and keep at it.

What if you see an article or newscast that should have quoted you or your book but didn't. Getting lizard-spit green with envy is only useful if it prompts you to act. Call whoever was responsible for the coverage. Introduce yourself as someone who is available as a source next time. Be prepared to offer them a new slant, a new idea on a similar or different subject in which you can be an integral part of the story. Don't stop there.

- Add the editor's e-mail address to your media list.
- Follow up with a letter outlining your ideas or expertise. Put your bookmark in the envelope.
- Watch the medium where you saw this piece. When you see something by the same writer, send a congratulatory note.
- When you land something big, let that editor know about it by sending her a copy of the media release you send to your local press and TV assignment editors.

-∞-

READERSHIP EXTENDING IDEAS are all around you. Here are suggestions for inexpensive battles you might wage with the preservation of your book in mind.

- Run a contest on your Web site, on Twitter, or in your newsletter. Use your books for prizes or get cross-promotion benefits by asking other authors for books; many will donate one to you in trade for the exposure. Watch the 99 Cent Stores for suitable favors to go with them.

> **Hint:** Any promotion you do including a contest is more powerful when you call on your friends to tell their blog visitors or Facebook pals about it.

- Barter your books or your services for exposure on other authors' Web sites.
- Post your flier, brochure, or business card on bulletin boards everywhere: In grocery stores, coffee shops, Laundromats, car washes, and bookstores.
- Offer classes in writing to your local high school, college, or library system. Publicizing them is easy and free. When appropriate, use your own book as suggested reading. The organization you are helping will pitch in by promoting your class. The network you build with them and your students is invaluable. Refer to this experience in your media kit to show you have teaching and presentation skills.
- Slip automailers into each book you sell or give away for publicity. Automailers are envelopes that are pre-stamped, ready to go. Your automailer asks the recipient to recommend your book to someone else. Your mailer includes a brief synopsis of your book, a picture of the cover of your book, your book's ISBN, ordering information, a couple of your most powerful blurbs, and a space for the reader to

add her handwritten, personal recommendation. Make it clear in the directions that the reader should fill out the form, address the envelope, and mail it to a friend. You may offer a free gift for helping out, but don't make getting the freebie too tough. Proof-of-purchase type schemes discourage your audience from participating.

- Send notes to your friends and readers asking them to recommend your book to others. Or offer them a perk like free shipping, gift wrap, or small gift if they purchase your book for a friend. That's an ideal way to use those contact lists you've been building.

- While you're working on the suggestion above, put on your thinking cap. What directories have you neglected to incorporate into your contact list? Have you joined any new groups since your book was published? Did you ask your grown children for lists of their friends? Did you include lists of old classmates?

- Though it may be more expensive than some ideas in this book, learn more about Google's AdWords and AdSense. Find these opportunities on your Google account page. Many authors of niche nonfiction or fiction that can be identified with often-searched-for keywords find this advertising program effective.

- Check out ad programs like Amazon's Vine review service. You agree to provide a certain number of books to Amazon and pay them a fee for the service. Amazon arranges the reviews for you. It's expensive, but it gets your book exposed to Amazon's select cadre of reviewers who not only write reviews for your Amazon sales page but also may start (or restart!) a buzz about your book.

- Some of your reviews (both others' reviews of your book and reviews you've written about others' books) have begun to age from disuse. Start posting them (with permission from the reviewer) on Web sites that allow you to do so. Check the guidelines for my free review service blog at TheNewBookReview.blogspot.com.
- Connect and reconnect. Start reading blogs and newsletters you once subscribed to again. Subscribe to a new one. Join a writers' group or organization related to the subject of your book.
- Record a playful message about your book on your answering machine.
- When you ship signed copies of your book, include a coupon for the purchase of another copy for a friend—signed and dedicated—or for one of your other books. Some distributors insert fliers or coupons into your books when they ship them for a fee.
- Adjust the idea above to a cross-promotional effort with a friend who writes in the same genre as you. He puts a coupon for your book in his shipments; you do the same for him in yours.
- Donate your book to contests run by other authors. In return they promote your book for you and provide links to your Web site or blog.
- Explore the opportunities for speaking on cruise ships. Many cruise ship lines have cut back on

the number of speakers they use, but your area of expertise may be perfect for one of them, anyway. I tried it, but found ship politics a drawback. Still many authors like Allyn Evans who holds top honors in Toastmasters and Erica Miner have used these venues successfully. For help with the application process from beginning to end, contact Daniel Hall at speakerscruisefree.com.

-∞-

STAY IN THE PROMOTION HABIT. The longer you stick with it the more productive each effort becomes.

Try new ideas. At the grocery check-out stand, Janet Elaine Smith, a woman with a saucy sense of humor who has written fifteen books of fiction, offers the back of her book instead of her driver's license as picture ID. If the checker says there is no number on it, Janet points to the ISBN. She says, "If they aren't convinced by the legality of this ploy, I still tell them about my book while I search for my driver's license." She then gives the checkers bookmarks and autographs them so they won't throw them away. She is the brassiest of promoters but, as you might guess, none of her many books have died inglorious deaths.

Smith has a more serious side, too. She sets aside a little time every weekday morning to call bookstore buyers. She asks if they have stock on her Irish-themed book for St. Pat's Day. She tells them about her new book. She builds relationships.

-∞-

PLUMB THE WEB AGAIN. The Web is the best tool of all for beginning promoters because it doesn't cost a single copper to learn what's effective and what's not. Here are some free promotion gizmos you can use to extend the reach of your published book:

- Link your Web site, your blog, your social networks—everything!—to each other and to other like-minded sites.
- Get your site listed on as many search engines possible. Go to ineedhits.com and addme.com. These sites lead you through a free-for-all listing spree at no cost.
- Learn a little basic HTML code to help you do more online promotion for yourself. It's faster than waiting for someone else to do it for you. And it's more frugal. MaAnna Stephenson's Blogaid site has a tutorial that's easy for learners: blogaid.net/jazz-up-your-site-with-simple-html.
- Learn to use a new Internet tool like Real Simple Syndication (RSS feeds) that lets you get widgets (little logos or pictures) that take your reader somewhere else on the Web with just a click. You often see widgets that let people join or comment on social networks easily. Learn more by searching on "RSS tutorial" or try guidesandtutorials.com/rss-tutorial.html.
- Use online calendars like Google's to list your events, then feed the HTML code to your Web site, blogs, and your social networks that accommodate it. That way you need only key in your public events once. When you spend less

time to reach more people, you increase your book's chances for success incrementally.

- Add the ability to use quick response codes (QRs) to your battery of techie tools. Some people think they look flowery…or like puzzles or computer chips…even Rorschach tests. They are a kind of barcode, but they can take people with smartphones to a Web page or video or even make a call for them—it depends on what the author chooses to put in the code. Use QRs  at book fairs, tradeshows, and book signings to let folks with smart phones scan whatever promotional gift or information you want them to have. You can put them anywhere: Your business cards, your ads, in your book, or on your printed tote bag. The leading maker of codes is Scanbury. Related to them is a program called Scanlife (scanbuy.com/web/handset-manufacturers). Get free codes made at qrcode.kaywa.com/. The example you see here takes you to the Writers' Resources pages on my Web site.

- Google Alerts has been around a long time, but authors often don't use it or a similar tool. Find Alerts (a little bell icon) on your Google account page. I use it to inform me when my name or titles have appeared anywhere on the Web so I can comment and send thanks. It's also useful for those who are doing research for a book by letting them know when pertinent keywords are mentioned.

- Make your book available for e-readers. Most e-book services including Kindle and Smashwords charge nothing to upload your book. Check out eBooks99cents.com, too. There is a charge only when your book sells. Now you have a published book, you are a retailer. Smart retailers take checks, cash, and credit and debit cards. Smart authors want readers to access their books in whatever way they prefer.
- Reexamine the keywords you use when you market on the Web. Some work better than others. You may be missing one that doesn't have much competition. That may be the one that puts your blog, Web site, article, or book at the top of a reader's search page. To find these keyword jewels, use Google's Keyword tool. You'll find it on your Google Account's homepage.

Appendix

Appendixes were invented by efficient little elves who delight in keeping trade secrets tucked away where only the most curious readers find them. ~ CHJ

Appendixes can be full of obscure resources, strict rules, and templates. Mine is not so heavy-handed. It more closely resembles a collection of ideas. When I interviewed literary agents for the chapters on query letters in *The Frugal Editor* (budurl.com/TheFrugalEditor), Stephanie Kip Rostan, an agent for Levine/Greenberg Literary Agency, Inc., said, ". . . don't slavishly follow a query letter template . . . . If you can't write a query letter on your own, I have to be concerned about your ability to write a book. Besides, it's just creepy."

Each book is different. Each occasion that calls for a query—anything from a request for representation to an appeal for a TV appearance—is different. Ditto for each occasion a media release is called for. Thus, I can only suggest.

Use the samples in this Appendix as guides so you don't stray into embarrassing territory, but, in the long run, it is *your* voice and the ambience of each circumstance that dictates how these samples should be used.

Hint: I annotated some of the Appendix entries to make it easier for you to see how to apply them to your needs.

APPENDIX ONE
SAMPLE QUERY LETTERS

Because query letters are important for many steps in the publishing and marketing processes, I include several examples for you to use as inspiration.

Sample query for an agent or acquisitions editor.

An author must carefully research an agent's or publisher's preferences. The construction of this letter works for most any query, but the tone would not be suitable if an agent represents only nonfiction or speculative fiction.

Dear Agent or Editor: **(Note: You will use a carefully researched name here.)**

Memory is subtle like the caress of a spider's web across one's face or the sweet scent of jasmine in the approaching dusk. It evokes emotion—the sweet, the painful, the frightening—one by one or all at once. It is our connection to the souls of others and to our own identity.

Harkening is a collection of creative nonfiction that does those things. It moves through the generations of a single, isolated family living in Utah. It touches on the repression of women, the pain of prejudice, the warmth of family. It moves lineally from the 20s to the present, revealing the lives of a dysfunctional but loving family. **(This is an example of a short soft-sell synopsis.)**

I have a varied background as a writer. I was a staff writer for *The Salt Lake Tribune* and am now a columnist for the *Pasadena Star News*. My novel, *This Is the Place*, was published by AmErica House in July of 2001 and is already an award-winning novel and has received favorable reviews like this one from *Library Journal*:

"Howard-Johnson strengthens her novel with behind-the-scenes details of Mormon life and history in a book suitable for all collections, particularly those where . . . Orson Scott Card's . . . books are popular." **(Here I used one of those all-important blurbs we talked about in this book.)**

I also have many years' experience as a retailer and, in that capacity, as a speaker at tradeshows and a contributor to industry magazines. **(Note: This letter is a sample from my early writing days. This paragraph shows how to plumb past careers for information about your ability to promote.)**

I am enclosing pertinent information including a brief biography, some promotional material, and my favorite story from *Harkening* based on a childhood experience. **(This letter was sent by USPS. It would offer these materials on request if it had been sent using e-mail.)**

I was impressed by your client list and hope you will consider representing my work. **(It would be better if you can be specific about the authors and titles on that client list.)**

Sincerely,
Carolyn Howard-Johnson

-∞-

Sample query for a National Public Radio (NPR) interview.

This letter, printed with permission from Christine Louise Hohlbaum, got results! It got her a gig on National Public Radio. Notice the different thrust of this query from the one before. It focuses more on establishing expertise.

Dear Ashlee: **(Note the friendly opening, the name correctly spelled.)**

Experts across the board agree that the first four years of a child's life are crucial. These crucial years are a time when the essential groundwork is laid for a child's future: Language acquisition, social skills, and rapid brain development all take place during this time. (Note that the author sets a professional tone, projects her expertise first thing.)

Parents are often so busy juggling career and family they find it challenging to give their children what they need, and sometimes feel isolated, discouraged, and helpless. (Here is a suggested consequence if parents don't take advantage of the author's expertise.)

How can parents nurture their children while still maintaining their work lives? Despite how it may sometimes seem, children do not always need to be with their parents. In fact, they thrive even more when they are with a different number of trustworthy people: daycare workers, relatives, family friends, etc. Exposure to many different settings can enhance a child's growth, not hinder it. (Here she suggests benefits for those who access her expertise; both benefits and consequences will be important for NPR's own audience.)

A playgroup is a great way for toddlers to first experience life outside of the home. I'd like to suggest a show about how to develop a toddler/preschooler playgroup as an easy guide for parents and child care workers to follow. (Ahhh. A specific angle!)

I have led numerous playgroups over the past few years in several languages. With over 140 published articles on parenting and child-rearing, I have the expertise to discuss parenting issues with authority and clarity. My debut collection of short stories, *Diary of a Mother: Parenting Stories and Other Stuff*, has also been well-received by a breadth of readers. (Here the author establishes her expertise with concrete credentials.)

I look forward to hearing from you about my show suggestion, "How to Develop a Toddlers' Playgroup in Five Easy Steps." I will be in Virginia at the end of May for six weeks in the event that you like your guests to appear at the station. (And here, Hohlbaum takes care of business—everything that Ashlee needs to make an interview a reality.)

Warm regards, (Hohlbaum's close is not overly formal or overly familiar.)

Christine Louise Hohlbaum

~Christine Louise Hohlbaum generously contributed this letter for *The Frugal Book Promoter*. An American author of *Diary of a Mother: Parenting Stories and Other Stuff* she lives near Munich, Germany. When she is not writing, teaching, leading toddler playgroups, or wiping up messes, she generally prefers to frolic in the Bavarian countryside. Visit her Web site at: http://DiaryofaMother.com.

-∞-

Sample query for magazine or newspaper feature stories.

This is a letter I wrote that targets media that specialize in senior readers. Most are interested in stories by, about, or of interest to people over fifty-five. It was printed on a letterhead with complete contact information in the header and award logos in the footer.

The Follies Footlighter
Joelle Casteix, Editor
128 S. Palm Canyon Dr.
Palm Springs, Ca. 92262

Dear Ms. Casteix,

What you at the Palm Springs Follies started is rather like a film of falling dominoes run in reverse—one domino after the other standing and marching into their older years with pride and gusto. **(Here the letter establishes a connection to the theater's demographic.)**

I attended your Follies many times when I lived in Palm Springs and owned a business there (Carlan's Fine Gifts in the Palm Desert Mall). In fact it inspired me to begin writing a novel at the age most are contemplating retirement. **(Here the letter establishes a local connection as well as a connection because of age.)**

It is pretty amazing to have one's first novel published at sixty-two, but I think my story is typical of aging America and I know you agree. We are not aging. We are rarifying.

Today as we approach fifty, we may have what was once a full lifetime to do something else. Start a new career. Fight intolerance. Help raise a grandchild. You name it. I have done or am planning to do all of those things.

My first novel, *This Is the Place*, is set in Utah at a time when that state is surely in the news. The 2002 Winter Olympics. Polygamy. Bombings on Temple Square. There was even a cover story on genealogy in *Time* magazine last year. My love of genealogy was one of the inspirations for my book. **(Here the letter establishes a connection with current events.)**

The media are finding it interesting that I started a new career at an age that many are considering retirement. In February the *Los Angeles Daily News* ran a story on me and I was also interviewed by a Los Angeles TV station. **(Here the letter establishes credibility.)**

If you need more information, find a picture, a bio, and the first chapters and prologue to *This Is the Place* by going to: howtodoitfrugally.com/this_is_the_place_excerpts.htm. Find reviews for it at howtodoitfrugally.com/reviews4.htm.

I am enclosing a first-person essay and a headshot in case you can find room for me on the pages of your *Follies Footlighter*. If I can do anything else to help you or we can work together in some other way, please let me know. Thank you so much for your time and consideration.

Sincerely,
Carolyn Howard-Johnson

APPENDIX TWO
SAMPLE MEDIA RELEASES

When you send a release by post, use quality 8 ½ x 11 inch plain white paper. It should be no more than one page. Use Times New Roman font for print and Verdana for a release that will be seen online. When you e-mail a release, use "Media Release: (subject of release here)" in the subject line.

Tailor the title of your release to intrigue the media segment you feel will be most interested in your news.

When you send your release by e-mail, use active links to your resources so your contact can click through to them easily. Because Web site links won't be active when you send your release by post, underlines are superfluous. Remove them to unclutter your copy.

At the end of your release, insert three pound signs. Your pound sign closure will be followed by a prompt to ask for support materials and will look something like this:

Support materials and a media release are available on request.

See several sample releases used for different kinds of promotion on the following pages.

–∞–

Sample media release for an event.

MEDIA RELEASE

Library Contact: Chuck Wikes,
Glendale Public Library Event Coordinator
Phone: XX
E-mail: XX

For Release March 06

Lecture Series Offers
Three Faces of Tolerance

Glendale, CA—Three authors known for their stand against intolerance will be guests of the Friends of the Glendale Public Library Wednesday, March 5, at 7 p.m. at the library's central branch auditorium. The theme for the evening is "Three Faces of Tolerance."

Carolyn Howard-Johnson is the author of two award-winning literary books, *This is the Place* and *Harkening: A Collection of Stories Remembered*. Both explore the corrosive nature of subtle intolerance. Dr. Alicia Ghiragossian is an internationally known poet who was nominated for the Nobel Prize. Of Armenian descent, she often writes of the Armenian Genocide. Stephen Veres' memoir, *A Light in the Distance*, tells his story of survival and triumph at the beginning of WWII in Budapest, Hungary.

Library Events Coordinator Chuck Wike is pleased that "these three exceptional local authors will discuss the intercultural challenges that face our community." Howard-Johnson and Ghiragossian are residents of Glendale and Veres lives in Burbank. The event is cosponsored by the Glendale Human Relations Coalition.

Howard-Johnson's poetry and short stories appear frequently in literary journals and anthologies and she has appeared on TV and hundreds of radio stations nationwide. She also teaches classes for UCLA Extension's renowned Writers' Program.

Learn more at http://carolynhoward-johnson.com.

###

Media kits, headshots, and other support are available upon request.

-∞-

Sample media release for the publication of a book.

With hundreds of thousands of books released each year, it is no longer news that a book has been published. You must hook your releases to the bandwagons of current news—political, technical, business, health, fashion—anything, really, that's being covered by news outlets in the moment. Or you might create news of your own. You might have developed a new genre, founded a critique group for your city's library, or instituted a scholarship for writers.

I am including this sample release because many first-time authors have trouble analyzing their own work for news angles. This one tells a little story about the writers that fits with media interest in globalization, the Internet, and social networking.

Note: This release is longer than most. Rules are made to be broken, but in order to fit the one-page rule, this release could be broken into several—one covering the Smashwords angle, one on the tradition of chapbooks, or one on the idea of small books of poetry as inexpensive greeting cards. These releases with different focuses could then be sent two to four weeks apart.

MEDIA RELEASE

CONTACT:
Carolyn Howard-Johnson
E-mail: HoJoNews@aol.com
Phone: XX

CONTACT: Magdalena Ball
E-mail: maggieball@compulsivereader.com
Phone: XX

For Immediate Release

Poets Digitize Towards
Deeper Understanding

World Wide Web—Award-winning poetry partners Carolyn Howard-Johnson and Magdalena Ball live on different continents. In different hemispheres.

That hasn't stopped them from collaborating on a series of poetry chapbooks designed to replace trite greeting cards with real sentiment. With their Celebration Series, the two have developed a new concept for inexpensive seasonal gifts.

Their chapbooks of poetry include *Cherished Pulse* (for anyone you love) with artwork from California artist Vicki Thomas and *She Wore Emerald Then* (for mothers on your gift list) with photographs by North Carolinian May Lattanzio. A new booklet titled *Imagining the Future* will be released in time for Father's Day and *Blooming Red*, a Christmas chapbook is in the works.

Chapbooks have been a tradition in the poetry world since Elizabethan times. The Celebration Series goes beyond the clichéd sentiments in most greeting cards—and does it for about the same price.

Now they're also available even less expensively as e-books on the high profile Smashwords.com site. Smashwords' unique technology allows the work to be available in every format used by millions of new e-book readers flooding the market. Even as hardware and software change, the author's words will remain available to readers. This is a revolution for Ball and Howard-Johnson, both of whom started their writing careers when the latest technology was a typewriter and carbon paper for copies.

Magdalena Ball runs the highly respected compulsivereader.com review site. She is the author of the poetry book *Repulsion Thrust*, published in December 2009 to unanimous five-star reviews. Her novel *Sleep Before Evening*, published in 2007, was a Next Generation Indie Book Award finalist.

Carolyn Howard-Johnson's poetry appears frequently in review journals. She is listed in *Poets & Writers* and her chapbook of poetry, *Tracings* (budurl.com/CarolynsTracings), was given the Award of

Excellence by the Military Writers Society of America. She is also an award-winning novelist and short story writer and instructor for UCLA Extension Writers' Program.

For more information on any of the chapbooks in this poetry series, contact either author or visit media rooms at howtodoitfrugally.com/poetry_books.htm or magdalenaball.com.

Support material available digitally or by post on request.

APPENDIX THREE
SAMPLE BLOG ENTRY

I gave you lots of ideas for blog posts in Chapter Twenty-One on blogging, but here's another one that L. Diane Wolfe, author of *Overcoming Obstacles with Spunk: The Keys to Leadership and Goal Setting*, came up with for Valentine's Day. All blog visitors are readers of one kind or another so she gave them Valentine gift ideas for storing their hardcopy books and media collections. Of course, she included images and links to where her visitors could buy them. Notice

how she editorialized to bring her own personality to the post.

Wood Bookcase/ Display Cabinet—The unique design of this bookcase gives you the option of positioning it vertically or horizontally. Is that not cool?

Walnut Five-tier Ladder Shelf— I've always wanted one of these. And a house with that much wall space . . .

Coffee Bean Book Case/Display Cabinet—This one is just too cute for words! Yes, I have a thing about bookshelves. One can never have too many.

And where's the best place to read but in a comfy hammock. Hand-woven 'Cool Lagoon' Hammock (Mexico). I really liked this one. I'll take the house it's in, too!

~Diane L. Wolfe blogs in a variety of formats like the ones suggested in this book at circleoffriendsbooks.blogspot.com.

APPENDIX FOUR
SAMPLE INVITATION
FOR TRADESHOW APPEARANCE

This is the invitation I sent to anyone on my contact list I thought might attend Book Expo America. That included authors, publishers, agents, book publicists, reviewers, those who blog on the publishing industry, librarians, and the media.

USA Book News Awards
cordially invites you to Book Expo America to meet

Carolyn Howard-Johnson
Author of
The Frugal Editor: Put Your Best Book Forward to Avoid
Humiliation and Ensure Success

The winner of our 2008 award for
Best Book in the Publishing Category,
she will sign free copies
Friday May 30
from
11 to 11:30
Booth Numbers 835 and 837
PMA Pavilion

Please drop by to chat or to
arrange an interview or event.

The Frugal Editor is also the winner of the
Literary Reviews Award
and the
New Generation Indie Award for Marketing

Make reservations for BEA at: bookexpoamerica.com. Learn more about the author and her award-winning HowToDoItFrugally series of books at howtodoitfrugally.com. *The Frugal Book Promoter*, first in the HowToDoItFrugally series, is also a USA Book News Award winner as well as a winner of the Irwin Award given for its outstanding publicity campaign.

Those who came by the USA Book News booth were given copies of participating authors' award-winning books. We also asked visitors to sign our guestbooks. We didn't want to lose a single name because people who attend these tradeshows are publishing industry professionals who can help authors get greater readership for their books.

APPENDIX FIVE
SAMPLE SCRIPT FOR PHONE PITCH

Here is how Raleigh Pinskey pitches the media by phone. She incorporates elements of a formal, written pitch. It seems long, but if you rehearse Raleigh's script out loud, it moves along so quickly it feels like three or four lines:

> Hello, I'm the author of *101 Ways To Promote Yourself: Tricks of the Trade To Take Charge of Your Own Success*. The book is published by Harper Collins/Quill and has sold close to 100,000 copies. **(Note how she establishes credibility.)**

> I show your audience how they can get more than just those fifteen minutes of fame plus money-making tips, and ways they can be a household name, online and offline, locally or globally. **(Here Raleigh lists benefits. Learn more about them by looking up "pitches" in the Index of this book.)**

> I've been helping business people to fame and fortune for twenty-five years. I've worked with Sting, McCartney, Blondie, KISS, *Chicken Soup for the Soul*, Fit For Life Solution, and hundreds of mouse and mortar businesses. **(Here she tosses in more credibility plus some razzle-dazzle.)**

> My name is Raleigh Pinskey and I would love to be a guest on your show so both of us can help take the members of your audience to their next level of success. **(Notice how she asks for exactly what she wants.)**

Raleigh told me, "I wait until the end to say my name because it's not important until they want to book me. Why take the chance of losing their interest in the beginning with unimportant information and small talk. I go right to the chase."

You may or may not yet have the glitzy platform that Raleigh has. Use what you have and what is appropriate. Some of your credentials may be vocation oriented. You'll gather more as you become more acclaimed.

~Learn more about Raleigh at PromoteYourself.com.

APPENDIX SIX
SAMPLE AUTOMATED E-MAIL SIGNATURE

Automated e-mail signatures are good little helpmates. Having one saves *you* time and gives your contacts the information they need so they don't waste *their* time. I break some of my own rules about the length of autosignatures because I like to give my readers access to as many of the free resources I provide for writers. I'm also trying to set an example that being shy about accomplishments is counterproductive to the health of your book.

> **Hint:** Though an e-mail address is in every e-mail one sends out, I include it in my signature as a service to those who copy and paste addresses to their contact files. It becomes a one-step process because they don't have to come back to a different part of the post to pick up the e-mail address.

> **Caveat:** Some e-mail services put up their little algorithm antennae for spam if you use too many links in your signature, so adjust your signature accordingly.

Here's what mine looks like:

Carolyn Howard-Johnson
Instructor for the renowned UCLA Extension Writers' Program
Web site: http://www.HowToDoItFrugally.com
E-mail: HoJoNews@aol.com

Award-winning author of the HowToDoItFrugally Series of Books for writers, including USA Book News award winners

The Frugal Editor http://budurl.com/TheFrugalEditor

The Frugal Book Promoter http://budurl.com/FrugalBkPromo

The Great First Impression Book Proposal
http://budurl.com/BookProposals

Great Little Last Minute Edits: http://budurl.com/WordTrippersPB

Banner courtesy of Nancy Cleary

Networking:
LinkedIn: http://www.linkedin.com/in/carolynhowardjohnson
Twitter: http://www.twitter.com/frugalbookpromo
Facebook: http://www.facebook.com/carolynhowardjohnson

Blogs for Writers:
http://www.SharingWithWriters.blogspot.com
http://TheNewBookReview.blogspot.com
http://www.TheFrugalEditor.blogspot.com

Tip sheets are one of the items authors can include in their media kits to help them get free ink or publicity. See Section III in this book for more on media kits and tip sheets. This tip sheet is a quick list of marketing tips for authors.

One Dozen Publicity No-Nos
or
How to Avoid Being a PR Numbskull

1. Don't assume your publisher will publicize for you.
2. Don't publicize your book. Brand yourself instead.
3. Don't ask an editor, producer, or host for publicity. They are not in business to do favors for you.
4. Don't send a publicity or a news release. Professionals use the term "media release."
5. Don't send material to media professionals who have been dead for over a year or were fired for showing preferential treatment to friends.
6. Don't avoid controversy. It may be your prescription for getting noticed.
7. Don't discard the word "ethics" from your campaign.
8. Don't pretend those who visit your Web site are only there to purchase your book.
9. Don't depend only on e-mails and faxes to get the word out to editors and booksellers.
10. Don't toss your how-to books on marketing into your Goodwill bag once your book has been launched.
11. Don't treat your writing career as if it were a hobby.
12. Don't believe everything you read on the Web about publicizing books (or writing them!). Consider the source. Check credentials.

Free poster series.

Writers & designers are intrigued by the ampersand. A stylish new poster series by Chaz DeSimone, entitled AmperArt, celebrates this curious & curvacious symbol. Each poster features the ampersand & a common phrase, set in a unique font & a clever layout. The posters are delivered as high quality printable pdfs, along with bonus tips for professional book design & brand identity.

Sign up for your free poster series at www.amperart.com

ADVERTISING

Advertise in future HowToDoItFrugally books. Contact Carolyn at HoJoNews@aol.com.

ADVERTISING

Advertise in future HowToDoItFrugally books. Contact Carolyn at HoJoNews@aol.com.

Index

About the Author

 Carolyn Howard-Johnson's several careers prepared her for promoting her own books and those of others. She was the youngest person ever hired as a staff writer for the *Salt Lake Tribune*—"A Great Pulitzer Prize Winning Newspaper"—where she wrote features for the society page and a column under the name of Debra Paige. That gave her insight into the needs of editors, the very people authors must work with to get free ink. Being familiar with the way news is handled helps her see how different books fit into different news cycles.

Later, in New York, she was editorial assistant at *Good Housekeeping Magazine*. She also handled accounts for fashion publicist Eleanor Lambert who instituted the first Ten Best Dressed List. There she moved from reading effective media releases (then called press releases) to writing them for celebrity designers of the day including Pauline Trigere, Rudy Gernreich, and Christian Dior, and producing photo shoots for clients.

She has also worked as columnist, reviewer, and staff writer for the *Pasadena Star-News, Home Décor Buyer*, the *Glendale News-Press* (an affiliate of the *LA Times*), Myshelf.com, and others and appeared in commercials and on dozens of TV and radio shows.

She learned marketing skills both in college (University of Utah, and University of Southern California) and as founder and operator of a chain of retail stores. That

415

helped her understand how authors might best partner with retailers to affect both of their bottom lines.

Howard-Johnson's experience in journalism and as a poet and author of fiction and nonfiction helped the multi award-winning author understand how different genres can be marketed more effectively. She has been an instructor for UCLA Extension's renowned Writers' Program since 2003 and has studied writing at Cambridge University, United Kingdom; Herzen University in St. Petersburg, Russia; and Charles University in Prague.

She turned her knowledge toward helping other writers with her HowToDoItFrugally series of books for writers. Her marketing campaign for the second book in that series, *The Frugal Editor*, won the New Generation Indie Best Book Award. She also has a multi award-winning series of HowToDoItFrugally books for retailers.

Howard-Johnson was honored as Woman of the Year in Arts and Entertainment by California Legislature members Carol Liu, Dario Frommer, and Jack Scott. She received her community's Character and Ethics award for her work promoting tolerance with her writing and was named to *Pasadena Weekly's* list of fourteen women of "San Gabriel Valley women who make life happen."

Born and raised in Utah, Howard-Johnson raised her own family in sunny Southern California.

Author Photo by Uriah Carr

13982043R00238

Made in the USA
Lexington, KY
02 March 2012